# *The* BUSINESS OWNER'S GUIDE
*to*
# Bankruptcy
# Insolvency
# LAW
*in*
# Canada

*The*

# BUSINESS OWNER'S GUIDE

*to*

# Bankruptcy
# Insolvency
# Law

*in*

# Canada

Jeffrey C. Carhart

John Wiley & Sons

Toronto • New York • Chichester • Brisbane • Singapore

## John Wiley & Sons Canada Limited

22 Worcester Road
Etobicoke, Ontario
M9W 1L1

## Canadian Cataloguing in Publication Data

Carhart, Jeffrey C.
    The business owner's guide to bankruptcy and insolvency law in Canada

Includes index.
ISBN 0-471-64122-7 (bound) ISBN 0-471-64121-9 (pbk.)

1. Bankruptcy - Canada.  2. Business failure -
Law and legislation - Canada.  I. Title
KE1499.C3 1995                      346.71'078       C95-931463-6
KF1524.C3 1995

## Production Credits

Cover & text design: JAQ
Electronic Assembly: Vesna Mayer
Printer: Tri-graphic Printing Ltd.

Printed and bound in Canada
10 9 8 7 6 5 4 3 2 1

*For Kathe and Peter*

# Contents

CHAPTER 16 – SOME FINAL OBSERVATIONS  187

# Canada's Corporate Bankruptcy and Insolvency Legislation

The law sometimes seems to pervade all aspects of our lives and an involvement with bankruptcy and insolvency law has proved to be almost unavoidable for businesspeople in Canada during the 1990s.

In simplest terms, corporate bankruptcy law provides a set of rules to prevent chaos among the creditors of an insolvent corporation. The legislation is complex in part because those creditors fall into so many categories—secured creditors, unsecured creditors, government creditors, and so on—each with its own special rights and interests in the bankruptcy process.

Canada's federal bankruptcy statute, the *Bankruptcy and Insolvency Act,* also deals with corporate receivership. A receivership is not the same as a bankruptcy. By the same token, a receiver is not the same as a trustee in bankruptcy. However, the two systems have a lot in common and a receivership of a corporation often occurs at the same time as a bankruptcy.

Corporations that have become insolvent can try to avoid bankruptcy and receivership by reorganizing their finances. The *Bankruptcy and Insolvency Act* deals with reorganizations and another federal statute, the *Companies' Creditors Arrangement Act,* may offer relief to some corporations. Some of Canada's biggest news stories of the past few years have concerned the attempts of major Canadian companies such as Olympia & York, Algoma Steel, Grafton Fraser, Woodwards, Westar Mining, and Birks, to complete reorganizations.

Canada went more than 40 years with essentially the same federal *Bankruptcy Act.* The statute became badly outdated, and successive governments attempted bankruptcy reform to some degree or other. However, the subject was never a burning political issue, and each time the process died. Finally, in November 1992, the *Bankruptcy and Insolvency Act* became law. It brought a host of changes to such areas as the following.

**Corporate reorganizations:** Under the old *Bankruptcy Act,* it was almost impossible for companies to reorganize. The new legislation has tried to add new life to restructuring efforts under this statute.

**Secured creditors and receivers:** Before the *Bankruptcy and Insolvency Act,* when a bank wanted to enforce security against a corporate borrower it would usually call the loan in its own way and appoint a receiver. To the extent that this process was regulated, it was essentially a matter of provincial law, and many people felt it was not regulated very thoroughly. Now the federal *Bankruptcy and Insolvency Act* regulates both the manner in which the loan is called and the receivership process.

**Government claims:** Many government liabilities can arise out of the day-to-day operation of a business. Prior to the 1992 bankruptcy reform, these government claims enjoyed a sweeping preferred status, which tended to mean that other creditors recovered little or none of the debt owed to them, on a corporate bankruptcy. There was a general feeling that this situation was unfair, and the *Bankruptcy and Insolvency Act* has largely redressed the imbalance by downgrading government claims (other than a few claims, including those relating to income tax, Canada Pension Plan and Unemployment Insurance withholdings) to ordinary status.

**Environmental legislation:** In the decade before bankruptcy reform, the federal and provincial governments expanded the scope of their environmental protection legislation. One of the results was that anyone who had control over a property with an environmental problem could be held liable for the cost of fixing the problem, even if they were not the ones who had caused it. Such persons could include receivers and the banks and other lenders who appoint them, as well as trustees in bankruptcy. The situation reached the stage where no trustee in bankruptcy would assume responsibility for two large insolvent companies in British Columbia and Quebec because the companies' assets included environmentally hazardous property.

The *Bankruptcy and Insolvency Act* introduced a modest degree of protection for trustees in bankruptcy but not for receivers. The Act protects trustees from liability for any environmental condition or damage occurring before or after their appointment "except where the condition arose or the damage occurred as a result of the trustee's failure to exercise due diligence." In other words, the trustee must show due diligence by investigating whether an environmental problem has occurred or is occurring (e.g., determining if a pollutant is being discharged into a river) at the time of accepting the appointment. The trustee must also continue to show due diligence during the term of the appointment in order to continue to enjoy protection under the Act.

**Unpaid suppliers:** Under the old *Bankruptcy Act,* many trade suppliers received little or no recovery on a corporate bankruptcy or receivership due to the abundance of claims that used to be accorded a status superior to that of trade suppliers. Legislators become particularly concerned about suppliers who were unpaid even though the product was supplied just days before the bankruptcy or receivership occurred. The *Bankruptcy and Insolvency Act* introduced a right for suppliers who ship product to a company that becomes bankrupt or subject to a receivership within 30 days. Essentially, the remedy is a right to reclaim the product. Unfortunately, the conditions that have to be satisfied in order for suppliers to exercise this right are so complicated that in practice the right is often unavailable.

This book is written from the perspective of an Ontario lawyer, and a number of the references to legislation are to Ontario law. However, the main statutes under review, the *Bankruptcy and Insolvency Act* and the *Companies' Creditors Arrangement Act,* are federal and thus apply across the country; as well, provincial legislation—except in Québec—is largely similar across the country.

My goal in this book is twofold. First, I attempt to explain the law in a clear, practical way. Insolvency issues, at any point in the process, have a way of erupting quickly, and (although I hope most of you will be reading cover to cover purely for interest's sake) if you ever have to rush off to an emergency insolvency meeting, this book will supply some quick reading to prepare you for what lies ahead. Although I try to avoid "legalese" and jargon, the use of some specialized terms is inevitable, and I encourage you to refer to the Glossary at the back of the book.

Second, I try to focus the discussion of insolvency legislation on how businesspeople can organize their affairs to avoid the major pitfalls of insolvency law and to take full advantage of opportunities that present themselves. Obviously, a bankruptcy or a receivership is a situation that leaves many people unsatisfied. However, I think that many businesspeople end up worse off than they need to in these situations. By laying out the rules of the game, I hope to help businesspeople plan ahead to reduce the negative effects of a business insolvency. I focus on such planning when I discuss the legal framework surrounding particular insolvency situations.

An example of a "pure opportunity" that may present itself in these turbulent times is the chance for a healthy company to buy the assets of a competitor that has gone into receivership. There is an art to negotiating such acquisitions, and again I hope that I can offer some guidance by discussing the law and practice in this area.

Of course, this book cannot substitute for legal advice specific to a real situation. Certainly, the material will give you an appreciation of the large extent to which the particulars of every situation must be considered carefully. However, I hope, too, that this book will give you a sufficient understanding of the basic legal principles surrounding bankruptcy and insolvency, to allow you to ask the right questions when examining a situation with your lawyer.

Jeffrey C. Carhart
May 1995

# Acknowledgements

I think most lawyers would have trouble writing a brief acknowledgement of all of the fellow lawyers, professors, clients, and colleagues who have helped them in their career because the nature of the profession is that one never stops learning and benefiting from an increasingly lengthy list of people. Certainly that is true in my case.

I must acknowledge my partners and associates at the law firm of Miller Thomson, where I am fortunate to work. In particular, I thank Ward Passi, John Chapman, and Hugh Dyer for reading all or part of the manuscript; and I thank Jim Proskurniak, Doug Moodie, and Steve Wesfield for their help concerning the agreements and other material in the Appendix. The Right Honourable John Turner of Miller Thomson and Steve Wesfield have done an extensive amount of work on the subject of director liability and the chart in the Appendix on this point is the product of much of that work.

I also particularly want to acknowledge and thank Karen Milner and Elizabeth Fowler at John Wiley & Sons Canada, Ltd. In addition to putting in countless hours on this project, they never stopped being a source of encouragement and support.

I would like to thank Janki Chowbay, Pat Gallo, and Sherry Piercey for their strong work in typing the bulk of the manuscript.

Finally, I would like to thank my wife Kathe. It is with great love that this book is dedicated to her and our son Peter.

# ONE

# Types of Creditors
# and Their Rights

# The Financial Structure of a Typical Corporation

T O UNDERSTAND HOW THE RECEIVERSHIP or bankruptcy of a corporation works and how a company might reorganize to avoid
bankruptcy or receivership, it helps to be familiar with the financial
structure of a typical Canadian corporation and with the fundamental rights of creditors. It is, after all, those rights that come into
play, and into conflict, in an insolvency scenario.

The classic debt structure of a Canadian corporation tends to be
made up of three types of credit. The first is an operating line of credit
from a bank, which is secured by a security interest over the corporation's inventory and accounts receivable. The amount of credit that
the corporation is entitled to draw on is linked to the amount of its
inventory and accounts receivable. Although the bank will have a
security interest over the corporation's inventory and accounts receivable, its security typically also includes a "general security agreement," which covers other assets of the corporation.

The second common form of credit is a term loan from an insurance company, trust company, or specialized term-lending institution.
The loan is secured by fixed assets such as equipment or real estate.
Again, this lender may also take a general security agreement as part
of its security.

Third, there is financing that pertains to specific assets of the corporation. For example, a corporation that already has a bank and a term lender may finance its vehicles, photocopiers, and fax systems through the individual vendors of those products or their affiliated finance companies. Such financing can be secured by a charge over the specific assets being financed.

Beyond these basic credit facilities, the corporation is indebted to various suppliers and other trade creditors. This indebtedness can be described as a use of "credit" only to the extent that some of these creditors may not require payment until after the debt arises, as is the case when a supplier requires payment within 90 days after receipt of goods.

If the corporation leases its premises, it has ongoing obligations to its landlord. Under modern commercial leases, these obligations extend well beyond rent and include responsibility to pay an appropriate amount of realty taxes, operating costs, and a share of the corporation's profits.

Also, the corporation will have various government liabilities, depending on the nature of its business. As mentioned, these liabilities might include federal income tax withholdings, Canada Pension Plan contributions, Goods and Services Tax, and provincial corporations tax.

Finally, any healthy company finances its business through shareholders' equity and perhaps shareholders' loans.

Each of these types of creditor is discussed in more detail in the following chapters.

# Secured Creditors

A SECURITY INTEREST IS A charge or an encumbrance over the assets of a borrower, in favour of a creditor, to secure the performance of the borrower's obligations to the creditor. An everyday example is the security interest contained in a residential mortgage to secure the obligations of the homeowner (the borrower) to the bank (the creditor); if the borrower defaults on payments, the creditor is entitled to sell the property or to pursue other remedies against the property. One of the fundamental aspects of bankruptcy and insolvency law, which will be stressed throughout this book, is that, generally speaking, creditors with security interests rank ahead of other (unsecured) creditors of an insolvent company, including a company that is in receivership or bankruptcy, or is reorganizing its finances.

There are, however, some unusual circumstances where a security interest may not come first. For example, sometimes certain government claims rank ahead of the security interests of private creditors, even when the private creditor's security agreement was put into place before the government liabilities arose. Also, sometimes a security interest can be "attacked," or set aside, because there is something sufficiently wrong with the way the security interest was given by the borrower or registered by the creditor, and it will not stand up when the creditor tries to enforce it. Banks and other secured creditors do their best to ensure that no one will attack their security and that it will protect them to the greatest extent possible if their borrower becomes insolvent.

In Ontario, three main statutes govern security: the *Personal Property Security Act* and the *Mortgages Act* (which are both provincial statues), and the federal *Bank Act*.

## PERSONAL PROPERTY SECURITY ACT

As its name implies, the *Personal Property Security Act* governs the taking and enforcing of security over personal property, which is anything that is not real estate. The following types of security agreements are typical under the Act: general security agreements, general assignments of book debts, and purchase money security agreements. Each of these agreements attempts to protect a creditor in different ways. Each will be discussed in detail below, but first let's take a look at the general rules and requirements for any type of agreement under the *Personal Property Security Act*. While these types of agreements can be very powerful in securing debts, they could be null and void if such details are not taken care of properly.

## "Attachment" and "Perfection" of *Personal Property Security Act* Agreements

Two of the most important concepts in the *Personal Property Security Act* are "attachment" and "perfection."

"Attachment" means that there is a signed security agreement that identifies the collateral; there has been an exchange of value between the secured party and the debtor; and the debtor has ownership rights in the collateral.

"Perfection" of a security interest basically means taking the extra steps, such as registration, explained below, that the *Personal Property Security Act* stipulates in order to make the security interest enforceable against third parties.

## Registration of *Personal Property Security Act* Agreements

The most common method of achieving perfection is for a creditor to register notice of a security interest. To do so, a "financing statement" must be completed and registered with the government (in Ontario with the Ministry of Consumer and Commercial Relations). Financing statements must set out basic information about the secured creditor, the various types of collateral over which security is held, and the term over which the registration is to remain effective. Statements can be registered electronically by inputting the data directly on a computer, without having to go to government offices.

A financing statement can also be registered before the security agreement is signed. For example, on January 15, ABC Products agrees to lend $300,000 to one of its customers, XYZ Sales, on the condition that XYZ signs a promissory note for the money and a general security agreement over all of its assets. On January 17, ABC's lawyers register a *Personal Property Security Act* financing statement against XYZ and forward the draft documentation to XYZ's lawyers. On January 25, the money is advanced at the same time as the promissory note and the security agreement are signed, with the security registration already in place.

Of course, in the real world, things may change, such as the debtor's name or the assets over which the creditor holds security. The Act provides for the filing of "financing change statements" on a timely basis to record such changes.

It is possible for anyone, such as someone considering extending credit to a borrower, to order a *Personal Property Security Act* "search" against a debtor. The search is a computer printout summarizing all of the registrations that have been made against that debtor. These printouts can be either "certified" or "uncertified." People may rely on the accuracy of certified results, whereas uncertified results are for information only.

The results shown on these *Personal Property Security Act* certificates are typically current to within a matter of hours of when they are issued. For example, ABC's lawyers could have obtained a *Personal Property Security Act* certificate on January 25, before the meeting to sign the documents and advance the money, which would have shown the registration by ABC against XYZ.

## Perfection by Possession

Not all security interests have to be registered in order to be enforceable against third parties. For example, the *Personal Property Security Act* provides that a security interest in certain types of personal property—such as shares in companies—can be perfected by possession of the shares.

A practical implication of this provision for any creditor taking a security interest in shares is that they should require the debtor to turn over the shares in question. Otherwise, even though they have registered their security interest by filing a financing statement, they will always be wondering if another creditor will come along and claim to have been holding the shares (e.g., as security for repayment of a debt) prior to the date on which the financing statement was registered.

## Registration of Security Interests in Fixtures

The term "fixture" refers to a piece of personal property, such as a piece of machinery, that has become "affixed" to the real estate on which it is located. More commonplace examples are built-in refrigerators or freezers in restaurants, or shelving installed for tenants in leased premises.

Suppose, though, that instead of a piece of machinery being affixed by three-foot shafts permanently sticking into the ground, it is simply bolted in place, and that the bolts can be removed and the floor restored to its prior condition in a matter of hours. Is the machinery still a fixture? Although the law is not perfectly clear, it is safe to say that a piece of personal property can be considered a fixture whether it is attached to the real estate in a permanent or temporary manner.

Because fixtures have a real estate element, it is not enough to register a security interest in them by registering a financing statement under the *Personal Property Security Act*. Instead, they must also be registered in the appropriate land registry office.

## The Scope of *Personal Property Security Act* Registrations

One of the important features of *Personal Property Security Act* registrations is that they can be used to cover more than one security agreement. For example, suppose a registration is made in 1992 for a security agreement that secures a specific debt of $35,000. That is, the security agreement specifically says that the *only* debt which it secures is the $35,000 and that once any of that debt has been reduced, it can't be "reborrowed." At that time, the registration is in first place because it is the only registration against that debtor.

Suppose in 1994 the debt has been reduced to $5000, but the same debtor wants to borrow another $50,000 from the same creditor and the debtor is willing to sign a new general security agreement, this time not limited to any particular debt. Since 1994, three other parties have registered financing statements against that debtor. However, because the first creditor can still rely on his 1992 registration to cover the new general security agreement, he or she does not have to "re-register" to stay in first place. This fundamental feature of the *Personal Property Security Act* was called into question in a recent case, but that case seems to be in error.

## Typical Security Agreements Under the *Personal Property Security Act*

Now that the general rules and requirements regarding agreements under the *Personal Property Security Act* have been covered, the individual types of agreements will be looked at.

### General Security Agreements

General security agreements are structured to amount to a charge, by the borrower, over all the borrower's property (including any acquired after the date of the agreement) in favour of a creditor, as security for all borrowings made by the borrower from the creditor (including borrowings made after the date of the agreement). The agreement is extremely flexible, allowing a borrower to draw (and repay) credit from time to time and to carry on business, while offering the creditor the assurance that it has a security interest over all of the borrower's personal property.

If the borrower commits an act of default (the most obvious being a failure to pay the debt on schedule), the creditor may take control over all of the property covered by the security agreement. In other words, as in the case of a residential mortgage, if the borrower defaults on payments, the creditor is entitled to sell the property or to pursue other remedies against the property. See Exhibit 1 in the Appendix for a form of a general security agreement.

### General Assignments of Book Debts

A general assignment of book debts is basically limited to a charge over accounts receivable and the personal property of a borrower necessary to convert those accounts receivable to cash. For an example of a general assignment of book debts refer to Exhibit 2 in the Appendix.

### Purchase Money Security Agreements

In a purchase money security agreement, a debtor (for example, a retailer) agrees to grant a charge over specific personal property (such as a line of inventory) to the creditor (such as the manufacturer of the inventory or a financier of some sort) who provided the financing to the debtor to acquire that property.

An example of a purchase money security agreement is included in the Appendix as Exhibit 3.

## Ranking of *Personal Property Security Act* Agreements

How is priority determined under the *Personal Property Security Act?* Subject to some important exceptions, the *Personal Property Security Act* codifies the basic principle that security agreements that have been completed properly are ranked in order of the date on which they were perfected, which in most cases means the order in which they were registered. In other words, if a company gave a general security agreement to its bank on January 15, 1990, and the security agreement was properly registered at that time and the company granted a second agreement on May 2, 1991, to one of the corporation's shareholders, the bank would generally rank first and the shareholder second on an insolvency of the company.

However, there are some of the exceptions to this general priority principle. One, which was noted earlier in this chapter, is that sometimes it is possible to attack security on the basis of the circumstances in which it was given by the borrower or the manner in which it was registered. This topic is covered in detail in Part 3.

Another exception to the general priority rule involves purchase money security agreements. If all of the special requirements are satisfied, the purchase-money-secured creditor will rank first with respect to the assets that have been financed under the purchase money security interest, regardless of the dates on which other types of agreements (such as general security agreements) were perfected.

The most important special requirement is that if the purchase money security interest relates to inventory of the debtor, the creditor must send a specified form of notice to any other creditors who have already registered notice of their security interest(s) against the debtor, before the purchase money security interest will become effective. This advance notice is not required where the collateral is equipment of the debtor.

For example, suppose that on July 1, 1993, a retailing company, Bob's Stereo Ltd., agrees to buy product from National Stereo Wholesalers Inc. on the basis that Bob's will pay for the product within 90 days of delivery and National would retain a security interest over all unsold product as well as the proceeds of any sold product to secure any unpaid balance owing, at any time, by Bob's to National. On July 3, 1993, National obtains a *Personal Property Security Act* certificate against Bob's that shows that Bob's has already granted security to: a bank, which has security over all of Bob's assets; a leasing company, which has financed Bob's fax machine and cash register; and the shareholders of the company, who have a security interest over all of Bob's assets that ranks behind that of the bank. National must properly deliver a purchase money security interest notice[1] to the bank, the leasing company, and the shareholders before shipping product to Bob's.

If the procedure is followed and Bob's declares bankruptcy on December 15, 1993, at a time when Bob's owes $45,000 to National,

---

[1] The *Personal Property Security Act* contains specific rules covering the way in which notices are to be sent.

National will have the ability to recover the unsold product in Bob's possession at that time, and the proceeds of any sold product, to help defray that $45,000 ahead of any rights of the bank, the leasing company, and the shareholders (and, for that matter, the trustee in bankruptcy or any other of Bob's creditors).

Suppose that the unsold product was worth $22,000 and the proceeds were worth $11,000. National would be at the front of the line for $33,000 to be applied towards its $45,000 debt—a position obviously preferable to that of an ordinary, unsecured creditor for whom recovery might be little or nothing.

### Purchase Money Security Agreements: Worth Fighting For

The special priority rule for purchase money security interest holders can often mean the difference between life and death for such creditors. Take, for example, the case of manufacturers selling their products to Canadian retailers over the past five years. As anyone who watches television or reads the newspaper knows, Canadian retailers have fared badly over these years. There are many reasons for such poor performance. However, many of those who failed (e.g., Etac, operators of the Alfred Sung and Brettons group of stores) or who have reorganized (e.g., Grafton Fraser, which operated the Jack Fraser chain of stores) had become overloaded with debt.

In such cases, ordinary unsecured creditors who had supplied product to the stores had little or no bargaining power when the insolvency of the company became unavoidable, while suppliers who had insisted on a purchase money security interest enjoyed substantial bargaining power in the insolvency proceedings.

Though not as widely reported as the main insolvency, the ripple effects of a major insolvency are devastating. A supplier to the insolvent company may have lost both a badly needed customer and significant accounts receivable. Such a blow might be enough to tip the supplier itself into insolvency. These concerns alone are reason enough to obtain and register purchase money security agreements wherever possible.

In most situations, however, suppliers have to fight to get purchase money security agreements. Obviously, no purchaser wants to give a purchase money security interest to a supplier. For one

thing, the purchaser's banker may be unhappy at receiving the purchase money security interest notice and may, as a result, question
the purchaser's financial well-being (since the purchaser's own suppliers are apparently too nervous to ship without getting security).
There is also the cost and delay always associated with the proper
taking of security.

The bargaining often degenerates to the point where the purchaser will say, "If you don't ship product to me on credit, without
a purchase money security interest, I'll take my business to your
competitor (who will do that for me)." The supplier then has to
think hard and even try to determine whether the purchaser is
bluffing. Each situation will be different.

## How Can a Creditor Collect on a Debt Under the Personal Property Security Act?

If a debtor defaults under a security agreement that has been
entered into under the *Personal Property Security Act,* the agreement and the statute provide the secured creditor with a variety of
methods of collecting the debt. For practical reasons the most commonly exercised remedy is to seize and sell the collateral. However,
other remedies are available, including retaining the collateral in
satisfaction of the debt and, in the case of accounts receivable, simply collecting the amounts otherwise payable to the debtor.

The Act governs and supplements the otherwise blunt remedies
written into the agreement so that, together, the legislation and the
agreement allow the creditor to act in a systematic way.

A strict statutory requirement imposed on creditors realizing on
*Personal Property Security Act* security (and, as will be seen, *Mortgages Act* and *Bank Act* security) is that the debtor and, in most
cases, other parties, *must* receive both prior notice of certain fundamental steps in the process and an opportunity to stop the process,
based on fair and appropriate terms.

### Notice of Intention to Enforce Security

The *Bankruptcy and Insolvency Act* requires 10 days' notice whenever a secured creditor intends to enforce security over all or

substantially all of the business assets of an insolvent debtor. This is a separate notice requirement found in a *federal* statute, which is distinct from the other notice requirements of the *Personal Property Security Act*. A sample *Bankruptcy and Insolvency Act* notice is included in the Appendix (Exhibit 12).

## Notice of Sale

Before selling collateral, a secured creditor must give 15 days' notice to the debtor, any secured creditors or guarantors, and others. Again, the essence of the information set out in the notice is that those parties have the opportunity to "redeem" the collateral by paying out the debt. A sample sale notice is included in the Appendix (Exhibit 6).

In certain circumstances, however, the notice is not required. These exceptions include cases in which the sale will be on a recognized market (such as a stock market), and where the sale is by a receiver and manager and occurs in the ordinary course of the debtor's business. Another situation where the notice is not required is one in which all of the parties who would otherwise be entitled to the notice agree to waive it.

## Standard of Care

Where a secured creditor takes possession of a debtor's property and proceeds to sell it to satisfy a debt, the *Personal Property Security Act* imposes a standard of care that consists of two basic duties: (1) while in possession, the secured party must use "reasonable care in the custody and preservation of collateral;" and (2) every aspect of any sale of the collateral—whether by public or private sale—must be "commercially reasonable."

This subject will be discussed further in Parts 2 and 3.

## Notice of Retention Under the Personal Property Security Act

In order to keep the collateral in satisfaction of the debt, a *Personal Property Security Act* secured creditor must deliver a proper notice, called a notice of retention (see Exhibit 4 in the Appendix), to the debtor, any other secured creditors, and any guarantors of the debt, giving each of them 30 days to stop the process. If one of them does stop the process, the collateral must be sold, instead of simply being retained.

Naturally, the debtor or another creditor will wish to stop a fore-closure or retention process where they feel that the value in the collateral is beyond the amount of the indebtedness owed to the creditor who wants to keep the collateral. For example, if the debt is $100 and the collateral is worth $5000, as a debtor, you would want to stop the process.

Note that only *business* assets can be retained in this way. Where the property is used primarily for personal, family, or house-hold purposes, the retention option is not available to a *Personal Property Security Act* creditor.

## Collection of Accounts Receivable

The *Personal Property Security Act* allows a secured creditor to gain access to a debtor's accounts receivable by sending notification to the people who owe the money, either before default (if that has been specifically agreed on) or after. A sample notice is included in the Appendix (Exhibit 5).

As with the sale of collateral, accounts receivable must be collected in a "commercially reasonable" way by a secured creditor.

## Notice to Remove Fixtures

As noted earlier in this chapter, special rules apply with respect to registering security interests in fixtures. Likewise, special notices are required to sell fixtures beyond the notices otherwise required by the *Personal Property Security Act*.

Specifically, the secured creditor must notify everyone with a reg-istered interest in the real estate at least 10 days before removing the collateral. A sample notice is included in the Appendix (Exhibit 7).

## MORTGAGES ACT SECURITY

This statute, in conjunction with other statutes such as the *Land Reg-istration Reform Act,* governs the taking and enforcing of security over real property. Security agreements covering real property are, of course, traditionally called mortgages, though for some legal purposes they are now also called a "charge."

For ease of reference in this book, I will use the term "mortgage" when talking about either a mortgage or a charge. The secured creditor under a mortgage is the "mortgagee" and the person who gives the mortgage (i.e., the debtor) is the "mortgagor."

## How Can a Creditor Enforce a Mortgage?

If a mortgagor defaults, the mortgagee has a number of possible courses of action. The most common remedies are (i) power of sale; (ii) foreclosure; and (iii) the hybrid remedy of judicial sale. Two other options, suing the mortgagor for the indebtedness and taking possession of the mortgaged property, are discussed in Chapters 4 and 6, respectively.

In pursuing the remedy of foreclosure, a mortgagee is seeking to acquire title to the land in satisfaction of the debt. In a power of sale, on the other hand, the mortgagee's aim is to sell the property and apply the proceeds towards the debt. If a shortfall remains after a proper power of sale proceeding, the mortgagee can sue the mortgagor for that shortfall. Once a foreclosure proceeding has been completed, however, the mortgagor is deemed to have accepted the land in full satisfaction of the debt.

Many factors are considered in determining which of these remedies should be pursued by a mortgagee (including the value of the property versus the debt, the timing of the process, whether there are other mortgages against the property). I will discuss some of these factors in Parts 2 and 3.

## Power of Sale

As already mentioned, with a power of sale the property is being sold in order to raise funds that will go against the debt. As simple as it sounds there are many steps associated with the power of sale process.

## *The Need for Default Prior to Power of Sale Notices*

A loan, of course, has to be in default before a secured creditor (including a mortgagee) can enforce security (such as a mortgage). However, in complicated commercial situations, it is not always easy to say how much notice a commercial debtor is entitled to before the secured creditor can act. The statutes give some guidance, but there is a significant gray area.

In the case of mortgages there is an important technical rule to the effect that a mortgage must have been in default for "at least fifteen days" before the mortgagee can issue a formal notice to proceed with the power of sale. In practice, most mortgagees interpret this requirement as meaning more than just the fact that the mortgagor missed a payment 15 days ago. Rather, the conservative view is that the mortgagor must receive a formal notice of the missed payment, and only when the mortgagor fails to respond to this notice does the mortgagee start counting the 15 days until the notice of sale can be issued.

A relatively long lead-up prior to a power of sale notice being issued is, therefore, not unheard of. For example, suppose that in 1980 General Products Limited borrows $700,000 from a bank and as part of the security for the debt, General Products grants a mortgage to the bank over the building from which it carries on business. Now suppose that General Products makes all of its monthly payments and the mortgage is renewed three times so that by mid-1994, $550,000 is still outstanding when General Products finally misses a payment on July 1.

In those circumstances, if the bank wishes to sell the property, it would probably not take the position that it could send the power of sale notice on July 16 (i.e., 15 days after technical default). Rather, the practice of most institutional lenders, in this case, would be to send a formal demand letter to General Products on July 3 or so, recounting the default and giving General Products a reasonable period to satisfy the debt.[2] Depending on the balance of the facts, a ten-day notice of intention to enforce security under the *Bankruptcy and*

---

[2] The subject of calling commercial loans (including what a "reasonable period" is, in this context) is discussed in more detail on pages 65 through 68.

*Insolvency Act* would probably be sent at the same time: in other words, the mortgagor would be given until at least July 13 or so to rectify the situation. If the mortgagor failed to pay the entire indebtedness on July 13, the bank would then count *another* 15 days (i.e., taking the process to July 28) before sending the power of sale notice.

## Notice of Sale

As with the *Personal Property Security Act* notice of sale discussed on page 14, the *Mortgages Act* power of sale notice sets out a clear, comprehensive statement of the outstanding debt and provides a final opportunity to bring the debt into good standing. The notice (a sample of which can be found in the Appendix as Exhibit 8) is sent to the debtor, to any subsequent mortgagees, and other designated recipients.

In the case of mortgages over commercial real estate, 35 days' notice must be given before the sale process can commence during which, according to the *Mortgages Act*, the mortgagee cannot take "further proceeding(s)" with respect to the sale, without leave of the Court. Examples of such further proceedings include engaging a real estate agent to sell the property, advertising the property as being for sale, and engaging appraisers to appraise it. The point, of course, is that the 35-day period is supposed to be a real opportunity for the debtor to redeem the debt without the amount being driven up by such additional costs.

However, in many situations there will be a need to "manage" the property during this period, if the debtor is hopelessly in default. This subject is discussed in detail in Parts 3 and 4.

## The Farm Debt Review Act

This federal statute, which came into being in 1986, was the product of intense lobbying by farmers who wanted greater restriction on the enforcement of mortgages on farming properties. The goal of the legislation is "to facilitate financial arrangements between farmers and their creditors," which, of course, is commendable if the system can afford it.

Unfortunately, the statute is not well drafted; it does not focus on the property in question but on whether the owner of the property fits the statute's wide definition of "farmer." Any degree of farming could bring an owner within the definition. Thus you get the absurd situation of mortgagees having to comply with the *Farm Debt Review Act* where, for example, the borrower is a lawyer or an accountant who spends a couple of days a month hobby farming on a different property than that which is the subject of the mortgage.

The *Farm Debt Review Act* requires the creditor to give 15 days' notice to the debtor, at the outset, of his or her right to apply to the Farm Debt Review Board for a "stay" (or suspension) of proceedings by creditors against the farm while the Board reviews the situation.[3] These stays run in 30-day segments for a total of up to 120 days, and during that time the board will, if it considers the case appropriate, set up a meeting between the debtor and the creditor to talk things out.

## *Standard of Care*

A mortgagee selling under a mortgage is obliged to act in good faith and to take reasonable precautions in order to obtain the true market value of the property at the time it is being sold. That is, while a mortgagee does not have to "wait out" a bad market and can sell in the market that presents itself when the mortgage falls into default, he or she must still make every reasonable effort to get the best value available in that market and not simply subject the property to a fire sale.

## Foreclosure

The remedy of foreclosure is cumbersome and lengthy. Prior to the early-1990s recession and the real estate market plunge in southern Ontario, most foreclosure proceedings took much longer than a power of sale proceeding, with respect to the same property, would have taken. However, because of the collapse in the commercial real estate industry it is harder than ever to find buyers, and many power of sale proceedings now take more than a year, eliminating

---

[3] It has been held by the courts that this notice may be sent at the same time as a power of sale notice.

the distinction. In other words, if you can acquire ownership of a property more quickly than you can sell it, you might as well acquire the ownership (because, from there, you have more options).

A foreclosure action begins when the mortgagee issues a statement of claim as part of a formal court proceeding. The relief sought is a final order that forecloses, or terminates, what is referred to as the mortgagor's "equity of redemption"[4] and names the mortgagee owner of the property. The other parties to the foreclosure action are the mortgagor and every person with an interest in the property subordinate to that of the mortgagee, (such as other mortgagees). Each of these parties may "defend" the action by filing a request to pay the mortgage, by requesting that the foreclosure action be converted to a judicial sale (discussed below) or by advancing a defence on the merits.[5]

Foreclosure obviously makes most sense, for a mortgagee, where the value of the land is significantly less than the amount of the mortgage. By the same token, in those circumstances, the mortgagor (and any other mortgagees) may not be motivated to stop the process. For example, suppose that a piece of land is worth $400,000 and the mortgages against it are as follows:

| Rank | Principal Amount | Mortgagee |
|------|------------------|-----------|
| First | $800,000 | Bank |
| Second | $200,000 | Private Investors |

In those circumstances, if the bank sold the property it would immediately realize a significant loss. Accordingly it might decide that it is better off simply to acquire title to the property (through a foreclosure) and wait and see if the property values picks up to more than $400,000. Given that there is so much of a gulf between the amount of the first mortgage and the value of the land, neither the mortgagor nor the private investors may try to stop the bank from foreclosing.

---

[4] In plain English this term means the mortgagor's right to get back the property by paying off the debt secured by the mortgage.

[5] For example, by challenging whether the debt is owing as stated in the statement of claim or whether there has been a default.

However, of course, if the numbers were different and the land worth, say, $1,500,000, the mortgagor and the private investors would want to stop a foreclosure by the first mortgagee.

Eventually foreclosure actions are settled in a court hearing, and if no adequate defence is raised there, an initial judgment for foreclosure will be entered and a final "redemption period" will begin to run. Generally these redemption periods are set at 60 days, but they can be lengthened or shortened by the court. If the defendants do not make payment within this time, a final order of foreclosure is issued, which can be registered on title. At that point the mortgagee has become the owner of the property with the ability to deal with it as he or she pleases.[6]

## Judicial Sale

A judicial sale is a hybrid of the power of sale and foreclosure remedies. In this process the property ends up sold, as with a power of sale; however, each step in the process is regulated by the courts, as with a foreclosure action.

As noted above, judicial sales often result when either the mortgagor or a subsequent mortgagee objects to an attempt by a first mortgagee to foreclose on a property. To continue the example just used, if the private investors felt that there was some possibility that the land was worth more than the $800,000 (plus interest and costs) owed to the bank, they might respond to a foreclosure action by the bank asking the court to supervise a sale of the property (instead of allowing it simply to pass to the bank, free of the interest of the private investors and the mortgagor). If the land fetches, say $1,100,000 there should be some money for the private investors even after the real estate commissions and other expenses are paid.

From the bank's viewpoint, there is some comfort in a judicial sale because the sale price is "approved" by the Court. In other words, the mortgagor (or "subsequent mortgagees" such as the private investors in our example) cannot challenge the adequacy of the price, which is an option with sales conducted under "power of sale."

---

6 Final orders for foreclosure are almost never reviewed by the courts.

## SECURITY IS NOT JUST FOR FINANCIAL INSTITUTIONS

The next section of this book deals briefly with *"Bank Act"* Security. As the name implies, it is available only to institutions that meet the definition of "Banks." However security agreements regulated by the *Personal Property Security Act* and the *Mortgages Act* are available to all creditors and that is a fact that all business people should appreciate.

For example, consider this scenario. In 1985 Roy Clemons incorporates a company called Roy's Machinery Ltd. At that time Roy and his wife each acquire 50% of the shares and Roy lends $100,000 of his savings to the company for its initial working capital.

The company prospers through the late 1980s through Roy's hard work and in 1989 the company is given a line of credit of $500,000 by a bank. Part of that bank money goes to acquire a piece of real estate to house the company's new production facility and, to help close the deal, Roy lends the company another $100,000.

The bank secures its loan by taking security against the company's personal property under the *Personal Property Security Act* and by taking security over the (new) real estate under the *Mortgages Act*. In order to generate the $100,000 which he loans to the company, Roy mortgages the home in which he and his family live.

Now suppose that in 1993, Roy's Machinery Ltd. is hit by a wave of bad luck: the land has plummeted in value, one of the company's biggest customers goes bankrupt and another of its customers is beset with a bitter strike which lasts for months during which Roy's Machinery receives no orders. Finally, one of the company's pieces of equipment fails to perform for a customer and the company is sued for $1,000,000 in damages.

One morning Roy sits down with his accountant and his lawyer and reviews the following numbers for Roy's Machinery Ltd:

**Assets**

| | |
|---|---|
| Land & Building: | $ 350,000 |
| Equipment: | $ 100,000 |
| Accounts Receivable: | $ 150,000 |
| Motor Vehicles: | $ 25,000 |
| Cash: | $ 25,000 |
| TOTAL: | $ 650,000 |

**Liabilities**

| | |
|---|---|
| Secured Bank loan: | $ 485,000 |
| Secured Loans | |
| (re Motor Vehicles): | $  15,000 |
| Loans to Shareholder: | $ 200,000 |
| Trade Payables: | $ 100,000 |
| Amount Payable | |
| (Due to Lawsuit): | <u>$1,000,000</u> |
| TOTAL: | $1,800,000 |

In those circumstances, if Roy's Machinery went bankrupt,[7] the $200,000 owing to Roy would rank no higher than the trade payables and the amounts due as a result of the lawsuit. On these numbers, there is only $150,000 left after the bank and the financier of the motor vehicles is paid.[8] In other words there is $150,000 to pay debts of $1,300,000 or 11¢ on the dollar. Thus Roy would only receive about $23,000 for the $200,000 which he legitimately invested in this company and to which he devoted his life for 8 years. $23,000 is, of course, not even enough to pay off the $100,000 mortgage which Roy placed on his home in 1989.

However, consider the difference if Roy had taken the following simple, relatively inexpensive steps. First, in 1985, Roy obtained a general security agreement from Roy's Machinery Ltd. and Roy registered it under the *Personal Property Security Act*. Then, in 1989 Roy obtained a mortgage over the land and buildings in compliance with the *Mortgages Act*. In order to keep the bank happy, in 1989 Roy also agreed that his security under both the *Personal Property Security Act* and the *Mortgages Act* ranked behind the bank. In those circumstances, as a secured creditor, Roy would receive the entire $150,000 or so left after the bank and the second creditor who financed the motor vehicles[9] are paid. Thus Roy receives $150,000 which is at least enough to pay off the mortgage on his house and to give him and his family something to start over again with.

---

[7] As discussed in Part 4, there are alternatives to bankruptcy in such a situation.

[8] For simplification I have not lowered the $150,000 by the legitimate costs associated with a bankruptcy and/or a receivership in these circumstances. This topic is discussed in Parts 2 and 3.

[9] Using, for example, a purchase money security interest.

There is absolutely nothing illegal, unethical or improper about a shareholder of a company taking security, from his own company, for moneys loaned to the company. It is simple prudent business practice. No one running a business has a crystal ball which enables him or her to foresee every calamity that could befall the company, so as to be able to discontinue operations just before any creditors get hurt.

In the real world companies go bankrupt and in most cases it is not due to dishonest, reprehensible conduct by the owners and operators; instead it is due to tough economic conditions. In those circumstances, if the owners have security to support the debts they are owed from their company, the law allows them to be paid ahead of the other creditors.

## SECURITY IS TYPICALLY ASSIGNABLE

Another fact to bear in mind in that most standard form security used by banks and other financial institutions is assignable. This fact can be very important when guarantees are involved.

For example, suppose that the story of Roy's Machinery Ltd. unfolded this way. In 1985 Roy established the company with no money of his own but with a $250,000 loan from the bank. In typical fashion, the bank required a personal guarantee from Roy and his wife (in whose name their family home was registered). In order to protect themselves even more thoroughly the Bank took a mortgage over the home.

Now suppose that in 1993 Roy's Machinery Ltd. has assets of only $100,000 and secured debt to the Bank of $225,000 and unsecured debt of $875,000. Remember that in this second example none of the debt is owed to Roy personally because he never invested any money. However, if the company's assets are liquidated in a bankruptcy, the bank will only receive $100,000 or so and they will be looking to Roy and his wife for $125,000 under their guarantees. Depending on their situation, Roy and his wife could lose their home.

However, suppose that Roy believes that if he could buy the assets of Roy's Machinery Ltd. through a new company owned by him and his brother-in-law he could make a success of the business. In addition, Roy's brother-in-law is prepared to lend Roy and his wife enough money ($225,000) to pay out the bank.

In those circumstances, Roy could take an assignment of the bank's security in exchange for paying the bank the money it is owed. By doing that Roy would then have "first call" on the assets of Roy's Machinery Ltd. and the right to sell the assets subject to the security agreements, the *Personal Property Security Act* and the *Mortgages Act*. Provided that all of those requirements are met, there is nothing to prevent the assets being sold to the new company incorporated with Roy and his brother-in-law. Thus, by taking an assignment of the bank's security, Roy has been able to preserve both his house and the opportunity to continue in business.

Again, absent any special circumstances, there is nothing illegal or unethical about this situation. In fact, with some slight variations, it happens quite often.

## BANK ACT SECURITY OVER INVENTORY

The *Bank Act* allows banks (and other institutions defined as banks) certain types of security not available to other creditors.

The most common type is called "section 427 security." According to this section of the Act, a bank can take security over all types of inventory, including raw materials, goods in progress, and finished inventory. (i.e., but not other personal property).

The *Bank Act* also provides for the bank to acquire a right over the inventory that is effectively the same as having legal title to the goods. The practical importance of this ownership interest is minimal in many situations, however, as the legislation also goes on to provide for sale and foreclosure powers and procedures not unlike those found in the *Personal Property Security Act* and *Mortgages Act*.

## Notice of Sale

The *Bank Act* requires that the borrower receive at least 10 days' notice of any sale made under *Bank Act* security. As with the *Personal Property Security Act*, there is no form of notice per se, although in the Appendix (Exhibit 9) I have quoted in full the section of the *Bank Act* that stipulates what information must be contained in such a notice.

## Standard of Care

The *Bank Act* requires banks to meet a standard of honesty and good faith in carrying out sales of inventory pursuant to the *Bank Act*. The Act specifically provides that such sales may be made by way of auction.

In a classic case involving *Bank Act* security, a bank was held to have fallen short of this standard in selling some cattle that had been pledged to it by a customer. One of the main attributes of the animals was that they were "disease-free," but this status could only be retained as long as the cattle remained on the customer's farm. The bank knew of this, but removed the animals from the farm to sell them at auction. The results were disappointing and the Nova Scotia Court of Appeal held that although banks are entitled to sell *Bank Act* security items at auction, they still must have regard to the nature of the property, which had not been done in that case.

When a secured creditor fails to meet such standards, a number of unpleasant results are possible. However, depending on how bad the error was, the result is usually either that the creditor cannot sue the debtor for any "shortfall" after the sale or that the creditor actually has to pay over money to the debtor.

## Priority Agreements

You will have gathered by now both that most business corporations have more than one secured creditor, and each secured creditor can have security regulated by several different statutes. Often these credit agreements are negotiated, and made available, at different times in the history of the borrower. It is not uncommon, therefore, for the secured creditors of a typical Canadian business corporation to enter into what is referred to as a priority agreement.

Such agreements set out an arrangement whereby each secured lender has priority over certain assets of the debtor, perhaps up to a certain dollar amount, regardless of how the technical statutory rules would set the priorities. Priority agreements can also regulate priority between a security agreement under one statute (say the *Personal Property Security Act*) and a security agreement under another statute (say the *Bank Act*).

Priority agreements may also set out a number of other provisions, including obligating creditors to share information about the borrower, and requiring any creditor who intends to enforce his or her security to give notice to the other secured creditor(s).

These agreements are important to both lenders and borrowers because they may impose obligations and restrictions on security enforcement over and above the technical, statutory rules that apply to these agreements. If you are a borrower, you should negotiate them as vigorously as any other agreement. For example, think carefully about the extent to which you would want one of your secured creditors talking to another secured creditor about your affairs. A priority agreement could mean that if you commit a minor default with your bank (and which you would prefer to be able to fix without anyone else ever knowing of the problem), the bank is legally obligated to notify your other lenders of the incident.

# Landlords

2

Although it is possible for a commercial landlord to be a secured creditor of a business corporation, in practice a landlord seldom holds a security agreement—general or any other kind—from a tenant. On the other hand, if the tenant starts experiencing financial difficulty, landlords enjoy special rights that may give them more power than ordinary, unsecured creditors, and sometimes even secured creditors.

When a commercial tenant breaches a lease (for example, by failing to pay rent when due), a landlord has a number of remedies available. In determining which remedy to exercise, the landlord must first decide whether he or she wishes to preserve the lease or terminate it. Naturally, if the rent under the lease is less than the prevailing market rent for the space, the landlord will leap at the chance to terminate the lease and re-lease the property at a higher rent. On the other hand, many leases signed in the boom years of the late 1980s are at rent levels significantly above prevailing market rents; in those circumstances the landlord will be slow to take any step that can be construed as a termination of the lease. However, that is not to say that where a tenant breaches a commercial lease that is at a rent level above market values, the landlord is without relief.

## IF THE LANDLORD WANTS TO PRESERVE THE LEASE

A landlord can utilize a number of options in the event that a tenant breaks a lease, and the landlord still wishes to preserve that lease. These options will be outlined in the following pages.

## Distress

When a tenant is behind in rent payments, the landlord can seize the tenant's property on the premises[1] and sell it to satisfy the rent arrears. This process, known as the remedy of "distress," is an old common law remedy used in many provinces in Canada and specifically provided for in Ontario's *Landlord and Tenant Act*.

There are a few important requirements for a distress action to be carried out properly. First, the landlord is supposed to give the tenant 5 days' notice of the landlord's intention to sell the goods. As a matter of practice, this notice is usually taped to the door of the premises.[2]

If the five days go by without the tenant's paying the outstanding rent, the landlord is then supposed to get two appraisals of the goods before proceeding with the sale. There is no required method of sale but the landlord must sell at a fair market price and, as a corollary, must not sell more than is necessary to satisfy the rent arrears. In other words, a landlord is not entitled to seize and sell brand new stereo equipment that would sell, at retail, for $25,000, in order to recover $9,000 in rent arrears.[3]

---

[1] Some (fairly unusual) types of property are, by law, exempt from the distress remedy. Also, in circumstances where the tenant has fraudulently removed the goods from the leased premises, the landlord can seize them in another location.

[2] Often what happens is that the locks are also changed by the landlord in order to gain control over the goods while the five-day period runs. I have always thought that this practice is inconsistent with the overriding requirement that a landlord can only exercise distress if he or she is willing to treat the lease as still alive; traditionally, when a landlord changes locks, it is evidence that he or she is terminating the lease. However, in practice, these notices tend to say something to the effect that the lease is still (technically) alive and that if the tenant wants access to the premises during normal business hours, he or she need only contact the landlord who will open the door (presumably with security personnel in attendance). The courts have allowed this practice.

[3] Even factoring in some costs for the landlord.

## Other Remedies

There are obvious risks to a distress action, such as the danger of seizing and selling something that does not belong to the tenant.

A landlord, therefore, might instead decide to sue a tenant either for rent arrears or, where the breach relates to something other than non-payment of rent, for damages suffered or costs incurred by the landlord because of the breach of the lease.

Two remedies available to a landlord and normally used where the breach relates to something other than non-payment of rent are to apply to court either for an injunction (to prevent the breach) or for an order for "specific performance," which, if granted, would require the tenant to do something positive to remedy the breach. An example of the latter type of order would be where the lease specifically provides that a tenant in a commercial mall is supposed to stay open until 9:00 p.m. and the court orders him to do that instead of closing at 4:30 p.m. every second day.

If the tenant has, in effect, acted as if he views the lease as being at an end—for example, by abandoning the location and telling his customers that he has relocated permanently—the landlord can nevertheless treat the lease as continuing by readying the premises for a new tenant and re-leasing it. As a matter of form, the landlord will re-lease "on behalf of the tenant" given that the original lease is still considered to be alive. The landlord can thus sue the tenant for any rental deficiency over the balance of the term of the lease.

## IF THE LANDLORD WANTS TO TERMINATE THE LEASE

When the tenant is in breach and the landlord wishes to terminate the lease, one remedy is for the landlord to simply re-enter and re-lease the premises. In other words, the landlord concedes that the lease is over—maybe because the tenant is not worth suing.

However, in what is only a slightly different scenario, the landlord can also give the tenant notice that although the landlord is treating the lease as terminated, he or she will still sue the tenant for any rental deficiency after re-leasing the property at the prevailing market rates. In other words, even if the lease is at a rent above market rates, sometimes the nature of the breach will be such that the landlord has really no choice but to act as if the lease is terminated and to sue the tenant for the loss. In a major Supreme Court of Canada case, a landlord was faced with such a situation when the biggest tenant in a strip mall suddenly abandoned the premises, which caused other tenants to leave as well.

## REMEDIES INVOLVING PERSONAL LIABILITY EVEN WHERE THE TENANT IS A CORPORATION

The *Landlord and Tenant Act* contains a section that can be devastating if it is ignored, yet even many lawyers are not familiar with it.

Consider this scenario: Sam Laidlaw is the sole shareholder and director of a company called Sam's Hardware Inc., which enters into a five-year lease for a 2000 square foot store in a mall, in January 1992. After some good months at the beginning of the lease, the company soon finds itself struggling and by January 1993, when a new superstore opens five blocks away, Mr. Laidlaw is convinced that he has to get out of the lease any way he can. The rent is $4000 per month and the company is two months behind in rent.

The landlord is aware that his tenant is unhappy but he is watching Sam's Hardware carefully because he has no other prospective tenants for the location. Sam knows all of this and decides that he must do a "midnight run." So he rents a truck and under cover of darkness loads up all of the assets of Sam's Hardware ($35,000 in inventory and $15,000 in equipment) and drives away.

What does the *Landlord and Tenant Act* say about this situation? Not only can the landlord sue Sam's Hardware for breach of the lease (as discussed in the previous section), but he can also sue Sam Laidlaw personally for $100,000—*twice the amount of the assets Sam removed from the premises.*

Specifically, the *Landlord and Tenant Act* provides that "any person [who] wilfully and knowingly aids or assists" a tenant (including a corporate tenant), who "fraudulently or clandestinely conveys away, or carries off from [leased] ... premises ... goods ... to prevent the landlord" from exercising the remedy of distress against those goods "shall forfeit and pay to the landlord double the value of such goods or chattels."

Obviously, this is a harsh provision, and, like the remedy of distress, it has its origin in old English law. However, it is still part of modern Canadian law, and the courts have not been receptive to arguments that the punishment is inappropriately strong.

Of course, the provision applies only if there are rent arrears, because a landlord can only exercise the remedy of distress for rent arrears. Modern leases, however, call for all sorts of payments by a tenant[4] all of which are typically described as "rent." Thus it is often not a simple matter to say, at a given moment, that there are no rent arrears.

[4] For example, as noted on page 4 tenants are routinely responsible for "their share of" realty taxes, hydro charges, business taxes, maintenance costs, and, often, "percentage rent," which is based on a percentage of the profits (as defined) or a percentage of sales (as defined) from the business carried on from the leased premises.

# Government Liabilities

T HE PRESENCE AND COST OF government are powerful forces for Canadian business people. Just consider this partial list of the types of government liabilities that arise in the day-to-day operation of a Canadian business: federally, there are income tax withholdings, Canada Pension Plan contributions and unemployment insurance contributions for employees, as well as goods and services tax arising from the sale of product and other corporate activities; provincial liabilities include retail sales tax, corporations tax and payroll deductions relating to workers' compensation and government health plan payments for employees. In addition, provincial statutory provisions impose obligations on corporations relating to any unpaid wages, vacation pay, termination or severance pay owing to employees. At the municipal level are realty taxes and business taxes.

One of the reasons that Canadian governments have been running deficits through good times and bad is that many companies that encounter financial difficulty do not pay, or are not capable of paying, what they owe to some or all of these governments over significant periods of time.

For insolvency lawyers, the fight by governments to maintain the upper hand in the struggle among the creditors of an insolvent company has been very interesting to watch over the last decade or so.

The subject of government liabilities has great bearing on receiverships, bankruptcies, and reorganizations and will be returned to throughout this book. However, at this point, a summary of the four basic approaches governments have taken to collect these debts would be most practical.

## STATUTORY LIENS

Unlike security interests (examined in Chapter 1), which are created voluntarily by private contracts between the parties, statutory liens are created by legislation. The indebtedness secured by a statutory lien is any shortfall in the corporate debtor's obligations to the government agency in question. In other words, if a company is supposed to pay $800 every week towards its workers compensation "dues," but it fails to do so, each week the statute in question gives the governmment a lien over the company's assets to the extent of $800.

Before the 1992 enactment of the *Bankruptcy and Insolvency Act,* the courts ruled on a number of disputes between private-sector holders of various types of security interests and government beneficiaries of statutory liens. One of the many objections that private-sector secured creditors had to statutory liens is that they were not subject to the detailed public registration requirements in the *Personal Property Security Act*, the *Mortgages Act*, and the *Bank Act*. In other words, creditors objected because the statutory liens could not be checked in public records.

The *Bankruptcy and Insolvency Act* introduced significant change to this area; in essence, the law now says that statutory liens will be valid only if the security has been properly registered prior to the commencement of legal proceedings under the Act.

## DEEMED TRUSTS

This collection mechanism is based on the fundamental (and logical) provision in both the old *Bankruptcy Act* and the new *Bankruptcy and Insolvency Act* that property held in trust by a bankrupt does not form part of the estate and thus cannot be divided among the creditors. That is, on a bankruptcy the beneficiary of a trust can claim his or her trust property, ahead of all creditors.

For example, suppose that in 1990 Bob agreed to hold $5000, given to him by John in trust for John's son, on specified terms including that the money be put in a bank account in the name of "Bob Smith, in trust." If Bob goes bankrupt in 1994 due to an overwhelming burden of debt associated with paying his sister's medical bills and the cost of hurricane damage to his uninsured business, the $5000 would go to John's son, as designated, and would not be one of the assets that Bob's creditors get to share.

This favourable treatment of trusts in an insolvency caught the eye of governments and many statutes came to provide that corporate debtors were "deemed" to hold the amount of certain statutory liabilities in trust for the appropriate government agency.

Unfortunately for governments, however, the traditional principles of trust law hold that a trust must meet the following three minimal requirements: certainty of intention (to create the trust), certainty of the persons or objects to be benefitted by the trust, and certainty of the subject matter of the trust. This last requirement of certainty of subject matter means that the trust property must remain identifiable or traceable. In other words, under a proper trust you must be able to identify, at all times, the fact that someone intended the trust to be created, who the beneficiaries of the trust are, and what the property is that is supposed to be in trust. If any one of these components is not clear or "certain" the trust will break down, in the eyes of the law.

In practice, of course, companies who are deemed to hold certain monies in trust do not segregate the money. Instead, everything tends to get lumped together in one or perhaps a few big "snowball" bank accounts. When the company starts to become insolvent it pays the creditors it deems most deserving of payment,[1] and, when some kind of formal insolvency occurs, whatever money is left in the bank is unlikely to be identifiable as the money deemed to be held in trust.

As such, for many years, the enforceability of these statutory deemed trusts was debatable, particularly where the trust had been established under provincial law and its terms could, therefore, conflict with the federally regulated bankruptcy process. This

---

[1] As discussed in Chapter 13, which deals with reviewable transactions, these payments may or may not stand up to later scrutiny.

uncertainty was resolved in 1987 by the Supreme Court of Canada in a case called *British Columbia v. Henfrey Samson Belair*. In that case the court held that a deemed trust established under provincial law would not be respected in a bankruptcy unless the traditional, common law requirements of a trust could be established and if the so-called trust property was not identifiable (as in that and most cases), the provincial government's trust claim would fail.

The *Bankruptcy and Insolvency Act* has codified this decision: Crown trust claims are now respected in bankruptcies only where the traditional common law requirements of trust law are established. However, this rule, in turn, is subject to an important exception in the case of deemed trust claims relating to *Income Tax Act* withholdings, Canada Pension Plan contributions, and *Unemployment Insurance Act* premiums. These three deemed trusts usually will be valid even where the "trust money" was not actually segregated. However, there are some secured creditors who may still win out. Who these creditors are will be discussed in a later chapter.

## GARNISHMENT

Many statutes stipulate that if a debt to a government agency is not paid on schedule, the agency can unilaterally notify anyone who owes money to the company that has not paid its government debt to pay the government instead. These statutory garnishment[2] provisions are a powerful tool and can be invoked much more quickly by governments than by "ordinary" creditors who first have to obtain a judgment through the cumbersome process of civil litigation. In most instances, governments simply have to certify the debt as due and owing before embarking on their recovery process.

## DIRECTOR LIABILITY

Ultimately, individuals run companies and over the years governments have introduced many statutory provisions that make directors personally liable for many of the governmental liabilities of their companies.

---

[2] Garnishment, in general, is discussed on page 59.

In a sense, director liability provisions go to the very heart of corporate law. One of the classic cases studied by all law students is the decision by the British House of Lords in 1897 in *Salomon v. Salomon.*

The case represented an early encounter between a corporation and a creditor of the corporation who could not accept the idea that when the corporation was unable to pay the debt he did not have recourse against the directors or the shareholders.

The House of Lords endorsed the principle that the liability of a corporation is limited to the value of its assets (hence the word "Limited" in the name of many companies) and, if those assets are depleted, the liability does not extend to third parties, such as shareholders or directors. In other words, the court held that a corporation is a distinct legal entity and the recourse of creditors who do business with a corporation is limited to the assets of the company.

Obviously, limited liability is essential to the functioning of commercial life. Many important business ventures in the century since the *Salomon v. Salomon* decision would never have been undertaken if the people with the original idea did not have the comfort to know that (as shareholders) their exposure, if the business failed, was limited to their investment in the company incorporated to carry on the business. One can also think of situations where a particular, perhaps very talented, individual would have wanted to act as the director of a company (and where many employees and other people would benefit from the person's leadership and abilities at the company's helm) only if they knew they would not be liable for the company's debts if the business failed. In a very real sense, limited liability is at the foundation of commercial life in the western world.

At the same time, disgruntled creditors are often left with a bad taste in their mouth when they find that their recourse stops at a company that cannot (and maybe never could) satisfy the obligations owed to them. In fact, sometimes other people besides the corporation that has incurred an obligation, are legally responsible to pay it.[3]

---

[3] See, for example, Chapters 7 and 13, which deal with the rights of unpaid suppliers and reviewable transactions, respectively.

In this regard, the phrase "piercing the corporate veil" has gained popularity, conjuring up images of courts rescuing poor, mistreated creditors by apprehending those people behind the ownership and operation of the company. I have always felt that this phrase is too vague; in other words, in this context, there is still no general legal principle which says that if you have not been paid money by a corporation which has no assets left with which to pay you, you can complain to a judge and ask that he or she "pierce the corporate veil" and declare the director(s) and/or shareholder(s) of the corporation liable to you as well.

However, it is perfectly valid for a statute to provide that, in certain circumstances a director of a company is personally liable for certain debts otherwise incurred by his or her corporation. If the corporation runs up just such a debt, the director is justifiably responsible and "piercing the corporate veil" is unnecessary. Rather, the liability is grounded in fundamental, understandable legal principles that were known (or should have been) to the director when he or she took the job.

The number and scope of these statutory liabilities of directors has simply exploded over the past 10 to 15 years. Exhibit 10 in the Appendix lists more than 40 statutes that impose liabilities on directors. Besides the numerous statutory provisions that make directors liable when companies fail to remit specific day-to-day tax obligations,[4] another notable ground for liability is the environmental protection legislation whereby directors may be liable for the (potentially enormous) costs associated with environmental damage caused by their companies.

Many people think that good, honest people are being discouraged from taking on the role of directors because they are afraid of personal bankruptcy if the business runs into any kind of trouble.

It is hard to agree with this view where a company is small enough to be run by one or two directors who can, or at least should, be familiar with all of the details of the day-to-day functioning of the company. If that day-to-day functioning involves the company discharging a pollutant into a river or failing to pay its retail sales tax liability, it seems fair and appropriate that the directors who allowed those things to happen should bear the responsibility.

[4] This subject is discussed in Chapter 12.

However, when companies get past a certain size it is not realistic to believe that each director can be familiar with all aspects of the day-to-day affairs. Many functions are delegated to officers, agents and employees of the company.[5] Corporate law has always recognized this necessity. For example, many of the statutory provisions imposing liability allow, in the same breath, a "due diligence defence." For example, suppose John as a director of Goldstar Mining Corporation, hires a nationally recognized accounting firm to oversee the payment of the company's tax liability and reviews the accountants' regular statements, which show the liability being discharged on an ongoing basis. John would probably—in the absence of other factors—have a strong "due diligence defence" if, at the end of the year, the accountants were found badly in error in their work and the liability was not discharged in full.

Another protective measure for directors in these turbulent times is "director liability" insurance, which is now being developed and marketed by some insurance companies. For anyone considering a corporate directorship this product should be carefully investigated.

Historically, Canadian legislation has been, in my view, weak in assisting companies in trouble. In Part 4, I discuss the long-standing inadequacy of the provisions in the *Bankruptcy Act* designed to enable companies to reorganize. In the last few years they have been bolstered by the stronger terms of the new Act. However, many statutory provisions remain that stand in the way of what one might call "rescue attempts."

One such provision is the restriction in the *Income Tax Act* on the extent to which tax losses of a company can be used by another company which acquires the first company. In very broad terms, the rules allow the acquiring company to use the tax losses only if it is engaged in the same type of business activity as was carried on by the company with the losses.

As a taxpayer, I am as interested as anyone in seeing that all companies pay their fair share of tax. However, if a company that is in the business of manufacturing hockey pucks wants to buy the

[5] In 1991, Ontario's NDP government contemplated making corporate officers (i.e., as opposed to directors) liable for certain corporate responsibilities in its Bill-70, which contained a series of sweeping labour law reforms. However, this idea was abandoned.

shares of a troubled personnel company with large tax losses, (and which also employs 15 people) in a genuine effort to repair and preserve both that company's business, and the jobs of its 15 employees, should it make a difference—all other things being equal—if the acquired company is in the personnel business?

As it stands, Canadian legislation contains many disincentives to rescue attempts, and one of the most daunting is the massive number of director liability provisions. For example, if a company is in serious difficulty, many months in arrears with its tax remittances, and also perhaps contributing to an environmental problem, why would anyone, given the director liability provisions, take on the position of a director of such a company? Their reluctance would be reasonable even if—and this is the irony—they were one of, say, three people in Canada with the brains and vision to take the company out of its tailspin and save jobs both in that company and in those others that are dependent on the continued existence of the first company. The penalty of personal liability if the effort fails is too high and the person will probably pass on the opportunity, the company will fall into receivership or bankruptcy, and many of the jobs will be lost.

While I can respect the basic philosophy of director liability provisions, there is an ebb and flow to the process of arriving at a fair balance that addresses all of the interests of society. At the moment, the pendulum may have swung too far in the direction of making directors liable for almost every sin their company commits.

# Unsecured Creditors

T RADE DEBT CAN ARISE IN a myriad of ways. Just think of the number of entities that provide the most basic goods or services to a typical Canadian company. Inventory and equipment suppliers, personnel agencies, courier and communications companies, and advertising agencies and carriers are but a few of them.

The fundamental supply and demand forces of competition will mean that in many situations a trade creditor will supply goods or services on an unsecured basis. Because this book aims to explain legal processes, the art of good credit or accounting policies for companies is not discussed. However, I do note that by carrying out searches of the various "registry systems" which are created by some of the statutes discussed in this book, it is possible to learn information about a company which is extremely useful in evaluating how much credit they should be given. For example, a *Personal Property Security Act* search (discussed on page 7), will tell you who the registered secured creditors of a company are (at least in terms of the company's personal property). Other searches that provide information about a company are identified in Exhibit 11 of the Appendix.

What recourse do "mere" unsecured trade creditors have when customers do not pay on a timely basis? Of course, the classic remedy is to sue the debtor. However, before taking that route, trade creditors may find that they qualify for a better remedy because certain legal provisions fit their situations.

The thinking behind some of these provisions is that a trade creditor who has somehow "enhanced the value" of a piece of property belonging to a debtor should not have to wait, unpaid, while other (secured or otherwise preferred) creditors of the debtor enjoy the benefit of that work. For example, suppose that Steve owes the bank $50,000 and the bank has a security interest over all Steve's assets, which are worth about $45,000. However, one of Steve's assets, a Corvette automobile, is badly in need of repair, and suppose that Steve has $7000 worth of repair work done to the car just before he goes bankrupt, without having paid his mechanic.

It would seem unfair if the bank were able to recover $52,000 from Steve's assets[1] while the mechanic went unpaid. Fortunately, this is one situation where the law is at least somewhat in line with common sense.

## REPAIR AND STORAGE LIENS ACT

As the name implies, this statute provides protection for unpaid "repairers" and "storers." While the Act is complex, it basically creates two types of liens: Possessory Liens and Non-Possessory Liens.

## Possessory Liens

This is the type of lien that applies when the article is held onto by an unpaid repairer or storer. In other words, in our example, if Steve's mechanic refused to return Steve's car until the repair bill was paid, the mechanic would have a possessory lien over the car. The amount of the lien is the amount that the parties agreed on or, if there was no such agreement,[2] the fair value of the services.

---

[1] That is, $45,000 plus the benefit of the $7000 of work on the car (and more if the work has increased the value of the car beyond what it was before the repairs) minus any legitimate expenses of the bank.

[2] In the case of automobiles, the *Motor Vehicle Repair Act* requires clear authorizations for work to be performed.

## Non-Possessory Liens

Even if a repairer or storer surrenders the asset, he or she can still retain a lien over the asset. However, in order to do so, the person must register the lien under the *Personal Property Security Act.*[3] Also, before releasing the asset, it is imperative that the repairer obtain a signed acknowledgment of the indebtedness from the customer.

Thus, Steve's mechanic could have returned the Corvette but also could have protected him- or herself by filing a notice of a repairer's lien that would show up when anyone carried out a search for security registrations against Steve.

## Collecting a Debt Under the *Repair and Storage Liens Act*

As with security agreements governed by the *Personal Property Security Act,* the two main ways of enforcing rights under the *Repair and Storage Liens Act* are to retain the article (in satisfaction of the debt) or to sell it.

In order to retain the collateral, a repairer or storer with a possessory lien must give 30 days' notice to the customer, to anyone else with a security interest registered against the customer under the *Personal Property Security Act,* and to certain others.

Repairers and storers with non-possessory liens can force the sale of the article if 60 days have elapsed since they were supposed to have been paid. At that point, the repairer can instruct the sheriff to sell the article, although a further notice must then be sent to the customer, other registered secured creditors, etc.

If all of the technicalities are observed, a lien under the *Repair and Storage Liens Act* will rank first among all claims to the goods whose value has been enhanced by the repairer or storer.

---

[3] For these purposes, a financing statement is used. Interestingly, while *Personal Property Security Act* registrations can be made electronically (as mentioned on page 7), *Repair and Storage Liens Act* registration forms must be typed and filed in person at government offices.

## CONSTRUCTION LIEN ACT

The *Construction Lien Act* is designed to provide a similar basic level of protection for people who enhance the value of real property through their services as the *Repair and Storage Liens Act* does for people who enhance the value of personal property. However, like the construction process itself, the *Construction Lien Act* can be complicated—some would classify it as one of the trickiest statutes on the books.

Basically, the Act tries to protect contractors through three mechanisms: (i) a trust entitlement, (ii) a holdback requirement, and (iii) lien rights.

To understand these three ideas, let us look at an example. Brockington Enterprises Ltd. hires an architect to design a new building for its head office, to be erected on a large piece of vacant land that it owns. With the architect's drawings in hand, Brockington Enterprises enters into an agreement with Gordon General Contracting Ltd. for the construction of the building. In order to fund the construction, Brockington borrows $10 million from a bank, to be secured by a mortgage and to be advanced in monthly stages, as the construction work is carried out.

Gordon Contracting in turn enters into a number of subcontracts to secure all of the different services required to erect the building. One of those subcontractors is Morris Electrical Services Inc., which will attend to all of the building's electrical work. To ensure that it has everything it needs, Morris Electrical enters into a subcontract with McNeil Wire Ltd..

## Trust Entitlements

As previously noted (see pages 36 to 37), trust property held by someone does not form part of the property that can be divided among that person's creditors. Thus, if that person becomes insolvent—by, for example, going into receivership or bankruptcy, as discussed in Parts 2 and 3—the trust property is effectively removed from the process and can be claimed directly by the person entitled to the benefit of the trust.

In our case, suppose that McNeil Wire billed Morris Electrical for $5000 during the third month of construction. For that same month,

Morris Electrical performed work worth $10,000 and so Morris presented bills totalling $15,000 to Gordon Contracting for that month. After the next advance of funds by the bank, Brockington Enterprises forwarded some of the money it owed to Gordon Contracting.[4]

However, what if Gordon Contracting is, at that exact moment, in financial difficulty? Unfortunately, many companies in the construction business got into trouble in the 1990s due to overexpansion when times were good. Let us suppose that the day after Gordon Contracting receives the money (and before it has done anything with it), it is placed into receivership by its main secured creditor, a bank.

In that situation, the *Construction Lien Act* stipulates that Morris Electrical's share of the money received by Gordon Contracting is held by Gordon Contracting "in trust" for Morris Electrical.[5] Thus, Gordon Contracting's bank cannot use that money, which is technically in Gordon Contracting's possession, to pay down Gordon Contracting's debt to that bank. Nothing in law is simple and, in practice, there can be problems with identifying trust property in these situations. (See the earlier discussion of identifying or tracing trust property on pages 37 to 38.) However the most entitlement is a powerful provision in the *Construction Lien Act*.

## The Holdback Requirement

The trust entitlement exists regardless of whether Morris Electrical or anyone else in the construction process does anything. However, the *Construction Lien Act* contains many other provisions that necessitate action and one of these is the holdback requirement.

In our example, Brockington Enterprises has to retain or "hold back" 10 percent of all the money billed to it by Gordon Contracting

[4] As discussed ahead, because of the "holdback requirement," as a matter of practice, the amount which Gordon Contracting would receive from Brockington would not be the entire $15,000.

[5] Note that the trust obligation of Gordon Contracting does not relate to McNeil Wiring, because Gordon Contracting did not have a subcontract directly with McNeil; however, if Morris Electrical obtains the funds from Gordon Contracting, Morris Electrical will hold McNeil Wire's share of the money in trust for McNeil Wire.

until those funds can be released in accordance with the *Construction Lien Act*.[6] The idea is that if Gordon Contracting goes into receivership or bankruptcy, a limited fund will be available for companies like Morris and McNeil to pursue if they are unable to recover what they are owed from Gordon Contracting. The fund is not supposed to represent a precise calculation of what their shortfall might ultimately be—it is meant to provide a rough measure of protection only.

If there is no difficulty with a project, the holdbacks are eventually released, usually shortly after the project is "substantially complete"[7] and according to the formula provided for in the *Construction Lien Act*. However, it is possible to get the money out earlier in cases where individual subcontracts can be certified as being complete.

## Lien Rights

There are two types of lien rights under the *Construction Lien Act*. The general contractor—Gordon Contracting, in our example—has a lien right over the entire project for the work performed. As that work is paid for by Brockington Enterprises, the lien claim is regularly "satisfied." However, if Gordon Contracting carried out a substantial amount of work without getting paid—say $900,000 worth, which should have been paid in three monthly payments of $300,000 each (minus the 10% holdback)—then Gordon Contracting would have a lien against the project for the whole $900,000.

[6] The *Construction Lien Act* contains some very esoteric provisions, and one of them contemplates holdbacks by more persons than just the owner of the real estate being worked on, and possibly more than 10 percent of the monies otherwise payable. In other words, in our example, Gordon Contracting might also have to comply with the holdback provision.

[7] That is, as the expression suggests, it is not necessary for every last lightbulb to be screwed in for the project to be substantially complete. Basically, the *Construction Lien Act* contemplates that the architect will "certify" that the project is substantially complete, as measured by the cost of the balance of the work required. At that point, an advertisement of the substantial completion is published, and a brief limitation period starts running after which—if no construction liens are registered against the project, as discussed in the next section—the holdback can be released.

The subcontractors—including Morris Electrical and McNeil Wire in our example—have lien rights over the project that are limited to the amount of the holdbacks just discussed. Again, these liens are a matter of academic interest only as long as everyone is getting paid regularly.

Construction liens are pursued in two stages: the first is registering notice of the lien on title and the second is launching a specialized type of lawsuit to substantiate the claim. There are strict deadlines for registering liens on title. (If no liens are registered, holdback monies can be released, as already mentioned, following substantial completion of the entire project or, in some cases, completion of an individual subcontract.) There is also a limitation period that begins on the last date on which the subcontractor supplied material or services.[8]

If all of the many requirements of registering the lien are met, a validly perfected construction lien will bind or encumber the land and ultimately a sale of the land can be forced by the party in whose favour the lien is. If the owner has not met all the applicable holdback requirements, the construction lien(s) can even take priority over any building mortgage used by the owner to pay out the sums that were supposed to have been held back.

## Stoppage in Transit

One of the more arcane remedies available to trade creditors in Ontario is the right of stoppage in transit, which is given to sellers under the Province's *Sale of Goods Act* when a seller learns that a buyer has become insolvent. As the term suggests, this right applies only if, at that precise moment, there are goods in transit from the seller.

Special rules may apply if the goods have been resold to a third party,[9] but if those rules do not limit the remedy, the supplier is entitled to stop delivery of the goods and to reclaim them.

---

[8] This limitation period is relevant only if the lien rights have not expired according to other rules.

[9] These rules are somewhat tricky and include consideration of the extent of the seller's knowledge of such a re-sale.

## SUING TO COLLECT A DEBT: THE LAST RESORT

A lawsuit is really the last refuge for someone trying to collect a debt and who cannot benefit from any of the rights or remedies set out so far in this chapter and in Chapters 1, 2, and 3.

In civil litigation, there are none of the advantages that are afforded by either contractual security agreements between companies or statutory privileges, such as those available to governments, landlords, or the beneficiaries of construction liens. Instead, the parties must simply battle it out, building their case step by step until they finally get their day in court.

However, even if the person who starts the lawsuit (known as the plaintiff) is successful in court and wins the case against the person he or she has sued, (that is, the defendant) that is only half the battle. The other half is recovering that money from the defendant's assets.

Certainly, the system of civil litigation is not perfect. It is slow, expensive, and the plain truth is that defendants often pay their lawyers to further slow down the process. At the same time, plaintiffs are not lily-white; there are also far too many frivolous lawsuits that clog up the system, and we all end up paying for them to one extent or other.

Yet our legal system is still the envy of most of the world. And, for those who are willing to commit the necessary time and effort, it does work: ultimately, defendants who owe money and who have no real defence will be made to pay.

## The Lawsuit: When and How to Begin

There is no limit to the ways in which debts can arise out of business dealings and there is no limit to the number of excuses that can be and are offered to explain non-payment. Each situation has to be analyzed on its own terms as to whether formal litigation is necessary. This evaluation must, of course, include an analysis of the cost of the litigation as well as the likelihood of success in executing the judgment (i.e., turning the judgment into money).

If a creditor decides to litigate, it is typical for his or her lawyer to send a comprehensive demand letter to the debtor. This letter would outline the creditor's version of the facts, call for payment, and indicate that a lawsuit will be commenced should the debtor fail to comply.

## The Statement of Claim

If no satisfactory response is received to the demand letter, the next step is completing a statement of claim, which sets out the facts that give rise to this cause of action for unpaid debt.[10] The statement of claim is filed with the court—in Ontario, the Ontario Court of Justice, General Division—unless the amount being claimed is less than $6000, in which case the more streamlined forum of the small claims court (or, as it is formally known, the Provincial Court, Civil Division) is available.

## The Canadian System of Costs

In the United States, both parties to a lawsuit essentially pay their own way. That is not the case in Canada where, generally speaking, the losing party will be responsible for most of the costs of the other party. In other words, suppose that Bob's Trucking Inc. sued TransNational Enterprises Ltd. for $400,000 for services rendered. If Bob's is successful, the court will rule that TransNational must pay Bob's the $400,000 plus interest *and* most of its legal costs. On the other hand, if the lawsuit was ill advised and the court dismisses the claim entirely, Bob's will probably be ordered to pay a portion of TransNational's legal costs.

In my view, the Canadian system of costs is a powerful deterrent to unnecessary litigation.[11]

---

[10] Of course, lawsuits are used to address all manner of disputes from defamation to slipping on a sidewalk. In this discussion, I am concerned only with litigation designed to collect payment of business debts. However, even within that category, no two pieces of litigation are exactly alike.

[11] The *Rules of Civil Procedure* even contemplate that, at the outset, a party being sued can challenge the other party's ability to pay costs if the lawsuit is eventually unsuccessful. I also note that, as of the date of writing, the long-established American system is coming under review.

## The Initial Deadlines in the Lawsuit

Once a statement of claim has been filed with the court, it must be "served on," that is, delivered to, the defendant. If the defendant makes a conscious attempt to avoid delivery, this process can be difficult. On the other hand, the process is a mere formality if the defendant has a lawyer who is willing to accept service on his or her behalf.

Once the statement of claim has been served, the defendant has 20 days to file a one-page form called an "appearance," signifying his or her intention to file a statement of defence. The statement of defence is required within 10 days of filing the appearance.

Although it can seem frustrating to plaintiffs, their lawyer will often suggest that the defendant's lawyer be given more than the minimum 30 days to file the statement of defence. This is because the defendant's lawyer often has a valid excuse for not being able to move that quickly. Also, in the course of a long, drawn-out lawsuit, the plaintiff will probably want some reciprocal courtesy from the defendant at some point.

## Default Judgment

If the defendant refuses to file a statement of defence, it is possible for the plaintiff's lawyer to move for what is called default judgment, which allows the plaintiff to proceed with the enforcement steps (i.e., actually collecting on the unpaid debt) discussed below.

## The Statement of Defence

While the statement of claim is supposed to set out the facts that give rise to the lawsuit, the statement of defence is supposed to answer those allegations. Neither the statement of claim nor the statement of defence should include the details of the actual evidence that will be used to prove either side's allegations.

For example, if the plaintiff says he was appointed the exclusive distributor of the defendant's products in Ontario, he should simply say that in the statement of claim and not go on to recite details of all of his agreements with the defendant on this point. Similarly, if the defendant disputes the plaintiff had any such appointment, he should deny it in the statement of claim and not go on to list, and quote from, twelve different letters and memoranda.

Unfortunately, in the real world, many statements of defence amount to delay tactics in that all sorts of allegations of improper conduct on behalf of the plaintiff are set out. A lawyer for the plaintiff often has to calm down a client who is infuriated by allegations in a statement of defence that, for example, his goods or services were defective.

## Summary Judgment

Sometimes, although one party is resisting the other party's position, the statement of claim or the statement of defence is, in plain terms, so bad that, even if every statement made in it were found to be true,[12] the relief requested would still not be granted. For example, suppose that a plaintiff tried to claim a real estate commission based on an oral agreement. Sometimes Courts will uphold oral agreements but there is a specific statute in Ontario[13] which says that an agreement to pay a real estate commission must be in writing. In such a case, the defendant could apply to the court for an order dismissing the claim at the outset. It can also work the other way around; that is, sometimes a plaintiff can move for summary judgment after the filing of a statement of defence which is inadequate even if every statement in it is potentially valid.

## Affidavit of Documents

After the statement of claim and the statement of defence (which are sometimes called "pleadings") have been exchanged, both sides have to prepare an affidavit listing all of the documents in their possession that relate to the lawsuit. Certain documents—such as correspondence between a client and a lawyer—may be considered "privileged" and do not have to be listed in the affidavit.

---

[12] Of course, many statements in statements of claim and statements of defence are ultimately found to be untrue at the trial.

[13] The *Real Estate and Business Brokers Act*. The statute goes on to deal with a number of other matters governing real estate brokers.

## Discoveries

In the discovery phase of a lawsuit, the plaintiff and the defendant must make someone with knowledge of the case available to be examined under oath concerning the action. The proceedings are tape-recorded, and a transcript of the answers is made available. Sometimes the person may not be able to give a precise answer to a question but can be required to follow up on the issue and to provide the results of that inquiry.

Many lawsuits are settled after the discovery because that is when the parties put their cards on the table. Put another way, it is difficult for a plaintiff or a defendant to change his or her story after the discovery because if they do so, they are destroying their credibility. For example, if a plaintiff admits at discovery that he really did not know if another company was responsible for a certain debt, he does not look very good if he tries to say at trial that he was, in fact, positive all along that the defendant took on this liability.

## The Trial

If they cannot settle things after the discoveries are in, the parties go to trial. Once in court, lawyers put months of painstaking preparatory work to use by:

- introducing the evidence through (non-leading) questions put to (well-prepared) witnesses;

- trying to break down the other side's case by cross-examination;

- objecting when the rules of evidence are not being respected, and, finally

- delivering argument to show why the judge should make certain findings of fact, and why, in turn, a particular legal result should follow from those findings.

In the type of lawsuit we are considering, that finding is that the defendant is liable to pay the plaintiff a certain amount of money.

## Small Claims Court Proceedings

Lawsuits are expensive and time-consuming. However, in Ontario there is some relief from both of these pressures when the amount at issue is less than $6000. Claims under that amount can be litigated in what is known as small claims court.[14] As with cases in the "regular" court,[15] the first formal document in a small claims court lawsuit is a statement of claim, to which the defendant, also as in a regular court, is supposed to respond by filing a statement of defence. However, the proceedings move more quickly in a small claims court, and there are fewer restrictions about what can or cannot be put into these documents. For example, often the statements, or pleadings, will include evidence—such as an unpaid purchase order. Also, there is usually no discovery process, although there will often be what is called a "pre-trial conference" in which the parties describe their case and how they intend to prove it to a court officer, with the goal of settlement.[16]

At the trial, less emphasis is put on technical rules of evidence, although the judges are experienced and know how to evaluate evidence.[17] Certainly, most parties presenting cases in small claims court will do so without a lawyer.

As with regular lawsuits, if the plaintiff is successful in a small claims court action, the result will be a judgment to the effect that the defendant is liable for the amount of the debt, plus an amount for interest and costs.

## ENFORCING A JUDGMENT: COLLECTING ON THE DEBT

Obviously, the point of the effort and expense put into obtaining a judgment against someone is to get access to enough of the debtor's assets, and, if necessary, convert them into money, so as to collect the amount of the judgment. The two main ways in which "judgment

---

[14] The proper name is the Provincial Court (Civil Division), as already noted on page 51.

[15] Properly called the Court of Justice (General Division), as noted on page 51.

[16] There are also "pre-trials" with some cases tried in the Court of Justice (General Division).

[17] In other words, if every single piece of evidence presented by one side is hearsay or is delivered in response to leading questions, the judge probably will not give that side's case much weight.

creditors" (i.e., creditors who have obtained judgments) can achieve that goal are: forcing the sale of one or more pieces of the debtor's property, or gaining access to amounts of money either belonging or payable to the debtor. Unfortunately for judgment creditors, however, those mechanisms are much more complicated than they sound.

## The Priority of Secured Claims and Other Claims

Basically, a judgment creditor can only enforce a judgment against what is left over and above the amount of any security interests, liens, deemed trusts, and so on which apply to the debtor's assets. This amount is often referred to as the debtor's "equity" in the property.

For example, suppose that Smith & Jones Advertising Ltd. provides $25,000 worth of advertising services for Capital Productions Inc. For some reason Capital Productions will not pay the bill, and Smith & Jones eventually obtains a judgment for the $25,000, plus interest and legal costs. At that point, Capital Productions owns the following assets:

1) A piece of real property, which might have been worth as much as $800,000 in the late 1980s but which is now worth about $350,000; and

2) Personal property with a total value of $155,000, consisting of: equipment worth $75,000, inventory worth $15,000, accounts receivable worth $50,000, and $15,000 in the bank.

There is a mortgage registered against the real property for $400,000 in favour of an insurance company, and there is also a construction lien against the real property for $30,000 relating to an addition put on the building 10 months ago.

Capital Productions also owes $50,000 to the same bank in which it has $15,000 invested, and the bank has a general security agreement, registered under the *Personal Property Security Act*, in support of the $50,000 debt. In addition, Capital's photocopier is subject to a purchase money security interest for $10,000, also registered under the *Personal Property Security Act*.

Capital Productions, then, has no equity in its real property, and its personal property is worth only $95,000 more than the secured debt against it. What if, in addition, most of the accounts receivable cannot be collected for one reason or other and that Capital Productions has not been withholding the income tax, U.I., and C.P.P. payments it was supposed to have withheld, and not paying all of its provincial sales tax and GST liabilities, so that various government claims now cover Capital Productions's assets? Furthermore, the deficiency in secured claims (the mortgage and construction lien) against the real property totals $430,000, but the value of the property is now only $350,000. Therefore, there is $80,000 in real estate debts that cannot be satisfied by the value of that real property. This means that both the insurance company and the construction lien claimant are going to be looking to join Smith & Jones in pursuing the personal property of Capital Productions, for the amounts they are not able to recover from Capital Productions's real property.

The difficulty a judgment debtor faces in trying to collect on debts ties into two points made elsewhere in this book. As was mentioned on page 43, it would have been possible for Smith & Jones to carry out searches for security registrations against Capital Productions at any stage during Smith & Jones's dealings with the company, in order to uncover the existence of creditors like the bank, the insurance company, and the construction lien claimant. Also, although in our example the security interests appear to be "legitimate," as discussed in Chapter 13, judgment creditors should always consider whether security that appears to rank ahead of them will, in fact, stand up to scrutiny.

## Judgment Debtor Examinations: Trying to Locate the Money

One of the primary ways in which a judgment creditor can gain information about a corporate debtor (such as what assets do they have? what assets are they going to have? and what assets have they disposed of?) is by examining an officer of the company under oath about the company's affairs. By law, a judgment creditor is entitled to conduct such an examination once after obtaining the judgment, and once a year thereafter.[18] Judgment debtor

18 The court can order the debtor company to make a representative available more frequently. Also, when necessary, the debtor company may be ordered to send a representative with better knowledge of the company's affairs than the one it initially sends.

examinations are a serious matter and if a representative of a corporate debtor persistently fails to show up on schedule, he or she can face spending some time in jail.

In the Smith & Jones example, suppose that the Capital Productions officer being examined under oath disclosed that, in addition to the assets listed above, Capital Productions had an art collection worth $70,000 and would soon have a good quality account receivable of $50,000 from a company in Ottawa. Suppose that the officer also indicated that the other receivables were also of good quality and that all government debts were fully paid.

These revelations would mean that things are looking up for Smith & Jones' collection efforts—but the work is still not over.

## Collecting on Debts by Selling the Debtor's Property

In order to sell the property of a judgment debtor, a creditor must first apply to the court for what is called a "writ of seizure and sale," which sets out the particulars of the judgment the creditor has obtained.

Writs of seizure and sale may then be registered against title to the debtor's real property and delivered to the local sheriff for purposes of binding whatever equity value there is in the debtor's personal property. Eventually, the sheriff can even be called upon to seize and sell the property, although this is an extremely slow and difficult process.[19] Also, because sheriffs are understandably cautious about seizing property that has no equity value, they will require the creditor who has filed the writ, and who has instructed them to initiate the sale process, to sign an indemnity agreement in favour of the sheriff, whereby the sheriff's costs are covered should he or she inadvertently trip over the rights of, for example, a secured creditor.

Thus, in our example, Smith & Jones would probably have to sign an indemnity agreement in favour of the sheriff, covering his costs for the attempted seizure of the real property. Smith & Jones will not recover any of the debt owed them from the value of the real property, since, in this case, the full value must go towards satisfying the debts to secured creditors. Smith & Jones would also

---

[19] Also, sheriff's sales tend to be perceived as "fire sales," and as such do not bring the best possible prices.

have to respect the position of the bank and other secured creditors in instructing the sheriff to seize and sell some of Capital Productions[20] personal property in order to satisfy the approximately $25,000 judgment that Smith & Jones has obtained.

Even after the assets have been sold, the sheriff will by law hold on to the proceeds for 30 days before distributing them to all creditors who have filed an appropriate notice of their claim.

## Garnishment of Income: Another Option for Reclaiming Debt

It is always better to gain access to money in order to satisfy any sums owed to you than to have to seize and sell assets. If a judgment debtor is supposed to receive money from a third party, a judgment creditor may intercept those monies by obtaining a notice of garnishment from the court that is then served on the person who owes the money to the debtor.

In our example, the Ottawa company that owes $50,000 to Capital Productions must pay the money to the sheriff and not to Capital Productions. Under the *Rules of Civil Procedure,* it must also do so on a timely basis. If it does not comply on both counts, the Ottawa company risks being liable to pay the money again.[21]

---

[20] In practice, there would be a lot of give and take between the various parties in this scenario. For example, if Smith & Jones pushed things this far, Capital Productions would likely reach into its pocket and just pay the debt, rather than risking its bank's annoyance (i.e., because its borrower's creditors were "executing" against its assets) and shaking its confidence in Capital Productions's ability to repay its loan. Also, the value of the photocopier subject to the purchase money security interest could be negligible and there might be no advantage in seizing it. In other words, there would have to be some attempt to seize and sell assets in a systematic manner, so as to look after the secured creditors before freeing up some equity value for the Smith & Jones judgement to attach to.

[21] Note that although the bank's security over the assets of Capital Productions includes a charge over its accounts receivables, until those "account debtors" (such as the Ottawa company) have received proper written notice in accordance with the *Personal Property Security Act,* as discussed on page 15, they are entitled to make payment in accordance with other legal requirements, such as their contractual relations with Capital Productions or a notice of garnishment.

# TWO

Corporate Receivership

I N PART 1 I TALKED about the legal framework within which security is obtained and the ways that the assets of a corporate debtor are sold pursuant to that security. However, general security agreements, mortgages, and *Bank Act* security also typically give the secured party the power to appoint a receiver over all of the debtor's property. Receivers do a lot more than mechanically sell assets; they usually operate the debtor's business to some extent and at least attempt to sell either all or part of the debtor's business as a going concern. The goal of receiverships is to maximize the recovery of the debt from sales pursuant to general security agreements, mortgages, and other security. Chapters 5 to 8 will discuss how that process works.

Many Canadian companies, both large and small, have gone into receivership over the past five years. The examples have become so numerous that many people believe that banks and other secured creditors are far too eager to put companies into receivership.

From my experience, this perception is not well founded. Think of it from the banker's point of view. By putting a company into receivership the banker loses the income stream from the loan. If the borrower is beyond a certain size, details of the receivership, including the fact that the bank initiated it, may be reported in the press. Also, the receivership will give rise to dozens of tough decisions that must be considered and addressed over a concentrated period when there will be lots of other demands on the banker's time. Does that sound like fun?

I believe that in the overwhelming majority of receiverships the borrower is given adequate time to avoid the receivership, and that it becomes the only option when that time runs out. However, that statement begs the question, what is adequate notice before a bank is entitled to put a company into receivership?

This question and others dealing with how to avoid receivership, the regulation and conduct of receivers, and the rights of unpaid suppliers will be discussed in the following chapters.

# The Law and Practice of Calling Loans

## BEFORE THE *BANKRUPTCY AND INSOLVENCY ACT*

At one time, receiverships in Canada often occurred in a breathtakingly crude manner. Even where a business debtor had dealt with a creditor for many years and with respect to a large amount of debt, it was the conventional wisdom that where the loan documentation said that the loan was payable on demand, the creditor had the right to "pull the plug" at any time and with virtually no notice.

Although it might sound unbelievable now, creditors would sometimes appear at the doorstep of their debtor with a demand letter and another person in their company. Once the debtor had read the letter and looked up from his or her desk, the secured creditor would ask the debtor if he or she could pay the debt immediately. If the debtor indicated that he or she could not (which would be understandable if the debt was large) the other person would then be introduced as the receiver who was now in charge of the company, in accordance with the security documentation that the debtor had signed.

This practice came to a screeching halt in the late 1970s with a major case called *Lister v. Dunlop*. What that case held, in essence, was that this way of calling a loan and appointing a receiver was unacceptable and that, according to basic English common law principles, a business debtor was entitled to a meaningful amount of notice before a business loan could be called and the security enforced (even where the loan documentation said that the loan was payable on demand).

What constituted reasonable notice became the next great legal question and lawyers, insolvency practitioners, creditors, and debtors agonized over it during the decade or so following the *Lister v. Dunlop* decision. Of course, other such cases ended up in court and eventually a number of factors came to be identified as relevant to making this decision.

In a case called *Mister Broadloom Corp. v. Bank of Montreal*, the Ontario Court of Appeal identified the following factors for consideration in assessing how much time a creditor should give a debtor in calling a demand loan:

1) the size of the debt;
2) the risk to the security holder of not being able to realize on its security;
3) the extent of the relationship between the creditor and the debtor company;
4) the character and reputation of the debtors, and whether they had misled, attempted fraudulent preferences, or similar acts; and
5) the chances that the debtor could raise the money.

Predictably the pendulum swung a bit over the years. First cautious lenders and their advisers gave extraordinarily long notice periods. But, after some court decisions maintained that in many circumstances only a few days' notice was required, notice periods began getting shorter. If there was one thing you could say about this sensitive subject of calling loans, it was that each case was different and had to be examined carefully on its own facts.[1]

---

[1] Of course, the consequences of a wrong call could be devastating for either side. The *Lister v. Dunlop* case was a strong example of where the creditor was found not to have given sufficient notice; and the ultimate judgment was that the appointment of the receiver was invalid and the creditor was liable for significant damages (including punitive damages, which are seldom awarded) for trespass. Where appropriate, the debtor would also have a (potentially huge) claim for, in broad terms, "destroying a viable business unnecessarily."

## THE EFFECT OF THE *BANKRUPTCY AND INSOLVENCY ACT* ON CALLING LOANS

What the 1992 *Bankruptcy and Insolvency Act* has brought to the process of calling loans is a *minimum* statutory notice requirement. The Act requires that "a secured creditor who intends to enforce a security on all or substantially all of the ... inventory ... accounts receivable or ... other property of an insolvent person ... used in relation to, a business" must send a notice, in a prescribed form, at least ten days prior to enforcing the security. A sample notice is included in the Appendix (Exhibit 12).

Note, however, that this *Bankruptcy and Insolvency Act* notice is a basic statutory requirement that does not replace the common law notice requirements discussed earlier in this chapter. This point is important because it means that the common law requirement of adequate notice is still very much alive and that, in some circumstances, the debtor may be entitled to more than just ten days' notice.

For example, suppose Acme Worldwide Enterprises Limited has been doing business with its bank for 35 years. Over that time, Acme has grown from being a small customer of the bank to being one of its 50 largest customers. Its business, which started out in a small town in Ontario with 10 employees, has grown to the stage where it is carried on in seven provinces and in the United States and now employs 900.

Acme has always been a good customer and has not only paid all of its bills but has also observed all of the numerous reporting requirements (such as, the delivery of regular financial statements, internal and audited) and performance requirements (for example, maintaining certain debt/equity and working capital ratios) imposed by its bank over the years. However, after years of profitability, Acme has lost money for the past two years due to a number of factors beyond its control and has begun making minor defaults in the use of its credit facilities.

If Acme's bank decided that it wanted to end its long relationship with Acme by calling the loan and appointing a receiver if Acme did not pay up, the bank would probably have to give Acme more than the minimum ten days' notice required by the *Bankruptcy and Insolvency Act*.

In summing up this discussion of calling loans, I would make the following points. First, one of the major consequences of the

*Lister v. Dunlop* line of cases is that there is now much more communication between banks and their borrowers. A good portion of this communication is informal, but much of it is also made up of very formal reporting by borrowers to their bankers.

Many borrowers chafe at these detailed reporting requirements because they are time-consuming and may be costly, but the desirable goal of all this communication is that the banker be on top of the borrower's situation so that any problems are known about at an early stage. By discussing problems early, the banker may even be able to help the borrower before it is too late.

Because of this increased communication, in most cases, the decision to call a loan and seek the appointment of a receiver no longer occurs suddenly, in a panicky atmosphere, and that is in the best interests of both borrowers and secured creditors.[2]

Banks (and their borrowers) were heading in the direction of this increased, steady communication before the introduction of the *Bankruptcy and Insolvency Act* minimum ten-day notice requirement, and so the introduction of the requirement has not radically affected the way secured loans are administered. Therefore, in most cases when the bank decides to call a loan and to seek the appointment of a receiver, the borrower cannot say that the bank's displeasure with the borrower's performance and the bank's desire to have the borrower pay back the loan and find a new bank have not already been discussed for some times.

Having said all that, when the decision to call a loan is made, in most cases the bank will not have to give more than the minimum ten days' notice required by the *Bankruptcy and Insolvency Act* before a receiver can be appointed. In other words, the example of Acme Worldwide Enterprises Limited is exceptional: most Canadian small businesses will not, in the final analysis, get more than the minimum ten-days' notice their banker is required by law to give.

---

[2] In the kind of hair-splitting analysis that characterizes the practice of law, it should be noted that a borrower could be in default in its loan arrangements with its bank but not yet legally "insolvent." As noted above, the ten-day notice requirement only applies when the debtor is "insolvent," so it is possible to imagine situations where the bank is so "on top of the borrower" that the ten-day notice is not required.

## Avoiding Receivership: Forbearance Agreements

Is there a middle ground between the debtor paying out the loan in full and the finality (some would say, brutality) of a receivership? The answer is yes, but only in some cases.

Occasionally, lenders are prepared to enter into forbearance agreements, which means they agree not to enforce their security (i.e., by appointing a receiver) for a stipulated length of time and on stipulated conditions. From the lender's viewpoint, these agreements are appropriate in situations such as the following:

- The debtor is prepared to admit, in writing and with the benefit of informed legal advice, that he or she has committed an act of default. That is important because the debtor is conceding, in an enforceable manner, that the lender does not need to go through the complex procedure of again calling the loan and enduring all of the delay (and cost) that goes with that process if, in the future, the debtor commits another defined act of default.

- Despite the fact that the debtor has committed an act of default, his or her situation has not deteriorated so badly that the lender has lost all faith that the debtor can continue in business, albeit under a tighter leash, in order to repay the loan over time. That is, a forbearance agreement will typically set out detailed reporting and performance agreements over and above those the debtor agreed to at the time of the original loan.

There is really no limit on what can go into a forbearance agreement. Lenders will, of course, try to obtain any number of commitments to bolster their positions. For example, if the individual shareholders of a corporate borrower have not previously been called upon to guarantee the loan, they may be required to do so as part of the forbearance arrangements. The lender will also probably require a forbearance fee.

The classic requirement that lenders also usually ask for in a forbearance agreement is for the borrower to allow a designated insolvency firm access to the borrower's operations for a specific amount

of time and on specific terms[3] to monitor the business and to prepare a detailed report on the debtor's business. From a borrower's
viewpoint, this clause is often seen as a "killer" for a number of reasons including the fact that the fee for the monitorship engagement
is usually quite steep—at, of course, a time when the borrower
needs to make optimal use of its funds. Also, most borrowers feel
that the results of the monitorship study will be a foregone conclusion: namely, a recommendation that the borrower's business is not
salvageable and that the borrower should immediately be put into
receivership (with, borrowers predict, the same insolvency firm as
receiver,[4] thereby allowing it to earn even more fees).

This perception on the part of borrowers is incorrect: the insolvency firms have too much to lose if they relax their ethical obligations and their professional standards by making an unwarranted
recommendation to put a company into receivership. The insolvency community is a small one, and no one file is worth developing a
bad reputation within that community. However, I am not suggesting that borrowers should not negotiate as strongly as possible over
the issue of whether a monitor be allowed on their premises,[5] and if
so, on what terms, as part of an overall forbearance agreement.

Even if the attempt to negotiate a forbearance agreement ends
in failure, from the lender's viewpoint, the effort may help show
that the lender was especially fair in the way it called the loan, and
that may help deter any litigation by the borrower over that issue.[6]
On the other hand, the borrower can try to make the negotiations
"off the record" (the legal term for which is "without prejudice")
and, in fact, in some circumstances the lender will also want the
discussions to occur on that basis.

---

[3] The insolvency firm's activities are always carefully set out in a description that
includes limits on how much they will do. For example, these agreements always explic-
itly state that the insolvency firm will not take part in the borrower's management activities nor will it conduct an audit of the borrower's business, although in many ways, an
investigation of this nature is more thorough than an audit.

[4] Some banks have a policy to the effect that a firm which has done monitorship work
with respect to a borrower, on behalf of that bank, cannot also act as receiver on behalf
of that same bank with respect to the same borrower.

[5] Even if they are not convinced that the monitor will recommend a receivership,

## Evaluating a Forbearance Agreement

A corporate borrower must ask itself the following two basic questions in evaluating a forbearance agreement:

1) In exchange for all of the consideration the lender wants from me, how much "forbearance time" am I getting? In other words, it is obviously a bad deal for a borrower and its owner to give up a personal guarantee and to pay a large forbearance fee if the forbearance period is only two weeks.

2) Although I have defaulted in my loan arrangements, which I am prepared to admit by signing the forbearance agreement, do I have a future with this bank or must I immediately start looking for a new source of financing? This question is obviously related to the first one in that if the borrower has to find a new bank, he or she must try to get as much forbearance time and as much scope to operate their business as they can in order to get the best possible financing terms from the new bank. In turn, how much time they are able to get will depend on a number of factors such as how badly the present bank's security position is eroding and, of course, how realistic it is to think that new financing will be available.

A borrower will need to muster all of his or her professional resources—accountants, lawyers, and possibly also an insolvency professional—to conduct forbearance agreement negotiations. It is also critical that these people be brought into the picture at the earliest possible time. There is not much that a lawyer or an

---

borrowers also typically think that, despite its large fee, the monitor will not tell the borrower (or the bank) anything that is not already known. In other words, borrowers in these situation often say, "Look, I know what my problem is; I lost two big customers, I have to cut some overhead, I have too much debt. I don't need to pay big fees for someone to produce a report telling me that." Sometimes it is true that the borrower has already identified all of his or her problems. However, in many cases the monitor's "fresh look" will uncover issues that neither the borrower nor the bank has seen.

6 A monitor's report can also serve this function if it endorses the idea that a receivership is inevitable.

accountant can do when they receive a call at 8:00 p.m. at home from a corporate client who is going to go into receivership the next day, and who would like to see if a forbearance agreement can be negotiated.[7]

---

[7] Reference may be made to Part 4; there, other options for troubled borrowers are also explored.

# Receivers: Private and Court-Appointed

## PRIVATE RECEIVERS: THEIR REGULATION AND CONDUCT

For many years the term "receiver" was not expressly defined in any statute. As noted in the Introduction, although receiverships were common in Canada, particularly during the recessions starting at the beginning and end of the 1980s, no one statute took on the subject of receiverships. Instead, many of them, including the *Personal Property Security Act* and the *Mortgages Act*, imposed obligations on secured creditors which, in turn, served to regulate receivers to some degree. But, in 1992, the federal government, seeing a need for more direct regulation of the receivership process, brought it within the scope of its new legislation, the *Bankruptcy and Insolvency Act*.[1]

The Act defines a receiver as including someone who has been appointed under a security agreement to take "possession or control" of "all or substantially all" of the inventory, accounts receivable, or property of, a commercial borrower. This definition probably conforms with the way most people picture a receiver.

---

[1] The name of the Act reflects the fact that a receivership is *not* the same as a bankruptcy, a difference to be discussed in Part 3.

A secured lender can appoint a receiver where

1) a security agreement gives the secured lender that power;

2) the debtor has not repaid the debt after receiving an appropriate opportunity to do so;

3) the debtor and the lender either did not enter into any kind of forbearance agreement or, if they did, default occurred under that agreement or the forbearance period expired; and

4) the debtor has not sought some form of protection from the courts to prevent the receivership, or the term of any such protection has expired.[2]

To examine the workings of the federal government's legislation with respect to receivers, let us take the example of a company called the Great Canadian Garment Corporation, which operates two manufacturing facilities, one in Toronto and one in St. Catharines. It owns the facility in St. Catharines, subject to a mortgage in favour of its bank, and leases the facility in Toronto. In addition, a few years ago, at the height of the real estate boom, Great Canadian borrowed more money from the bank to acquire a large piece of raw land in Oakville, which was to be the site of a new manufacturing and factory outlet facility.

Great Canadian has about 200 employees, most of whom are unionized. The company has gross sales of several million dollars per year, with hundreds of different customers, both domestic and international. Although it has been intending to standardize its sales agreements, the agreements Great Canadian has with these customers are a patchwork quilt of agreements with varying arrangements concerning when goods must be paid for, and so on. Currently, the company has accounts receivable of $700,000.

Great Canadian has sewing and other manufacturing equipment that it values on its books at $350,000, and it has a variety of miscellaneous assets such as delivery trucks and other motor vehicles, a computer system, office equipment, and rights to certain intellectual property such as the right to manufacture clothing and uniforms, in Canada, under certain well-known international trade names and on behalf of certain corporate customers.

---

[2] Some of the ways in which the debtor can seek such protection are discussed in Chapter 5 and in Part 4.

Besides the mortgages on its real property, Great Canadian granted a general security agreement and an assignment of its accounts receivable to the bank.

If Great Canadian defaults in its loan arrangements with the bank and the bank appoints an insolvency firm to take control of all of the company's different assets, clearly that insolvency firm is acting as a receiver according to the *Bankruptcy and Insolvency Act*.

## What Is Required in Reporting a Receivership?

One of the most common complaints about the way receiverships were conducted before the *Bankruptcy and Insolvency Act* became law was that too much secrecy shrouded the process. A receivership could often be well under way before a variety of interested parties such as landlords, suppliers, or other creditors knew that the receivership had even occurred.

The *Bankruptcy and Insolvency Act* now requires all receivers to file notice of their appointment with the Superintendent of Bankruptcy, a federal civil servant who maintains a record of such notices, which is open to the public. This notice must be filed within ten days of the receivership, and the receiver must attempt to identify every creditor of the borrower and to deliver that notice to them as well. Thus, in our example, the receiver would have to notify all of Great Canadian's creditors of the fact of the receivership almost immediately after taking control of the assets.

## The Receiver's Role in the Operation of the Business

In large commercial insolvencies a receiver must have the power to operate the borrower's business in order to preserve the "going concern" value of as much of that business as possible.[3] However, operating a business involves an endless string of tough decisions. How is the receiver required to act in handling those decisions?

The *Bankruptcy and Insolvency Act* requires a receiver to "act honestly and in good faith ... and to deal with the property of the

---

[3] The going concern value of a business represents something more than the breakup or liquidation value of all of the individual assets which are used in the business.

[borrower] ... in a commercially reasonable manner." Obviously each situation a receiver faces in trying to operate a debtor's business will test his or her ability to meet that standard. However, while no receiver or receivership company will have experience in every conceivable type of industry, part of what a secured creditor is paying for in a receiver is the tremendous depth of experience many of them have in dealing with a variety of difficult business problems in just such a manner.[4]

## Dealing With Employees

One of the most difficult tasks for a receiver is dealing with the debtor's employees. Typically, the receiver will desperately need the services of a relatively small number of senior management and sales personnel, at least on a short-term basis, to help the receiver understand the intricacies of the business and to continue collection of accounts receivable, sales efforts, and so on. The receiver will also probably want to retain the services of some, but not all, of the other employees to finish production of any inventory that was still in progress when the company went into receivership and, where appropriate in terms of maximizing value, to produce fresh orders during the receivership. For example, in the Great Canadian situation, the receiver might decide it is best to shut the leased facility in Toronto and let 40 of the 50 employees who work there go; at the same time, it may be commercially reasonable to continue to employ 140 of the 150 employees in the St. Catharines facility to continue to produce clothing.

However, in grappling with these decisions, the receiver must be very careful not to take on unwanted liabilities to the employees.

## Wage Claims

Generally speaking, if the employees' wages are in arrears at the time the receiver is appointed, that claim will rank behind the claim

---

[4] As discussed in Part 1, the *Personal Property Security Act* and other statutes also require a standard of commercial reasonableness.

of the secured creditor who appointed the receiver.[5] However, the receiver will often pay wage arrears out of necessity where the receiver wants the services of those same employees continued.

By the same token, since most employees will not work for too long without being paid, the wage arrears will not be very far back in most cases—which also improves their chances of being paid by the receiver.

## Successorship and Union Claims

Most provinces have legislation that contains "successor employer provisions" (in Ontario, the governing statutes are the *Employment Standards Act* and the *Labour Relations Act*). In effect, these laws state that purchasers of businesses will be bound by union agreements entered into by the previous employer, and that the seniority and other status of the employees under the previous owner with respect to matters such as vacation pay, holiday entitlement, pregnancy leave, and termination of employment will be carried over to employment under the new employer.

These provisions have been a source of great concern in receiverships. On the one hand, receivers contend that since they are merely trying to preserve the business while a new owner is found, it is unfair and inappropriate for them to be saddled with the responsibilities contained in, for example, a union agreement. Employees, unions, and the Ministry of Labour, on the other hand, predictably take a less restrictive view of receivers (and the secured creditors who are standing behind them), and the law reports are full of cases in which receivers have had to defend their actions against charges by governments, unions, and/or employees that receivers who use employees in the operation of a business in receivership are considered successor employers with respect to that business.

Unfortunately the decisions by judges in these cases are somewhat muddled: some say that receivers can be successor employers and some say the opposite. As a result the battle has continued to rage, and both sides have attempted to improve their position.

---

[5] This issue is not black and white, however, and each situation must be considered in terms of the security agreements that apply.

Typically, one of the receiver's first acts will be to terminate all employees by a formal, written notice. Immediately after delivery of this notice, the receiver will attempt to hire those workers who are still needed for a stipulated term. In this way, the receivers try to establish and document that there has been a break in employment and that the receiver has not just stepped into the shoes of the former employer.

Also, sometimes the initial receivership appointment will be by court order, and often these court orders will specifically provide that the receiver is *not* a successor employer. Despite this measure, however, unions and the Ministry of Labour have been known to fight to classify even these receivers as successor employers.[6]

The relationship between a receiver and employees can indeed be a thorny one. The strain of a receivership is hard on all employees, no matter how junior or senior. I have never stopped being impressed by the class most people show in continuing to perform their duties—sometimes doing even more than they were required to do before the receivership—in an atmosphere of great stress where they do not know what the future will bring.

The goal of a receivership is to *save* as many of the jobs as possible for as long as possible, by trying to keep the viable core of the business alive so as to give the time necessary to find a purchaser who will take on responsibility for the employees (and for the rest of the business). What is regrettable about many of the attempts by unions and government labour officials to pin increased responsibility on receivers is that if they are ultimately successful, receivers will decide that it is probably better just to shut a facility down completely, letting all of the employees go and turning out the lights, than to try to keep the jobs alive. That approach will neither maximize the recovery on the assets nor increase the chances that someone else will come along to re-employ the employees (on a long-term basis).

Both receivers and their advisers on the one hand, and unions and government labour officials on the other, must strive to communicate earlier and more often with one another. For example, if a receiver is seeking a court order to the effect that the receiver will not be

[6] Court-appointed receiverships are discussed later in this chapter.

bound by the terms of a union contract, the union should be given notice of that effort at the earliest possible date. Maybe through such communication it would even be possible to solve the problem without litigation.

## Security Enforcement

All of the receiver's skills are brought to bear in applying the somewhat mechanical rules described in Chapter 1 to the task of realizing on the business assets.

### Security Enforcement Notices

As noted in Chapter 1, the *Personal Property Security Act* does not require that notice be given to sell assets "in the ordinary course of the debtor's business." Thus, in the Great Canadian example, the receiver could immediately sell clothing, since doing so is normally part of the business. However, in order to collect the existing accounts receivable and sell "fixed" assets such as equipment, land, and even inventory "out of the ordinary course," the various notices described in Chapter 1 must be sent out.[7]

### How Is the Collection of Accounts Receivable Carried Out?

Among the first people to get security enforcement notices will be those people who owe money to the company in receivership. Many of these people, however, tend to have some reason or other for not paying. The excuses are endless, though a common one is a variation on "Gee, there was a problem with the product which, coincidentally, we were just about to bring to the attention of the company."

In collecting the accounts receivable in a commercially reasonable way, the receiver must cut through all of these excuses and strive to make deals only where it is warranted. In the Great Canadian example, the receiver will have to deal not only with Canadian

---

[7] Unless, as is discussed in Chapter 1, one of the relatively uncommon exceptions from the notice requirements is available.

customers but also with international customers who may not hesi-
tate to invoke legal provisions applicable to their jurisdictions.
Again, the receiver must become familiar as quickly as possible,
with the overall terms of the sales arrangements between Great
Canadian and, say, a customer in Thailand to see if the Thai customer's refusal to pay all of the accounts receivable is justifiable.

## Appraisals and Advertising the Business for Sale

While the receiver is running the viable core of the business and
collecting accounts receivable, he or she will also engage professional appraisers to evaluate the assets.[8] Different appraisers may
be used, depending on the types of assets; wherever possible, two
appraisals will be obtained with respect to each major asset so that
an acceptable range can be established. For example, with the Great
Canadian Garment Corporation, two real estate appraisers might
appraise only the piece of raw land in Oakville, while two companies with expertise in the garment industry might appraise the
inventory, the accounts receivable, and the production machinery.

At the same time, the receiver will be working hard to put
together an "information package" on the company's assets that
are to be sold. Typically, this information package will break the
assets into categories such as real estate, inventory, accounts
receivable, trade marks, and so on.

When the results of the appraisals are in, the receiver will decide
on its selling strategy. Often that strategy will involve advertising for
tenders on the assets.[9] Interest in tendering will be solicited in a
variety of ways, including advertising in the business sections of
newspapers and by mailing invitations to view the information package to other people known to be involved in the business. Obviously,
the goal is to attempt to tap into as much potential interest in the
assets as possible.

---

[8] Subject to any statutory requirements that appraisals be postponed as discussed in
Chapter 1, on page 18.

[9] This is a generalization; in some cases the receiver will sell, or attempt to sell, the
assets in a different sequence than described here.

## Confidentiality Agreements

People who express interest in acquiring the assets being sold are normally asked to sign a confidentiality agreement before the full details of the information package are released to them. Information packages will typically say that although the information concerning assets being sold by a receiver has been assembled with care, it is nevertheless based largely on the company's own international information and, accordingly, the prospective purchaser must conduct his or her own investigation before submitting an offer to purchase.[10] Usually the information package also contains a preferred form of offer to purchase (an agreement of purchase and sale).

## Tenders

Ideally, the receiver will try to create a "bidding atmosphere," whereby several companies will want to buy some or all of the same assets at the same time.

Many sales are structured so that tenders will be called for, based on the information package, by a certain date and on certain minimum terms—such as a minimum deposit. In those cases the receiver will, on the designated date, open and compare all of the tenders.

In the real world, however, not every receivership results in a heated bidding war and even where tenders are called for by a certain date it is not unheard of for each tender package to be unacceptable to the receiver, for some reason. In such cases, the receiver will have to reject all of the tenders and begin more focused discussions with the most attractive bidder in order to kindle the best deal.

## Selling the Business by Auction

Sometimes no one wants to buy the business as a going concern, and in those cases the assets are typically sold by auction. Obviously, the value of the assets is diminished when sold in this manner but

---

10 These investigations (called "due diligence enquiries") are discussed in Chapter 8.

in no sense are auctions an excuse for receivers to be lax about their duty to achieve the most commercially reasonable price for the assets.

In one reported case, the assets being auctioned were pieces of photographic equipment owned by a company and subject to a security agreement in favour of a bank. The company's debt had been guaranteed by two people. Appraisals of the equipment were obtained, and an auction was advertised in newspapers. What was achieved at the auction fell short of the secured debt by about $50,000.

However, when the bank tried to sue the individual guarantors for this shortfall, the guarantors fought back. They said the auction had not been advertised or conducted properly, and the court agreed. Specifically, the court said that the newspaper ad did not make clear how sophisticated this particular equipment was, so that the ideal buyers for such equipment would not be likely to attend. The court went on to criticize the auction itself, saying that the people in charge did not appreciate, and therefore did not convey to the audience, how good the equipment really was; that the means by which prospective buyers could have tested the equipment at the auction were not provided; and that the overall presentation at the auction was "haphazard." In that case, the bank was held to be liable for damages that were roughly equal to the shortfall. Thus, the basic result was that the bank was unable to recover the full shortfall. However, depending on how badly a secured creditor fails to meet the standard of commercial reasonableness, the creditor might actually have to pay money to the debtor.

## Access to the Courts

With the amendments to the *Bankruptcy Act* in late 1992, that legislation was expanded to allow receivers, creditors, and other parties affected by a receivership increased and more direct access to the courts in order to obtain clarification as to whether certain steps in the receivership process were being conducted properly. These provisions are broad enough both to allow a receiver to seek the court's advice as to whether a proposed course of action is in accordance with the standards which a receiver must meet, and a creditor to seek a court order against a receiver, as a result of some action taken by the receiver, for failing to meet those same standards.

## The Receiver's Final Report

After the receiver has completed all of his or her duties, he or she must file a final report including a statement of accounts with both the Superintendent of Bankruptcy and the company itself, and give copies to any creditors who request them.

## COURT-APPOINTED RECEIVERS: THEIR REGULATION AND CONDUCT

Receivers are not always appointed privately under the powers contained in a security agreement. The other major way in which a receiver may be appointed is by court order.

In Ontario, the *Courts of Justice Act* allows a secured or unsecured creditor of a company to apply to the court for an order[11] appointing a receiver of that company on the basis that it is "just or convenient" to do so. These three simple words, "just or convenient," have been the subject of many heated court cases but, practically speaking, court-appointed receiverships have tended to be used mainly by two classes of creditors.

The first type is the secured creditor who is encountering difficulty in enforcing his or her security. An example of such a situation would be where a debtor simply refuses to grant access to a properly appointed[12] private receiver. In those circumstances, the receiver will usually report the difficulty to the secured creditor, whose lawyer will then seek a court order appointing the receiver. If the debtor still refuses to grant access, he or she is in contempt of court, which can result in a fine or jail term, or both.

A secured creditor might also seek the court appointment of a receiver when the security covers most of the assets of a debtor's

---

[11] From a procedural viewpoint, the party seeking the receivership order must already have started a broader action against the debtor (i.e. for recovery of indebtedness). Seeking the receivership order is then done as an interim (or "interlocutory") motion.
[12] That is, the debtor received all of the proper notification that the receivership was coming, including a proper notice of the calling of the loan and a notice of intention to enforce security.

business—for example, a mortgage over the real property and a security agreement over most of the personal property—but, for one reason or other, does not contain the power to appoint a receiver.

The second major applicants for court-appointed receivers tend to be government agencies. Typically, these appointments are made in accordance with the terms of the statute governing the business in question. For example, if a travel agency or a real estate brokerage is found to be sufficiently in breach of its responsibilities to do things like keep client trust funds segregated, the government may move to take over the business through a court-appointed receiver.

## Duties of a Court-Appointed Receiver

Court-appointed receivers are "officers of the Court." As such, their duties are grounded first and foremost in the court order under which they are appointed. Thus, anyone doing business with a court-appointed receiver is well advised to obtain and review a copy of the court order, which is a public document.

Also as a general rule, court-appointed receivers will owe a somewhat broader duty to *all* creditors than do private receivers. The distinction is fairly subtle in that, as already discussed, privately appointed receivers are supposed to act honestly and in good faith and to deal with the debtor's assets in a commercially reasonable way. However, this broader regard for all creditors can make itself felt in specific situations, and it is why, along with the added costs of court-appointed receiverships, secured creditors would usually rather use private receivers.

## The Court Order

A court order appointing a receiver will deal with the receiver's power to take possession of the assets and to carry on the business. Normally, the order also deals with the sale of the assets.

However, the order can go on to deal with any number of other matters and sometimes a court-appointment receivership is sought because of a creditor's need to address such an issue. For example, a serious environmental problem related to the property can be addressed in a court order. As mentioned in the Preface, with the recent expansion of environmental protection legislation, anyone who takes control of an environmentally hazardous property can become liable for the clean-up cost and other amounts, and receivers obviously take control of a debtor's property. Thus, typically, receivership orders will attempt to protect receivers from such liability.[13]

As mentioned in the discussion about the position of employees in a receivership, the effectiveness of court orders is generally dependent on the extent to which the parties affected by the order are given an opportunity to participate in the proceedings.

Certainly, this principle has proven true in the case of environmental problems where the court order will often contain a set of terms that have been negotiated by the receiver and the Ministry of the Environment. For example, one major case involved a chain of gasoline stations. (Among the many environmental problems that can go with such a business is the risk that an underground storage tank starts to leak. As one might guess, that is not a cheap problem to fix.) The court order required the receiver to dedicate a set percentage of the revenue from the receivership to a fund to be used for any environmental clean-up costs associated with the property. That arrangement was the result of vigorous negotiation between the receiver and the government.

## Reporting

The initial court order appointing a receiver will often provide for periodic reporting as to the status of the company in receivership and the sale or other treatment of its assets. The *Bankruptcy and Insolvency Act* requirements as to a final report (discussed on page 83) also apply to court-appointed receivers.

---

[13] The need to deal with an environmental or other delicate situation can be seen as another example of a secured creditor having a "problem" enforcing security, as discussed on pages 83 to 84.

# The Rights of
# Unpaid Suppliers

I N CHAPTER 5, I TALKED about how receiverships generally occur only after extensive dialogue between a debtor and his or her bank or other secured creditor(s). However, when a receivership hits, it is often a severe jolt to many people who have been doing business with the debtor. High on that list of people are those who supplied product to the company just before the receivership without getting paid.

Suppose that Bob and his wife, Mary, own a company called Bob's Sporting Goods Ltd., which operates a chain of five sporting goods stores. The company obtains a $200,000 line of revolving credit from the bank in 1991, and the bank, being cautious, requires (and receives) a personal guarantee of the company's borrowings from both Bob and Mary. Suppose also that the bank takes a mortgage over the (very nice) house in which Bob and Mary live, in support of any obligations they might ever have under the guarantee.

Now suppose that in 1994, after three good years, Bob's Sporting Goods falls on hard times for various reasons. In fact, the situation is so bad that the $200,000 credit line is fully drawn and the only assets the company has are:

| "hard assets" (e.g., cash registers, furniture, shelving) | $ 25,000 |
|---|---|
| cash on hand | 10,000 |
| inventory | 110,000 |
| Total | $145,000 |

Bob and Mary review these numbers one night and realize that if the bank appointed a receiver tomorrow, the most the receiver would realize would be $55,000 less than the $200,000 debt of the company.[1] That would mean the bank would then call on the guarantees, and Bob and Mary would either lose their house or have to refinance it.

Bob and Mary have lost faith in the viability of the company, but they are also ruthlessly determined not to lose or refinance their house. So, the next day Bob's Sporting Goods orders $95,000 worth of sporting equipment. As soon as the goods are in the stores, Bob and Mary go to the bank and consent to the immediate receivership of Bob's Sporting Goods. (In the vernacular, Bob and Mary "hand the keys" to the bank.) Because the value of the company's inventory has suddenly swollen to $205,000, there will be enough recovery from the receivership to pay the bank in full (and the bank will not need to pursue Bob and Mary on their guarantees).

While I am not sure how often this pattern of events actually occurred over the past decade or so, I do know that many people felt that it was occurring frequently and that it was something that had to be addressed as part of bankruptcy reform.

## PROTECTING UNPAID SUPPLIERS: BEFORE THE *BANKRUPTCY AND INSOLVENCY ACT*

Before commenting on how the *Bankruptcy and Insolvency Act* does protect suppliers, I want to point out that before the new legislation there were (and continue to be) a number of other statutory provisions designed to deal with the problem. For example, as discussed

---

[1] Not taking into account the legitimate costs of the receivership. This example also assumes that there are no other creditors who rank ahead of the bank.

in Chapter 1, any supplier shipping product to a business (such as Bob's Sporting Goods) can obtain a purchase money security interest over the goods. With this protection, the proceeds from the sale of any such product ordered on credit on the eve of the receivership would not go to reduce the bank debt but would go directly to that (otherwise unpaid) supplier. In Chapter 4, I discussed another remedy: the relatively rare, but still significant, right of stoppage in transit.

Most importantly, however, what Bob and Mary did in my example amounts to fraud. In simplest terms, they induced their suppliers to ship product to their company knowing that it would never be paid for. Under the old *Bankruptcy Act* and under the new *Bankruptcy and Insolvency Act,* it was and still is an offence when a bankrupt "obtains credit or property by false representations" or when a bankrupt "fraudulently conceals" its indebtedness.[2] The *Bankruptcy and Insolvency Act* also prohibits a company from improperly disposing of property that has been obtained on credit.

These statutory provisions address many of the more outrageous instances of debtors who, on the eve of bankruptcy, and in a state of insolvency, induce suppliers to ship product to them, only to have the product then be made available to the debtor's secured creditors[3] when the bankruptcy occurs shortly thereafter.

At the same time, the *Bankruptcy and Insolvency Act* (as it did under the previous statute) provides that an officer, director, or agent of a corporation may be found liable of a bankruptcy offence where the offence was technically committed by a corporation but the person in question directed, authorized, assented to, and acquiesced or participated in the commission of the offence. A jail term may result. Thus, if Bob's Sporting Goods were to be declared bankrupt, as well as in receivership, Bob and Mary could be fined and even go to jail for what they did. However, I acknowledge that

---

[2] As discussed in Chapter 12, a receivership often occurs in conjunction with a bankruptcy. A civil lawsuit, based on misrepresentation, is also possible and see the discussion of criminal fraud on page 156.

[3] Even if there is a surplus after the secured creditor(s) is or are paid, the surplus in a bankruptcy is shared equally among all creditors, instead of being paid to the one unfortunate creditor who supplied the product that may have been mainly responsible for the surplus.

these provisions may do nothing to put any money back into the pocket of, or return goods to, a supplier who has shipped goods to a debtor who promptly goes bankrupt before they are paid for.

## PROTECTING UNPAID SUPPLIERS: THE IMPLICATIONS OF THE BANKRUPTCY AND INSOLVENCY ACT

For those who think that the banks in Canada can dictate the ways in which business and law are carried on, consider this: though the Canadian Bankers' Association strenuously objected to the introduction, into the *Bankruptcy and Insolvency Act,* of a right in favour of unpaid suppliers to recover product shipped to companies in receivership and/or bankruptcy, the provision was not only introduced but also enhanced and strengthened while the legislation was under review.

By now you will have detected some sympathy on my part towards banks, and in this case, I was again on their side. There was—at least to me—a good reason for the banks' opposition to this provision: namely, it would limit the ability of Canadian businesses (particularly small businesses) to obtain credit based on a security interest over their inventory. In other words, because, at any time, a portion, perhaps a significant one, of a company's inventory would now be subject to being reclaimed by the unpaid suppliers, the company would not be able to borrow from its bank on the security of that inventory. Canadian businesses have difficulty getting access to credit at the best of times for many reasons (some of which are well beyond the scope of this book) and one questions how much room there really is to cut back on the availability of credit to a lot of companies.

## Repossessing Unpaid Goods

The right to repossess can be exercised by a supplier who is unpaid when the purchaser of the goods is either bankrupt or in receivership. It *cannot* be exercised if the purchasing company is attempting to reorganize its business pursuant to either the *Companies' Creditors Arrangement Act* or the *Bankruptcy and Insolvency Act* (as discussed in Part 4). In those circumstances, generally speaking, all creditors are prevented from exercising any remedies against the debtor until the proposal or plan either passes (and becomes binding on all the creditors) or fails, in which case it may still be possible to exercise the right of repossession. As a practical matter, such proceedings usually take many weeks, so a reorganization process may entirely defeat a right to repossess product.

It is possible that as part of a reorganization process, a special court order may be made giving a particular supplier, or suppliers as a whole, protection akin to the unpaid supplier remedy. However, without such a special order, no right will arise.

The right itself is exercised by filing a "demand for repossession of goods" with either the trustee in bankruptcy or the receiver. The prescribed form is straightforward, and a copy is included in the Appendix (Exhibit 13).

## Limitation Periods

There are two limitation periods to bear in mind regarding the repossession of unpaid goods. First, the right applies only to goods that have been delivered in the 30-day period preceding the delivery of the demand for repossession (i.e., *not* 30 days prior to the date of the bankruptcy or the receivership).

Second, the right to repossess the goods itself expires very quickly: ten days after the supplier is notified that the trustee or receiver admits the right, subject to any mutual agreement to extend the period. Also, a supplier *cannot* repossess any goods that are sold by the trustee in bankruptcy or the receiver during the period of 30 days after the receivership or bankruptcy has started, unless they are sold after the delivery of the demand for repossession. Therefore, unpaid suppliers should exercise the right of repossession immediately on being notified that their customer has gone bankrupt or into receivership.

To take a simple example, suppose a supplier delivered 400 lamps to a customer on December 1. On December 15 the supplier learns that the customer has gone into receivership. On that date 350 of the lamps are still in the possession of the receiver. If the supplier filed the demand for repossession immediately (by fax, for example) and the other requirements of the *Bankruptcy and Insolvency Act* could be satisfied, all 350 lamps could be recovered.

However, if the supplier, for whatever reason, did not file the demand for repossession until December 21 and on that date there were only 270 lamps left in the possession of the receiver because he had sold 80 of them in the course of operating the business in receivership, the supplier would be able to recover only 270 lamps, even though the demand for repossession was technically delivered on time.

## Requirements as to the Condition of the Goods to be Repossessed

This is where the statutory provisions get very picky. Without quoting the pertinent section of the *Bankruptcy and Insolvency Act* in full, the statute requires that the goods have the following characteristics at the time the supplier wants to repossess them.

1) they are "identifiable;"

2) they are "in the same state as they were on delivery;"

3) they have not been "resold at arms' length;" and

4) they are not "subject to any agreement for sale at arms' length."

When lawyers and insolvency practitioners saw this language in the draft legislation, they immediately commented on how difficult it would be to use in practice. For example, if a supplier delivered 90 blue dresses to a customer 100 days before a receivership, 50 more blue dresses in the same style and range of sizes 40 days before the receivership, and another 50 blue dresses 20 days before the receivership, and there are 75 blue dresses in the possession of the customer on the date of the receivership, how can one "identify" 50 of those dresses as being the ones shipped within the 30 days prior to the receivership? Doesn't one blue dress look like another?

Fortunately, after some time with the legislation in force, some helpful experience is emerging. For example, in the receivership and bankruptcy of a large tire chain in Ontario, there were many suppliers who had shipped the same product inside and outside the 30-day period. Again, one tire looks like another. However, after some investigative work by both the receiver and the suppliers, it was discovered through the internal accounting records that the inventory of the company in receivership was at a low ebb approximately 30 days prior to the bankruptcy/receivership. Therefore, the suppliers were able to establish that a relatively high percentage of the (otherwise indistinguishable) tires on hand at the date of the bankruptcy had been shipped within the preceding 30 days, and so, were "identifiable."

Similarly, in another recent case, the supplier had delivered product to a customer both inside and outside the 30-day period preceding receivership. However, by a stroke of good luck, the receiver took an inventory on the morning of the receivership before the next shipment of product arrived later that day. Accordingly, a large portion of the product that the receiver had on hand a few days later could be identified when the demand for repossession was filed, even though it was the same in appearance as product shipped more than 30 days before the receivership and that also had not been paid for.

Another issue arose in a case where a company had supplied industrial glue to a customer who went into receivership within 30 days. The glue was shipped in a large drum and at the date of the receivership the lid on the drum had been removed and part of the glue had been removed. However, the amount of glue that was left was worth enough to fight over. Initially, the trustee in bankruptcy took the position that because the container had been opened, the glue was not "in the same state as on delivery." Eventually, however, the trustee accepted the argument that although in some cases (such as in food packaging) the packaging would be such a critical feature of the product as to be relevant to the issue of whether the goods were in the "same state" on bankruptcy/receivership, in other cases the packaging itself was irrelevant. The trustee also agreed that this was such a case: the state of the packaging did not have any great bearing on the quality of industrial glue; the product was deemed to be essentially "in the same state as on delivery" and, therefore, eligible for repossession by the supplier.

## Ranking of the Thirty-Day Goods Right

Subject to all of the problems and issues identified, the 30 day goods claim ranks ahead of other claims by secured creditors and certain government agencies.

## Taking Security Interest Versus Exercising Repossession Rights

As you will have noticed by now, the 30 day goods right is picky and difficult to work with. Also, the right is very limited: at best, it protects only what has been delivered in those critical 30 days. If suppliers can raise themselves above this fray, they should do so. One way is to obtain a valid, enforceable security interest in the product sold on credit, as outlined in Chapter 1. Subject only to some very uncommon exceptions, a trustee in bankruptcy and a receiver cannot stop a secured creditor from acting on valid security and such action can include repossession of the products.

# Purchasing Assets From a Receiver

A NYONE WHO IS INTERESTED IN buying assets from a receiver has probably had some experience in purchasing a business that is not in receivership. While there are similarities between these transactions, there are also fundamental differences and only someone who appreciates these differences will be successful in dealing with receivers.

## WHAT IS INVOLVED IN NEGOTIATING WITH A RECEIVER?

In order to understand the unique quality of a receivership sale, it is easiest to return briefly to first principles. There are two common ways to buy a business in ordinary circumstances: you can buy the shares of the company that owns the assets used in the business (and which employs the employees) or you can buy the individual assets (and employ the employees yourself[1]).

Each of these approaches has advantages and disadvantages, but the way in which both the buying and selling parties try to deal with

---

[1] As discussed on pages 77 to 79, by law, the seniority of most employees with the old employer will generally carry over to their employment with the new employer. There are other, less common, ways of acquiring a business, such as by an amalgamation.

all of the complications is by negotiating comprehensive "asset purchase" or "share purchase" agreements that cover a host of issues.

The centrepiece of those agreements is usually a long list of
representations and warranties given by the seller after much negotiation with the buyer. Depending on whether the sale is structured
as a sale of shares or assets, such representations and warranties
will deal with one or more of the following aspects of the company
whose "business" is being sold:

- the company's incorporation, its share capital structure, and the
  details of how all shares have been issued to date;

- the ownership of the shares and whether they are subject to
  securty interests or other adverse claims;

- details about the company's financial performance over a stipulated period of time, including reference to its (audited or unaudit-
  ed) financial statements;

- the company's liabilities,[2] whether in the form of contracts,
  pension plans, lawsuits, governmental claims, or otherwise;

- the company's standing under various agreements relating to
  its business;

- the condition and adequacy of the assets used in the business;

- the company's title to those assets;

- the company's arrangements with its employees;

- the company's contracts with its customers; and

- the status of the company's inventory and accounts receivable.

Each of these issues is a legitimate concern for a buyer, and
where the purchase is between a buyer and a seller who are both
solvent and whose relationship is at arm's length, both will usually
take the time and resources necessary to negotiate them properly.

However, virtually all of that kind of thinking goes out the window
when the vendor is a receiver. Because the receiver has not had ownership and control of the assets for long, he or she will simply refuse to
give any kind of representation or warranty on many of these, admit-

---

2 This subject is vital with a share purchase since all liabilities associated with the business will accompany ownership of the shares in that business.

tedly important, matters. In other words, a receiver is not going to give a representation and warranty about the working capital ratio of the company over the past three years, or the condition of its delivery trucks, because the receiver has no first-hand knowledge of these facts.

Instead, in acquiring something from a receiver, buyers must generally satisfy themselves as to what they are getting. Of course, the people interested in those assets are often competitors of the company that has gone into receivership, and a receiver will take the position that, as such, the prospective purchaser knows the industry and knows what to look for, perhaps better than the receiver.

In fact, there is still a form and protocol to dealing with receivers and the agreement is invariably in writing; however, these agreements look different from normal sale agreements and are negotiated in a much different manner.

## SPECIFIC CONSIDERATIONS IN THE PROCESS OF RECEIVERSHIP SALES

There are many things to consider when purchasing assets from a receiver. These include the sale process, due diligence enquiries, dealing with landlords and employers, and the role of the courts. The remainder of this chapter will discuss these topics and more in further detail.

## The Sale Process

Essentially, anyone purchasing assets from receivers should start with the idea that the receiver does not want to give the purchaser any representations and warranties and that the receiver will simply convey "all of his or her right, title, and interest, *if any*" to the purchaser on an "as is/where is" basis.

Is it possible to get a receiver to move from that position to any degree? The answer is that receivers may be prepared to give (perhaps limited) representations and warranties on such issues as the basic circumstances of their appointment and the sale process. Ideally, such representations and warranties would attest to the following facts: (1) that the borrower gave good, valid, and enforceable security to a lender; (2) that default occurred under such security and that the borrower was given all notices required with respect to such default, so that appointing a receiver became a legitimate option for the lender; and (3) that all notices of sale required under the security—such as *Personal Property Security Act* or *Mortgages Act* notices—have been given. However, some receivers will resist giving even this much and will take the position that buyers should just examine the appointment of the receiver, the security, and/or the sale notices in order to satisfy themselves.

Sometimes a purchaser can get a receiver to give a representation and warranty that at least confirms the receiver has no knowledge of such things as adverse claims against the business that is in receivership. In other words, the receiver might be willing to say something amounting to "In the six weeks since my company has been receiver of XYZ Ltd., I personally have not become aware that any of the customers of the business have challenged the quality of XYZ's products; however, I have no knowledge of the relations between XYZ and those customers for the six years during which they did business prior to the receivership." Receivers do not like getting into representations and warranties even of that nature, though, and they may respond to such requests by saying that purchasers should reflect their concerns in the price that they are willing to pay and/or that they do their own investigation.

## Due Diligence Enquiries: Legal

Inevitably, someone who is buying from a receiver will have to do a certain degree of investigation, or due diligence. Sometimes this "going the extra mile" will make all the difference.

At the legal level, certain basic enquiries must be carried out on every file, starting with a thorough corporate and security search of the company that is in receivership. Among other things, what these searches will show is the ranking of the various security interests granted by the company; this, in turn, will determine the effects that a sale by a receiver of that company will have on the security holders and on the purchaser.

For example, suppose that Jackson Hardware Stores Limited learns that Clarke Hardware Stores Limited, one of Jackson's competitors, has gone into receivership. Jackson is very interested in purchasing the assets of the two hardware stores Clarke operated, so

Jackson's president contacts the receiver who offers Jackson some basic information about what is for sale and confirms that they have been appointed receiver of Clarke by Central Canadian Bank.

Suppose further that Jackson's lawyer carries out a range of searches against Clarke that shows there are three parties with general security interests against Clarke. In order of priority those secured creditors are: (1) Central Canadian Bank, (2) Northern Insurance Company, and (3) Mr. Robert Clarke, the owner of Clarke's. In addition to these three registrations, there is a registration by a motor vehicle finance company that described the collateral as limited to two vans.

This is vital information for Jackson because it means that if the receiver can demonstrate that the *Personal Property Security Act* notices of sale have been sent, by Central Canadian Bank to Northern Insurance and to Mr. Clarke, and neither of those parties has exercised its right to redeem the collateral, Central Canadian (through its designated receiver) can sell the assets of Clarke free and clear of any claim by Northern Insurance or Mr. Clarke. In other words, Mr. Clarke and Northern Insurance are cut out of the sale process, and their only claim is to any surplus left after the bank has been paid. For example, suppose that the debts (ignoring interest) to the three secured creditors are:

| | |
|---|---|
| Central Canadian Bank | $400,000 |
| Northern Insurance Company | $100,000 |
| Mr. Clarke | $250,000 |

and that the assets were sold for $550,000. The bank would receive $400,000 plus its costs for the receivership (say $30,000); $100,000 would then go to Northern Insurance, Mr. Clarke would get only $20,000 and Jackson, the buyer of the assets, would acquire them free and clear of any claim by Mr. Clarke.

Note that in these circumstances there is no need for Jackson to obtain a discharge of any of the *Personal Property Security Act* registrations—particularly those of Northern Insurance and Clarke—because they are effectively wiped out "by operation of law" or, in other words, by the sale process. That would *not* be the case, based on these facts, if the person appointing the receiver (and under whose security the sale was occurring) was Northern Insurance. Because

Northern is only in second position, its sale would *not* wipe out the first secured creditor and thus there would be a requirement to ensure that the amount of the purchase price is sufficient to pay out the first secured creditor. The way in which that fact is documented is for the creditor—Central Canadian Bank—to provide a payout statement in favour of Jackson and for Jackson to ensure that a sufficient portion of the purchase price is paid to the bank in exchange for which the bank discharges its *Personal Property Security Act* registration(s).

Note also that I did not suggest that the registration against the motor vehicles is discharged by a sale, even by a first-position general secured creditor. As discussed in Chapter 1, it may be that a creditor has a purchase money security interest, which provides a first claim on those specific assets.[3] If that is the case—and, again, purchasers usually find these things out by doing their legal due diligence homework—the purchaser will either not want to include those assets in the purchase price or, if they do, they will have to cut a specific deal with the motor vehicle finance company.

There are numerous other "legally-based" due diligence enquiries a prospective purchaser from a receiver should carry out, though sometimes the information that can be uncovered is limited. For example, although ten or fifteen years ago few people thought about environmental problems, particularly when dealing with urban properties, routine enquiries are now made with the Ministry of the Environment to see if there is any record of a property's having an environmental problem. Where appropriate, the purchaser may want to do his or her own environmental testing to see if there is a problem that has not yet come to the attention of the government.

Other legal due diligence enquiries include looking at government claims[4] against the assets being acquired and finding out whether the receivership was private or by court order. In the case of a court-appointed receivership, the purchaser should become familiar with the court order[5] and ensure that the sale is in compliance with that order.

---

[3] One possible situation is that although the vans were originally financed on a purchase money security basis, the loan has been paid in full; in that case the vans would fall under the bank's first ranking general security agreement and would be included among the assets the bank can sell.

[4] See Chapter 12.

[5] Note that the court file with respect to a court-appointed receivership will contain much

## Due Diligence Enquiries: Business

Obviously, a prospective purchaser from a receiver should carry out as many business-oriented enquiries about the company in receivership as possible. The problem is really one of how much can reasonably be done in the time available.

For starters, the purchaser should go and inspect the assets. To continue the hardware store example, perhaps Mr. Jackson would find that much of the hardware inventory in the Clarke stores consists of outdated and/or slow-moving product. Or he might find that the cash registers in one store do not work properly. Anything that is discovered from these due diligence enquiries must be reflected by the purchaser in the purchase price because he or she is not going to get a representation or warranty (saying, for example, that the cash registers are in perfect condition) that can be sued on later.

## Dealing With Landlords, Employees, and Other Third Parties

Of course, the purchaser's due diligence enquiries should include, to the greatest extent possible, contact with the people with whom the company in receivership did business.

An obvious example is the landlord, if the premises of the company in receivership are leased. First, it may be that the lease is not assignable and a new lease must be negotiated.[6] However, another

---

information besides the order appointing the receiver. For example, there will probably be a detailed affidavit by the creditor outlining why the relatively harsh relief of a court-appointed receiver should be granted. Ideally, all of this material should also be examined because it may contain information about the debtor's business that would be helpful to the purchaser.

[6] As discussed in Chapter 2, a landlord's desire to preserve or renegotiate a lease will largely depend on the state of the market at the time at which the default—and receiverships constitute a default under most commercial leases—arises. Also, as discussed in Chapter 12, it is possible, through a bankruptcy, to eliminate a landlord's control over the assignability of the lease(s) of a company in receivership.

important reason for having a discussion with the landlord is to clarify what the landlord views as constituting fixtures. For example, Mr. Jackson might think that he is buying and is therefore willing to pay for, the shelving in the Clarke stores, whereas the landlord may be right in thinking that he owns those shelves because they are fixtures. Again, whereas this matter might be the subject of a specific clause in an arm's-length asset purchase agreement that can be relied on after the sale, a sale agreement with a receiver will give no comfort to the purchaser on this and many other issues.

A prospective purchaser must also meet with the employees (including any union representatives) in order to make sure that he or she understands the scope of any employee obligations that are being taken on. Such enquiries would include an investigation of any company pension plan and the extent, if any, to which it is overfunded or underfunded.

Employees of a business are, of course, also a tremendous source of information about the company. They were there when the company started to struggle financially, and many of them will know the extent to which those difficulties have had an impact on the company's relations with its customers. I am not suggesting that it is appropriate, or even that there may be sufficient time, for a prospective purchaser to fish for juicy stories among the employees. However, used judiciously, due diligence enquiries of employees can yield useful information.

Other parties to whom the purchaser should try to make due diligence enquiries include guarantors of the debt that is owed to the secured creditor who appointed the receiver. To continue the Jackson/Clarke hardware example, suppose that Mr. Clarke signed a personal guarantee of the debt of Clarke Hardware Stores. It is possible that Mr. Clarke will have a dispute with Central Canadian Bank—for example, about the way they called his loan—but, on the other hand, he may be very motivated to help the sale to Jackson go through because that will mean that Mr. Clarke's guarantee will not be called on.

Under the circumstances, Mr. Clarke himself might be willing to give some of the representations and warranties that Jackson cannot get from the receiver. I am not suggesting that this practice occurs in many cases, but it should at least be considered.

Another category of people with whom a purchaser should conduct due diligence investigations is the people who owe money to the business. In one case, a bank appointed a receiver but specifically instructed the receiver *not* to make contact with any of those account debtors. A relatively hasty sale by the receiver was arranged, and the purchaser, who did not make any due diligence enquiries of those people, paid the receiver a significant amount for the accounts receivable, which were on the books of the company that was in receivership. As usual, the agreement of purchase and sale contained absolutely no representation or warranty about the quality of the accounts receivable.

In due course it was found that the accounts receivable were completely worthless. That is, the people listed as owing money to the company in receivership owed nothing, and the books contained lies.

A long, expensive lawsuit followed in which the receiver was held to be totally blameless. In a somewhat shocking development, though, it turned out that one of the officers of the bank did know that the receivables were uncollectible and thus the bank was held liable to a degree. But, if the purchaser had made some enquiries of its own, the problem would have been uncovered and the purchaser would not have had to pay the purchase price and then wade through a long lawsuit. Also, of course, if the bank had been innocent, the purchaser would have had no compensation whatsoever.

## The Sale Documentation

As noted on page 81, in larger receiverships, where a tender process is used, the receiver will suggest a form of agreement of purchase and sale that is very limited in scope. The agreement will typically be signed and then later, at the time of the "closing"—that is, when the purchase price is paid—the receiver will execute a similarly limited bill of sale. In smaller transactions, or where the sale is by way of an auction, only a bill of sale may be used.

Examples of a receivership agreement of purchase and sale and a receiver's bill of sale are included in the Appendix (Exhibits 14 and 15).

## The Role of the Courts

With a court-appointed receivership, the sale is usually approved by a formal court order, called a "vesting order." In some situations this order can be extremely helpful in solving problems. For example, suppose that there is a dispute among the secured creditors of the company in receivership as to who has priority over certain assets. Understandably, the purchaser's attitude will be that he or she is willing to pay a certain price for those assets in exchange for which he or she does not have to be party to any such arguments.

In those circumstances, a vesting order could provide for the passing of clear title to the purchaser. The order might go on to provide that the purchase money be held in trust while the secured creditors carry on their dispute but the point is for the order to help along the completion of the sale, which it is in no one's interests to risk losing.

However, as noted in Chapter 6, the court is now generally available in all (even private) receiverships if anyone affected by the receivership requires directions or the aid of the court. Thus, for example, an order of the kind just described could be obtained in a private receivership as well as in a court-appointed one. Similarly, if a receiver had a question about whether a specific aspect of a receivership was in accordance with the standards of commercial reasonableness, he or she could seek the court's guidance.

Since going to court costs time and money, the courts are not, in practice overused in relation to receiverships. However, in sticky situations they can provide invaluable help.

# Corporate Bankruptcy

# INTRODUCTION

A s DISCUSSED IN THE PREFACE, corporate bankruptcy law is designed to bring order to the affairs of an insolvent corporation.

Even though a company can go bankrupt in various ways, and there are various procedures—such as a receivership—that can continue at the same time as the bankruptcy of a company, once a company has been declared bankrupt the essential process is always the same.

Even though there are others, there are three fundamental repercussions of the bankruptcy of a corporation: the vesting, or passing, of property; the stay, or shopping, of proceedings; and the ranking and final satisfaction of all claims.

Every corporate bankrupcty is run by a federally licensed trustee in bankruptcy.[1] Somewhat like court-appointed receivers, trustees in bankruptcy are seen as officers of the court. In practice, that means that they must act in an evenhanded manner, and in the interests of all of the creditors.

A trustee in bankrupcty must do a number of things in every bankruptcy. These duties are discussed in this Part.

---

[1] There are both individual and corporate trustees in bankruptcy. The trustee in bankruptcy might be Anderson & Jones Inc., with Bob Jones being the individual handling the file.

# The Three Fundamental Effects
## of Bankruptcy

## Vesting of Property in the Trustee in Bankruptcy

*All* of the property of the bankrupt company vests in, or passes to, the trustee in bankruptcy. That is not to say that the trustee receives this property free of any rights affecting the property. For example, as will be discussed in more detail in Chapter 12, if the debtor has granted a valid security interest over some of its property, the trustee will take the property subject to that interest. Or suppose that the bankrupt corporation is the owner of a well-known trademark, but it previously entered into a valid contract to allow another company exclusive use of that trademark in Canada. Although title to the trademark would pass to the trustee, he or she would have to respect the continued use of the trademark by the other company, subject only to the terms of the contract.

The bankrupt corporation, in short, loses the legal ability to deal with its property, and the power to do so is transferred to the trustee.

## Stay of Proceedings

The second major effect of bankruptcy is that all proceedings that may be in progress against the bankrupt company are stopped, or stayed. There are two exceptions to this rule:

1)  A creditor may obtain a court order allowing such an action to continue. Such orders are relatively rare.

2)  Secured creditors are entitled to continue the enforcement of valid security, unless the trustee obtains a court order to the contrary.[1]

This stay of proceedings is essential to bring order to the situation and to protect the creditors who are pursuing those proceedings. For example, suppose that Stockton Enterprises Inc. has overdue debts to 12 unsecured creditors that total $600,000. No one creditor is owed more than $100,000 or less than $10,000, and each one is at some stage in the long process of civil litigation (described in Chapter 4), trying to collect the debt. However, Stockton's assets are worth only $300,000, and there is no reasonable prospect that it will regain its solvency.

In these circumstances, there is obviously just not enough money to pay all of the creditors and, in a sense, each of those creditors is making things worse for themselves by incurring more costs (i.e., on legal fees) in pursuing the claim. At the same time, the directors of Stockton are probably under tremendous pressure to deal with all of these lawsuits, making it difficult for them to concentrate on the business of the company, and the legal fees Stockton is having to pay are draining its scarce resources.

Bankruptcy is designed to help everyone in such a situation by putting a stop to all of the frantic, expensive attempts to "get at" what is left of the company and granting a measure of relief for the debtor company and the people running it.

## Ranking and Final Satisfaction of All Claims

All of the claims of the creditors are satisfied through the bankruptcy. In other words, whatever is available from the company's assets must go towards the claims of the creditors, and those creditors have no further recourse after the bankruptcy is completed.[2]

---

[1] See the discussion on this point in Chapter 12.

[2] That result follows because, except in exceedingly unusual situations, companies are never discharged from bankruptcy or, in other words, a company almost never resumes

Also, every creditor's claim is ranked. As mentioned on page 36 of Chapter 3, the first claims to be satisfied in a corporate bankruptcy are the claims of people for whom the bankrupt was holding property in trust. That property never legally belonged to the bankrupt and so it was never part of the "estate in bankruptcy," which is the term for what gets divided among the actual creditors.

The next to be paid are the secured creditors and/or the government "super priority claims." After the secured creditors and these government claims, come the "preferred claims," discussed and listed in Chapter 11. Finally, at the end of the chain, are the "ordinary, unpreferred claims."

activity after having been bankrupt. In contrast, individuals who go bankrupt are dis-charged, though certain types of debts—such as debts incurred by fraud and alimony obligations—are *not* extinguished as a result of bankruptcy. Also, the discharge of an individual bankrupt can be made subject to a number of conditions.

# The Voluntary and Involuntary Bankruptcy of a Corporation

T HERE ARE THREE WAYS FOR a company to go bankrupt. The two most common are: it chooses to do so or its creditors force bankruptcy upon it. The third and least common way for a company to go bankrupt is for it to attempt a commercial reorganization that fails (discussed in Part 4).

## VOLUNTARY ASSIGNMENTS IN BANKRUPTCY

A company can make what is called an "assignment" in bankruptcy fairly easily. In fact, in this era of fax machines, the paperwork can be processed within a matter of hours and consists of the following:

1) a resolution by the board of directors,[1] to put the company into bankruptcy;
2) a consent (i.e., to act as trustee) by the trustee in bankruptcy; and

---

[1] There is case law to the effect that the shareholders do not have the right to participate in this decision. If the shareholders were specifically given that right in a shareholder's agreement and the directors ignore it in making the assignment, the shareholders might have a cause of action against the directors, but it would not be grounds for annulling the bankruptcy.

3) a "statement of affairs," which lists the company's creditors, and the amounts owing to them.

This material is filed with the local office of the Official Receiver, a federal government agency administered by the Superintendent of Bankruptcy.

The only real requirement for a company to go bankrupt voluntarily is that it be insolvent. Generally, the *Bankruptcy and Insolvency Act* defines an insolvent company as one that has ceased paying, or is unable to pay, its obligations as they become due or whose property is not of a value that would allow it to pay all of its obligations.

## PETITIONING A COMPANY INTO INVOLUNTARY BANKRUPTCY

Chapter 4 discussed how an ordinary civil lawsuit is initiated and works its way through the court system. When a creditor wants to force a company into bankruptcy, the process is similar. However, in the case of bankruptcy proceedings, everything happens much more quickly.

## The Decision to Pursue Bankruptcy

When I say that the bankruptcy process moves much more quickly than a normal civil lawsuit, I know that many readers might be tempted for that reason to pursue bankruptcy whenever they are having trouble collecting a debt. However, things are just not that simple: many factors have to go into an evaluation of whether a company that is owed money by another company has the proper standing, and is well advised, to petition the other company into bankruptcy.

The first point to bear in mind is that if an unsecured creditor is successful in having a debtor declared bankrupt, the creditor will have ensured that he or she will have to share whatever is available for the unsecured creditors on an equal basis. That recovery could turn out to be zero, or not much better than that.

For example, suppose that Blackford Holdings Ltd. is owed $15,000 by one of its customers, Johnson Enterprises, Inc. Johnson owes its secured creditors $300,000 and it has debts to unsecured creditors of another $300,000 (among which is the $15,000 owed to Blackford). Suppose that all of Johnson's assets are worth only about $400,000 and that Johnson also has certain other debts that will have preferential status in a bankruptcy.

On those facts, if Johnson were declared bankrupt tomorrow, after the secured creditors were paid their $300,000, there would be, at most, $100,000 left for all of the other claims. If there were preferred claims of $50,000, all of the unsecured creditors would have to share the remainder, $50,000 equally.

Assuming that all $300,000 of the unsecured claims were advanced in the bankruptcy,[2] each creditor would get a "dividend" of $1 for every $6 owed, in full and final satisfaction of the claim. Thus, Blackford would get only $2,500 for its $15,000 claim.

Closely aligned with this practical reason for not pursuing a bankruptcy if you are an unsecured creditor is the fact that in many decided cases judgments have included the view that the bankruptcy process is not to be used as a collection agency. That is, the courts have held that it is an abuse of the process for a creditor to petition a company just to try to collect a debt.

## The Requirement of an "Act of Bankruptcy"

Obviously, there is a fine line to be drawn here because a company must owe debts in order to be eligible for bankruptcy. The *Bankruptcy and Insolvency Act* lists ten acts of bankruptcy; and the debtor, in order to be eligible, must have committed at least one of them within the six months prior to the date on which the bankruptcy proceedings began. By far the most commonly used act of bankruptcy is that the debtor "ceases to meet his liabilities generally as they become due." Typically, then, it will be necessary to show that the debtor has failed to pay other creditors in addition to the creditor who starts the bankruptcy proceedings.[3]

---

[2] The procedure for proving a claim is discussed in Chapter 11.

[3] Less commonly used grounds for forcing a company into involuntary bankruptcy include a written admission of insolvency to a meeting to creditors and improper dealings with the company's assets. Also, it is possible for a single creditor to establish that a company has ceased to meet its liabilities generally as they become due where there are suspicious circumstances in the way that the company has dealt with its assets, or other unusual factors.

## The Petition

The "petition" in an involuntary bankruptcy proceeding is the rough equivalent of a statement of claim in a civil lawsuit. In the petition, the "petitioning creditor"—that is, the creditor who is seeking a court order of bankruptcy against a company—alleges that the company committed an act of bankruptcy. Unlike a statement of claim, the petition is accompanied by an affidavit given by the petitioning creditor. [4]

## Selecting a Trustee in Bankruptcy

The petition also has to name a trustee in bankruptcy who has agreed to act as such. (In this regard, the petitioning creditor and the designated trustee must make an arrangement as to how the trustee's fees will be paid should the debtor have no unsecured assets with which to pay those fees.)

## Obtaining a Receiving Order by Default

The petition is filed with the court[5] and the Official Receiver's office. It must then be served on the debtor at least eight days before the petition is scheduled to be heard. If the debtor does not fight the petition, the Registrar of the Court will issue the order of bankruptcy, which is known as a receiving order. (This name is confusing to some people because although it sounds like it should relate to the appointment of a "receiver," it has nothing to do with receivers or receiverships, and is concerned only with bankruptcy.)

## The Corporate Debtor Fights Back: Notice Disputing Petition

On the other hand, if a corporate debtor decides to contest the attempt to put it into bankruptcy, he or she can file a Notice Disputing

---

[4] Where the petitioning creditor is a corporation, the affidavit is given by an officer of that organization.

[5] In Ontario, the court is the Court of Justice (General Division) in Bankruptcy.

Petition (the rough equivalent of a statement of defence in civil litigation), which will challenge the facts set out in the petition.

In addition, before the trial, the debtor has the opportunity to cross-examine the person who swore the affidavit in support of the petition. However, the petitioning creditor will *not* have an opportunity to examine an officer or director of the debtor before the trial. This set of rules has an obvious advantage for the debtor. From a creditor's viewpoint, it means that the creditor should have his or her case well thought out before filing the petition.

## The Trial of a Bankruptcy Petition

A trial of a bankruptcy petition unfolds much like a normal civil trial. The petitioner presents his or her case through witnesses who are subject to cross-examination by the debtor's lawyer. The debtor's lawyer then calls whatever witnesses he or she feels are appropriate and those witnesses are in turn subject to cross-examination by the petitioner. The lawyers then sum up the case and the judge renders a verdict.

## THE FAILURE OF A PROPOSAL

The least common way for a company to go bankrupt is for it to attempt a reorganization of its finances under the *Bankruptcy and Insolvency Act* and have it fail. This reorganization of finances is also called a "proposal" and will be discussed further in Chapters 14 and 15.

# The Bankruptcy Process

## THE FIRST MEETING OF CREDITORS

If a corporate bankruptcy occurs, the first major event in the proceedings is the initial meeting of creditors. The meeting must be called promptly after the trustee takes up his or her appointment, and every known creditor is entitled to a written notice of the meeting by registered mail. The meeting is also advertised in the newspaper.

The meetings typically take place at the Official Receiver's office, although sometimes they are held at the trustee's office or, in very large bankruptcies, in places such as hotel conference rooms.

### Mandatory Proceedings of a First Creditors Meeting

A representative of the Official Receiver's office acts as chair of the first meeting of creditors. Typically, he or she will read the results of their examination of an officer of the bankrupt corporation. A list of the mandatory questions to be put to such an officer is included in the Appendix as Exhibit 16.

At the first meeting of creditors, the Official Receiver will ask for a resolution from the creditors affirming the trustee's appointment.[1] It is very rare for a trustee's appointment not to be confirmed.

---

[1] Resolutions are carried by a majority of votes; however, in order to substitute a new

The other mandatory item of business at the first meeting of creditors is the appointment of "inspectors" from the body of creditors. Inspectors serve to assist the trustee in bankruptcy, as discussed below.[2]

## Attendance of a Creditor

The first meeting of creditors can be a good opportunity for creditors of a bankrupt company to obtain information. As a review of the list of mandatory questions to be addressed by an officer of the bankrupt[3] shows, a creditor may be able to learn something about the reasons for the bankruptcy and any unusual transactions involving the debtor in the period just before the bankruptcy.

On the other hand, the first meeting of creditors is held at a relatively early stage in the bankruptcy proceedings and chances are the trustee will both want and need to do a lot more work before being able to offer any kind of definitive analysis of the bankruptcy, including any information about expected returns to the creditors.

One important reason for a creditor to attend the first meeting of creditors is to stand for election as an inspector, if he or she wants that role.

## Filing a Proof of Claim

A proof of claim is written proof of a debt that must be submitted by a creditor in a bankruptcy. Filing a proof of claim before the first meeting of creditors gives you the right to vote for inspectors. If a proof of claim for a debt is completed and filed after the first meeting of creditors, the creditor will share in any distribution that is payable after the claim is filed.[4]

---

trustee, a "special resolution" of a majority in number representing three-quarters of the dollar value of the claims must be passed.

[2] Inspectors may be elected after the first meeting of creditors, although that rarely happens.

[3] See Exhibit 16 in the Appendix.

[4] Naturally, the *Bankruptcy and Insolvency Act* allows the trustee in bankruptcy to review and, where appropriate, disallow claims. Ultimately, disputes over the validity of a claim can end up before the Courts.

There are two types of proofs of claim: those used by someone claiming trust property and those used by someone claiming repayment of a debt. Copies of both forms are included in the Appendix (Exhibits 17 and 18).

## INSPECTORS

The trustee must go to the inspectors of the estate for approval to make many of the fundamental decisions involved in the administration of the estate of a bankrupt corporation. Ideally, the inspectors will be able to provide some real measure of assistance to the trustee through their knowledge of the industry in which the bankrupt company operated. In other words, if the bankrupt company was in the oil and gas business, the chances are that the body of creditors will include a number of people who know a lot about that business and can help the trustee when it comes to, say, selling a piece of highly specialized drilling equipment.

Up to five inspectors may be appointed. Trustees tend to prefer an odd number so that a deadlock over an issue that requires a vote of the inspectors can be avoided.

Technically the inspectors do not have to be creditors, but invariably that is the case. It is also typical that the inspectors represent the largest creditors.

## The Duties of Inspectors

Inspectors are supposed to act evenhandedly towards all of the creditors of the estate. Because most inspectors represent creditors of the bankrupt company, sometimes situations arise in which an inspector will have a conflict of interest with respect to a particular transaction that requires approval, and the inspector will have to abstain from voting on that issue.[5]

In specific terms, there are numerous individual items that inspectors potentially have to consider. I have already given the

---

[5] The *Bankruptcy and Insolvency Act* contains specific provisions dealing with, for example, inspectors buying assets of the estate. Also people who are a party to "any contested action...by or against the estate of the bankruptcy" are not eligible to serve as inspectors.

example of approving the sale of a piece of equipment. Other matters which an inspector could be asked to approve include:

- Approving the trustee's recommendation to settle a claim by the bankrupt company for money owing to it by another company at less than 100¢ on the dollar.

- Carrying on certain aspects of the bankrupt's business with a view to increasing the recovery for all creditors.

Even in cases in which there are few other matters to consider, the inspectors must at least review the trustee's bank records and accounting statements relating to the bankruptcy.[6]

## The Creditor as Inspector

One should not seek to be an inspector for the money: the *Bankruptcy and Insolvency Act* contemplates a fee per inspector per meeting of between $10 and $40, depending on how much money is in the estate.[7] As such, it can prove to be an impractical use of the time of many creditors.

However, in situations where the creditor has concerns about the way in which the bankrupt managed his or her affairs, being an inspector is a good way to stay close to the trustee in bankruptcy and his or her investigation of the bankrupt.

## THE ASSETS OF THE BANKRUPT CORPORATION

In addition to the property of the bankrupt on the day of bankruptcy, all property acquired after that date vests, in or passes to, the trustee in bankruptcy. For example, if a company made a voluntary assignment in bankruptcy on January 10, 1994, and on April 15, 1994, the federal government determined that it owed the bankrupt company a $10,000 tax refund, that money would vest in the trustee.

---

[6] The Act allows the trustee to get court approval instead, where no inspectors are available.

[7] Forty dollars per meeting covers all estates of $100,000 or more. A provision in the *Bankruptcy and Insolvency Act* allows a special fee to be paid to inspectors for providing highly specialized services for the estate.

## The Trustee's General Duty to Recover Assets

Closely aligned with this basic vesting principle are two other ideas. First, the *Bankruptcy and Insolvency Act* gives the trustee the power to recover a variety of assets that may properly belong to the bankrupt but that, for one reason or another, were allowed to get away or have not yet been converted into money. Second, the trustee is now obliged to expend money from his or her own pocket in order to make such recovery.

For example, suppose that on the day Maitland Enterprises Ltd. goes bankrupt its assets consist of some equipment, its accounts receivable, and the right to sue a company in Philadelphia for copyright infringement. The trustee reviews the files relating to this lawsuit, which is being carried on in Philadelphia, and determines that if it is successful, a court would probably award damages of US$150,000. However, it is going to cost $40,000 in legal fees and two years of effort in order to, *perhaps,* recover that money. The equipment and the accounts receivable are worth only about $10,000, and there are various legitimate expenses connected with the estate that are going to cost almost that much.

## Taking an Assignment of the Trustee's Right to Recover Assets

There is no obligation on the Maitland trustee to fund the legal fees necessary to pursue the lawsuit in Pennsylvania. However, the *Bankruptcy and Insolvency Act* does provide that one or more of Maitland's creditors can take up the action, at their own expense, but also for their own benefit.

The way in which this process works is that one or more creditors bring a motion (on notice to the trustee only) to the court for an order allowing the continuation of the action. In the Maitland example, suppose there were fifteen creditors, one of whom, Oxford Developments Ltd., was owed $90,000 and the rest of whom were each owed between $5000 and $20,000. Obviously, Oxford has the strongest interest in recovering assets so it might be the one to start the proceedings. When and if it does the other fourteen creditors need not receive notice that the process has been started. However, if Oxford receives the court's permission to pursue the lawsuit, Oxford must then notify the other creditors and give them an opportunity to share both the cost and any benefit from the proceedings.

## Reviewable Transactions

One of the ways for a trustee in bankruptcy to recover assets is by overturning certain transactions which the bankrupt may have entered into before having gone bankrupt. This subject is discussed at length in Chapter 13 but it may be noted here that one or more of the creditors may also take an assignment of the trustee's powers in this regard in the manner just discussed.

## PURCHASING ASSETS FROM A TRUSTEE IN BANKRUPTCY

As previously discussed, if a valid receivership is occurring at the same time as a bankruptcy, any sale of the assets of the bankrupt company will likely occur through the receivership. Accordingly, many bankruptcies do not include a sale of the assets by the trustee in bankruptcy.

Nevertheless, trustees in bankruptcy can sell assets. In this regard, many of the observations made in Chapter 8, "Purchasing Assets from a Receiver," apply when the vendor is a trustee in bankruptcy. That is, the purchaser must forget about getting any kind of detailed representations or warranties, and should instead do his or her own due diligence investigations, and reflect any concerns that those investigations bring up in the price he or she is willing to pay.

However, some aspects of a sale by a trustee are unique to the bankruptcy process. For example, as already noted, the sale must be approved by the inspectors or the court. Also, when the bankrupt's assets include land, the trustee will register a copy of the receiving order or assignment in the appropriate land registry office. That way, when a purchaser subsequently receives a deed from the trustee, there is a suitable "chain of title" showing how the transferor (the trustee) came to have the ability to sell the land to the transferee.[8]

---

[8] The registration of notice of the bankruptcy is also important in preventing any improper dealings with the land. Receivers generally do not register evidence of their appointment on title, although a deed from a receiver will recite his or her authority to deal with the land.

Although the trustee has the ability to sell assets by private contracts, many sales by trustees in bankruptcy are conducted by tender. The rules pertaining to the tender process are set out in detail in the *Bankruptcy and Insolvency Act*.

## DISTRIBUTION OF THE ASSETS

As has been said, for those cases in which a trustee has funds available for distribution to creditors, the *Bankruptcy and Insolvency Act* sets out a scheme for how the various creditors rank.

After any trust claims, secured creditors claims, and government "super priority" claims, have been satisfied, the "preferred claims" in a corporate bankruptcy rank, in descending order, as follows:

1) the costs of the administration—that is, the trustee's fees and the estate's legal fees;

2) a levy payable to the Superintendent of Bankruptcy with respect to any assets sold by the estate;

3) a claim for up to $2000 of wages owed to employees who rendered services to the bankrupt company within the proceding six months;

4) municipal taxes that do not constitute a lien on the bankrupt's real property, limited to the value of the property in respect of which the taxes were imposed;

5) a landlord's claim for up to three months' rent arrears and three months' accelerated rent;[9]

6) the legal fees and costs of the first creditor who started some form of enforcement proceedings—either by garnishment or by filing a writ of execution—pursuant to a judgment against the bankrupt; and

7) claims resulting from injuries to employees of the bankrupt, to the extent that the bankrupt receives monies to compensate for those injuries.

Only after wading through all of these preferred claims would there be anything left for the unsecured creditors.

---

[9] This preferred claim is subject to further limitations, as discussed in Chapter 12.

# The Relationship Between Receiverships and Bankruptcies

**M**ANY COMPANIES ARE BANKRUPT AT the same time as they are in receivership. In fact, the same company or person may act simultaneously as both receiver and trustee in bankruptcy of a company.

That situation may strike some readers as odd, but there is nothing inherently illegal, unethical, or unusual about it—provided that certain basic steps are taken. Very good strategic reasons often exist for a bankruptcy to be combined with a receivership.

In order to understand the relationship between a corporate receivership and bankruptcy, it is necessary to focus on some of the major effects of bankruptcy on the ranking and rights of the creditors, particularly secured creditors (who appoint receivers), government creditors, and commercial landlords.

## THE RIGHTS OF SECURED CREDITORS IN A BANKRUPTCY

The position of a secured creditor in a bankruptcy can be summarized in the following five basic principles:

1) As noted in Chapter 9, a secured creditor is generally not subject to the stay against proceedings by creditors the comes into effect on bankruptcy. Thus, in most circumstances a secured

creditor can continue enforcing security against a company notwithstanding that the company has passed into bankruptcy.

2)  The trustee in bankruptcy has limited power to stop a secured creditor from acting on (or enforcing) his or her security, in accordance with the first principle. One situation where the trustee might try to stop the secured creditor is where the secured creditor's security is worth much more than the amount of the secured debt. For example, suppose that a secured creditor was owed $10,000 and that as security for that debt, he held security over a piece of equipment that was worth $30,000. In those circumstances, the trustee might wish to be allowed to "buy out" the secured creditor's position by paying $10,000 so as to create $20,000 of value for all of the other creditors of the bankrupt company.

3)  As a corollary to the first two principles, a trustee in bankruptcy has a basic right to inspect property subject to security in order to determine whether there is surplus value in it, and to require a secured creditor to place a value on his or her security. On the other hand, a secured creditor can "foreclose" on his or her security by asking a trustee whether he or she wants to pay out the secured creditor or force a sale of the collateral.

4)  Another way for a trustee to stop a secured creditor from enforcing security in the face of a bankruptcy is to challenge the validity of the security. There are numerous grounds on which the security could be proved invalid.

    For example, there are the various registration requirements that apply to security discussed in Chapter 1. Those registrations are required to make security effective not only vis-à-vis other secured or unsecured creditors, but also against trustees in bankruptcy, who effectively represent all of those unsecured creditors. A relatively simple error in, say, a financing statement under the *Personal Property Security Act,* (such as typing "Miller" instead of "Milner") may result in a security registration being invalidated.[1]

---

[1] The *Personal Property Security Act* contains a number of provisions which permit errors in registrations to be fixed. However, corrected registrations will be subject to other registrations made before the error is corrected. Also, the *Personal Property Security Act* provides that it is too late to fix a registration when the debtor has become bankrupt.

Another basis on which trustees can attack security is if there is something improper about the way in which it was given. This subject is discussed further in Chapter 12.

5) Conversely, however, if a secured creditor's security is valid and enforceable, there is no reason why one firm or one individual cannot act as both receiver under that security, and as trustee in bankruptcy of the company that gave the security. There may even be much gained, in avoiding duplication of effort, in having one company fill both roles.

Before the *Bankruptcy and Insolvency Act* came into effect in 1992, the practice that most trustees in bankruptcy followed before accepting such "dual" appointments was to get a legal opinion from a law firm, independent from the firm being used by the secured creditor, to the effect that the security under which the receivership appointment was to be made was good. The *Bankruptcy and Insolvency Act* now contains a specific requirement to that effect.

## STRATEGIC REASONS FOR COMBINING A BANKRUPTCY AND A RECEIVERSHIP: DEALING WITH COMMERCIAL LEASES

Chapter 2 discussed the arsenal of remedies a landlord has when a commercial lease is breached. These remedies can be a thorn in the side of a receiver.

## Terminating the Landlord's Remedies

A bankruptcy is often combined with a receivership for the purpose of stopping the landlord's use of any of these remedies due to the general stay of proceedings against all creditors of the bankrupt.

For example, suppose that Weatherfield Holdings Inc., a corporate tenant that operates a T-shirt manufacturing and sales business is behind in rent and is also in default in its bank loans.

The bank has security, so it is in a position to appoint a receiver. However, suppose that before the bank has had a chance to get a receiver in place, the landlord has started to exercise his right to seize and sell Weatherfield's equipment and inventory on the premises to satisfy the rent arrears.[2] Suppose further that the lease is at a below-market level of rent and that, therefore, the landlord's plan is to terminate the lease—on the basis of Weatherfield's default—as soon as the distress action has been completed.

This plan of attack by the landlord is perfectly legal, but it obviously puts a crimp in the bank's plans to conduct an orderly receivership of Weatherfield, including operating Weatherfield's business, from the leased premises, for an appropriate period of time, while as much of the inventory as possible is completed and sold off.

If Weatherfield, on the other hand, were to go bankrupt, the bank could proceed with its plans for receivership because by "operation of law"—that is, by virtue of the legal effect of the bankruptcy—the landlord would lose the right to distress and other remedies such as the right to terminate the lease.

In this type of situation, the corporate tenant will often make a voluntary assignment in bankruptcy because the shareholder and/or directors of the company have signed guarantees in favour of the bank, and thus they want to ensure that the bank recovers as much as possible from the company.[3] However, if necessary, the bank or another creditor can petition the corporate tenant into bankruptcy.[4]

## Limiting the Landlord's Claim

In exchange for losing its substantial remedies, a landlord is given a limited preferred claim in the bankruptcy. This preferred claim is for:

1) up to three months' rent arrears; and

---

[2] This is the remedy of distress, discussed in Chapter 2.

[3] Usually, the directors of the company will have no liability to the landlord and, therefore, will not be troubled by the inconvenience of the bankruptcy to the landlord. However, that is not always the case: see the discussion of guarantees to landlords on pages 187 to 188. Also, whenever directors are called on to cooperate by allowing their company to make a voluntary assignment in bankruptcy, they should consider the effect of that bankruptcy on their personal liability under the various director liability statutory provisions.

[4] Special rules apply when the petitioning creditor is also a secured creditor. In those circumstances, the secured creditor must concede that there is some unsecured portion of the debt.

2) up to three months' accelerated rent if the lease provides for that.

However, this preferred claim is subject to three major qualifications. First, it ranks below certain other claims, including the claims of secured creditors.[5] Second, it is limited to the value of the property on the premises.[6] Finally, no matter what happens to the lease as a result of the bankruptcy, case law indicates that a landlord does not have a right to submit a proof of claim for anything beyond the preferred claim. In other words, the landlord, cannot submit a potentially enormous claim for the loss of the lease.

## The Trustee's Right of Occupation

The trustee in bankruptcy has a right to occupy premises leased by a bankrupt for up to three months after the date of bankruptcy.[7] Of course, trustees do not *have* to occupy the premises but if they do, they must pay "occupation rent" equal to the value of rent under the lease for the time of occupation.[8] Any occupation rent paid goes to reduce the landlord's secured claim.

To bring all of these ideas together, let's return to the Weatherfield Holdings example. Suppose that: the monthly rent under Weatherfield's lease was $500 and that at the date of going bankrupt, the company was two months behind; the lease allowed the landlord to claim three months' accelerated rent on the bankruptcy of the tenant; the property on the premises at the date of bankruptcy was worth $2000; and the trustee paid the landlord to occupy the premises for one month following the bankruptcy.

The landlord's preferred claim in the bankruptcy of Weatherfield would be calculated as follows:

---

[5] The ranking of preferred claims in a bankruptcy is discussed in Chapter 11.

[6] This limitation ties the preferred claim into the non-bankruptcy remedy of distress, which is only useful to the extent that the tenant has property on the premises.

[7] This right is contained in the Ontario *Landlord and Tenant Act,* which works in conjunction with the *Bankruptcy and Insolvency Act* in this area.

[8] Although there are some conflicting decisions on this point, it seems that the trustee is personally liable for such occupation rent (i.e., regardless of whether there are any assets in the estate to generate money to pay for it).

1) $1000       (for two months in arrears)
   + $1500     (for three months' accelerated rent)
     $2500

2) however, the $2500 would be reduced to $2000 because that is the value of the property on the premises; and

3) the $2000 figure would be further reduced to $1500 because it still contains a component representing accelerated rent (i.e., anything over $1000) that must be reduced by the amount of occupation rent ($500) paid.

## Disclaiming a Lease

Within the three-month period following the bankruptcy of a corporate tenant, the trustee in bankruptcy must decide what to do with the lease. One choice is to terminate the lease—which is known as "disclaiming the lease." In the event of a disclaimer, the landlord is free to look for a new tenant because the trustee has no further interest in the lease.

## Forcing an Assignment of a Lease

If the lease is an attractive asset—because, for example, it is at a below-market level of rent—the trustee can elect to preserve, or "retain," the lease within that same three-month period and to assign it to a third party who wishes to buy the assets of the company in bankruptcy (and possibly also in receivership[9]).

Although a landlord can attempt to fight such an assignment, the *Landlord and Tenant Act* and the case law provide that the court will allow the assignment to go through as long as it can be established that the new tenant will honour the lease obligations, and that he or she will make a fit and proper use of the premises.

Receivers cannot similarly force an assignment of a lease. Thus, bankruptcy can be a powerful tool to facilitate a sale of *all* the assets of a company in receivership as a going concern—that is, on terms whereby the purchaser can just take over occupation of the same premises from which the company in receivership operated.

[9] The ability of a trustee in bankruptcy to assign a lease exists even if the bankrupt company is not also in receivership.

Of course, in facilitating the transfer of a lease in this way, the trustee can be performing a valuable service for the secured creditor who appointed the receiver. Therefore, as a matter of practice, the secured creditor typically makes some form of payment to the trustee for facilitating the assignment in this way. That money then goes to the general body of creditors, not including the secured creditor.

## GOVERNMENT CLAIMS IN BANKRUPTCY AND RECEIVERSHIP

Chapter 3 looked at how federal, provincial, and municipal governments try to collect their debts from insolvent companies through the use of garnishment, director liability, statutory liens, and deemed trusts. Many of these statutory liens and deemed trusts are designed to give the appropriate government agency priority over some secured creditors—even in a receivership.

But as was mentioned in Chapter 3, one of the major consequences of a bankruptcy is that many of these government claims lose their priority vis-à-vis secured creditors. Thus, another reason for combining a bankruptcy with a receivership is to reverse the priorities in this way.

Not every government claim is affected by bankruptcy, and so it is always necessary to consider each claim individually. What follows is a brief discussion of how some of the most common types of debt owed by corporations to government agencies are affected by bankruptcy. From the viewpoint of the individuals who run companies, it should be noted that directors can be liable for all but a few of these government claims.[10] Thus, if the government is defeated in its attempt to collect the money because of a "strategic bankruptcy," it is all the more likely that the government will come after the directors of the company, in an effort to collect the money.

### *Income Tax Act* Withholdings, Canada Pension Plan Contributions and Unemployment Insurance Contributions

These liabilities still make up the "big three" of government debt in the sense that the obligation to satisfy them continues to be accorded the highest priority.

---

[10] See the chart of statutory director liability provisions in the Appendix (Exhibit 10).

The legislation imposes both a statutory lien and a deemed trust over all of the property of an insolvent company, to cover monies that were supposed to have been set aside to fund these payroll obligations. These deemed trusts (which are established by federal rather than provincial legislation) also survive in a bankruptcy even where the money was not specifically set aside.

Also, the debt may be collected by the government through the use of a "super garnishment" collection power, which is not stayed by a bankruptcy. In practice, though, Revenue Canada will typically work with the trustee in bankruptcy to ensure that the monies are collected in an orderly way. That is, often Revenue Canada will allow the trustee in bankruptcy to collect the funds, provided that Revenue Canada's priority is respected.

There have been many cases dealing with, and government pronouncements of one form or another on, how these deemed trust and super garnishment powers relate to the rights of secured creditors of the company that was supposed to, but did not, make the payments to the government. The one principle that seems fairly clear is that a fixed charge security interest (that is, a security interest in a "fixed asset" such as a piece of equipment or real property) which is taken before any *Income Tax Act*, CPP or UI arrears have arisen, will take priority over the federal government's interest in the same asset as a result of the owner's failure to make its payroll withholdings for those amounts. Less clear is how a floating charge, such as a security interest in a company's accounts receivable or inventory, relates to these government deemed trust and super garnishment claims, although overall (and especially in light of a very recent amendment to the *Income Tax Act*) it seems that the federal government will win out over a secured creditor with such security.

However, the point is that, unlike most government claims discussed in this chapter, the mere bankruptcy of the debtor company has no impact on the government's rights concerning these claims.

## The Goods and Services Tax

The statute that imposes the GST is the *Excise Tax Act,* and it gives the federal government both deemed trust and garnishment powers to collect unpaid GST. Through these powers, the government is able to gain priority over certain secured creditors of the same debtor—such as creditors with security over floating assets including receivables and inventory. However, it appears that this priority is lost if the company is declared bankrupt.[11]

## Provincial Retail Sales Tax

Provincial sales tax, in Ontario and in other provinces, is a classic example of a government claim that is the subject of a deemed trust that will take priority over certain secured creditors[12] outside of bankruptcy (including cases in which only a receivership is under way), but which will rank as a mere, unsecured claim after bankruptcy has occurred.[13]

## Provincial Claims for Unpaid Wages

In Ontario, the *Employment Standards Act* confers a limited priority on employees, over other creditors, for $2000 worth of unpaid wages per employee. As discussed in Chapter 6, there is case law to the effect that this claim ranks behind secured creditors. But in practice, receivers often choose to pay the wage arrears in order to ensure a good relationship with the employees during the receivership.

In a bankruptcy, this wage claim ranks behind the claims of secured creditors, although, as a preferred claim, it is ahead of the claims of ordinary, unsecured creditors.[14]

---

[11] The GST legislation is not particularly well drafted in this area. On the one hand, it contains provisions that specifically say that the garnishment powers and the deemed trust do not apply in a bankruptcy. In other words, the deemed trust does not fail in bankruptcy because of the general requirement that the trust property be identifiable; it fails because it does not apply even in bankruptcy. However, another provision in the *Excise Tax Act* speaks of the trustee being liable for GST outstanding at the date of bankruptcy. So far, in practice, it seems that Revenue Canada will concede priority to secured creditors after, but not before, the bankruptcy of a company that has failed to pay all of its GST liabilities.

[12] The provincial legislation also contains a statutory lien.

[13] Unless the company actually held its provincial sales tax money in a separate, identifiable account.

[14] In Ontario there is also a specific "wage protection fund" which will pay up to $5000 per employee with respect to unpaid wages owed by an insolvent company. In other words this fund operates independently of a bankruptcy and/or receivership process whereby the assets of the insolvent company are dealt with and distributed.

## Provincial Claims for Unpaid Vacation Pay

The *Employment Standards Act* creates a deemed trust and a statutory lien for unpaid vacation pay. Under both the case law and, since 1989, the *Personal Property Security Act,* these claims can take priority over certain secured creditors in a receivership scenario. However, they will fail, and rank below those of secured creditors, once bankruptcy occurs unless the statutory lien has been properly registered or the deemed trust property is identifiable.

## Provincial Claims for Termination Pay/Severance Pay

Termination pay and severance pay obligations are, in my experience, often confused with each other and/or misunderstood.

Under the *Employment Standards Act,* termination pay can arise in two situations, which are commonly referred to as "mass" and "individual" terminations. Subject to limited exceptions, mass termination occurs when an employer terminates 50 or more people within a four-week period. In such circumstances, the following termination pay obligations arise:

| Number of Employees | Pay Obligations |
|---|---|
| 50–199 | 8 weeks |
| 200–499 | 12 weeks |
| over 500 | 16 weeks |

In a non-mass termination, an employee terminated is generally entitled to the following termination pay, based on length of service:

| Length of Service | Pay Obligations |
|---|---|
| 3 months–1 year | 1 week |
| 1–3 years | 2 weeks |
| 3 years | 3 weeks |
| 4 years | 4 weeks |
| etc. | to a maximum of 8 weeks |

In contrast, severance pay obligations arise out of the termination of an employee with five or more years of service where either:

1) the annual payroll of the employer was over $2.5 million in either of the past two fiscal years; or

2) 50 or more employees have their employment terminated within a six month period, due to a permanent discontinuance of all or part of a business.

An employee can work off the termination pay (or notice) obligations, but not the severance pay obligations. In other words, adequate written notice from an employer will satisfy the termination pay obligations.

The provincial government's only tool in collecting unpaid termination and severance pay is a garnishment power that does not rank ahead of secured creditors with an interest in those same receivables, properly registered under the *Personal Property Security Act*. Although it is rarely done, the government may also launch a prosecution for contravention of the *Employment Standards Act*. With an insolvent company such a prosecution will have limited effect. Also, this garnishment power will be stayed as soon as a bankruptcy occurs.

Moreover, according to a recent decision of the Ontario Court of Appeal, employees do not have a claim for termination pay, severance pay or vacation pay under the *Employment Standards Act* merely as a result of their employer being involuntarily declared bankrupt. That is, a receiving order does not result in a deemed termination of employment for these purposes.

## Realty Taxes

Realty taxes are collected by the municipality in which a debtor company owns real property and are protected under the *Municipal Act* by a special lien. This lien does not have to be registered on title in order to enjoy priority over every type of security—including a mortgage that is registered before the realty taxes go unpaid—encumbering the property. In other words, as anyone who has ever bought a house knows, the lien for realty taxes has to be satisfied "off the top."

This priority status for realty taxes continues even through a receivership or a bankruptcy.

## Business Taxes

Business taxes are also collected at the municipal level, but they do not enjoy the same protection as realty taxes. In fact, the municipality's only statutory collection power is one of distress.

The most recent case law in Ontario is to the effect that this right of distress ranks ahead of the rights of secured creditors. It is stopped by a bankruptcy but it enjoys a limited preferential status in a bankruptcy.[15]

## Health Taxes

With the changes in the mid-1980s to the way Ontario's Health Insurance Plan is funded, employers became liable for payroll premiums. If the payments are not made, the provincial government can simply register a writ against the employer's property, which can ultimately result in the sale of the land. In other words, without having to go through the cost and process of a formal lawsuit the government can obtain in an instant the results that ordinary creditors must work for through the litigation process as discussed in Chapter 4.

These powers do not take priority over the rights of a duly registered and perfected secured creditor and are stayed as a result of bankruptcy.

## Workers' Compensation

Under the *Workers' Compensation Act,* if an employer fails to pay its assessments, the Ontario Workers' Compensation Board can file a certificate with the local municipality to collect the debt when it collects taxes. Alternatively, the certificate can be filed with the local sheriff as a "first lien" on the employer's property, subject only to municipal taxes.

---

[15] As set out in Chapter 11, on page 125.

There is case law to the effect that this lien will not have priority over a proper fixed charge (or a floating charge which has crystallized[16]). Also, it will be stayed by bankruptcy.

## Corporations Tax

The Ontario *Corporations Tax Act* gives the provincial government the right to register a lien against the real property of a company that has failed to pay corporations tax. This lien will not, however, take priority over the claims of creditors who have properly registered security interests in the land before the lien is registered.

The government's claim for unpaid corporations tax will simply rank as an unsecured claim in a bankruptcy, unless the lien has been properly registered.

---

[16] Generally speaking, a floating charge that has crystallized is one that has become enforceable.

# Reviewable Transactions:
# Uncovering Hidden Assets
# and Improper Dealings

O NE OF THE CORNERSTONES OF debtor-creditor law in Canada is a detailed web of legislative provisions designed to prevent debtors from improperly "hiding" assets from creditors. The dealings that give rise to both suspicion of, and legal action against, such attempts to hide assets are, in general, called reviewable transactions. This term is also used specifically to refer to transactions in which property has been dealt with at a price conspicuously more or less than fair market value (discussed on pages 154 to 155).

A number of the legislative provisions designed to prevent reviewable transactions are contained in the *Bankruptcy and Insolvency Act,* but obviously those provisions are only available when the debtor has been declared bankrupt. However, many are also found in other statutes (both federal and provincial), which are designed to be used both before and after bankruptcy. For a long time, many insolvency lawyers thought that the provincial legislation in this field might be unconstitutional because it was thought that only the federal government had the power to legislate in this area. However, in a 1977 case called *Robinson v. Countrywide Factors Ltd.,* the Supreme Court of Canada upheld the validity of some of this provincial legislation and, since then, it has enjoyed renewed life.

When you combine this web of legislation with those provisions of the *Bankruptcy and Insolvency Act* that allow individual creditors to take an assignment of the trustee's rights to an action designed to recover assets of the bankrupt, the following general points can be made:

1) Outside of bankruptcy, a debtor can be attacked by one or more of his or her creditors if he or she attempts to "hide" or otherwise improperly deal with assets in a number of ways.

2) Once that debtor goes bankrupt, the trustee in bankruptcy comes to represent those creditors and the trustee can pursue all of the claims available before the bankruptcy, plus an additional set of potential remedies, as a result of the application of the *Bankruptcy and Insolvency Act*.

3) If, for some reason—such as lack of funds—the trustee in bankruptcy is unwilling to pursue the full arsenal of remedies, any one or more of the creditors can take an assignment of the trustee's rights, including the rights that arise only as a result of the *Bankruptcy and Insolvency Act*.

So, what are the types of transactions that can be "reviewed" in this way? In this chapter, I will briefly discuss transactions that can be attacked by trustees in bankruptcy or, when applicable, by groups of creditors, under the following statutes: The Ontario *Bulk Sales Act,* the Ontario *Assignments and Preferences Act,* the Ontario *Fraudulent Conveyances Act,* the Ontario *Business Corporations Act,* the *Canada Business Corporations Act,* the *Criminal Code of Canada* and, of course, the *Bankruptcy and Insolvency Act*.

## BULK SALES

The *Bulk Sales Act* is designed to prevent a debtor from selling assets "in bulk," unless certain conditions, designed to protect that person's creditors, are met.

For example, consider this basic situation: Mario's Furniture Limited manufactures a line of furniture that it sells, on a wholesale basis, to a string of retailers. Suppose that Mario's assets are approximately as follows:

| | |
|---|---|
| equipment | $ 90,000 |
| inventory | $ 50,000 |
| accounts receivable | $ 60,000 |
| goodwill | $ 20,000 |
| Total | $220,000 |

Mario's buys from ten unsecured trade creditors, and its debt to those trade creditors has reached almost $200,000. In addition, Mario's has a government grant of $50,000 and has not paid its rent of $10,000 per month for two months. It also owes about $15,000 to each of the federal and provincial governments for taxes.

Suppose that one day Mario's contacts one of its customers Metropolitan Furniture Ltd. and offers to sell all of its assets to Metropolitan for $180,000 in cash.

Notice that, on these facts, no secured creditors would show up if Metropolitan were to carry out a series of corporate searches (as discussed on page 43) on Mario's. So, after having carried out those searches, Metropolitan decides that $180,000 is a pretty good price for these assets and completes the deal (without any consideration of the *Bulk Sales Act* or any other legislation).

Suppose that over the course of the next week the owner of Mario's removes the $180,000 from the corporate bank account and is last seen boarding a plane for a South American country that has no extradition treaty with Canada, following which the various creditors of Mario's learn about the sale.

In these circumstances, the nightmare Metropolitan will face is that they will have to return the assets for which they have paid (for the benefit of Mario's creditors) and will have no legal means of recovering that money. This is an extreme example, but I hope that it demonstrates that the *Bulk Sales Act* is a very powerful piece of legislation.

Basically, the *Bulk Sales Act* concentrates on sales of "stock," which is widely defined as goods, wares, merchandise, chattels, or fixtures[1] "in bulk." The phrase "sale of stock in bulk" refers to a sale of all or substantially all of the seller's stock "outside the usual course of the seller's business." In other words, when Mario's made

---

[1] In Ontario, the definition does not include intangible assets like goodwill and accounts receivable.

a routine sale of ten pieces of furniture to one of its customers a week before its sale to Metropolitan, that was not a bulk sale, because it was made in the ordinary course of business. However, the sale to Metropolitan was definitely a sale of stock in bulk and, because the *Bulk Sales Act* was not complied with, the creditors of Mario's can apply to have it set aside.

So, how do you comply with the *Bulk Sales Act*? In other words, if you are ever offered an attractive deal of the kind offered to Metropolitan, how do you complete it legally?

The *Bulk Sales Act* sets out three "proper" ways of completing such a sale:

1)  The sale may be approved by the court. This often occurs where the seller is a relatively large company and—although it wants to sell assets out of the ordinary course—the value of the assets being sold represents a relatively small percentage of the seller's assets. In those circumstances, it is possible to satisfy a judge that no creditors are going to be prejudiced by the sale.

2)  A majority of the unsecured trade creditors may consent to the appointment of a trustee who will receive the purchase funds and distribute them among the creditors.

3)  The most common way for the *Bulk Sales Act* to be complied with is for the seller to provide an affidavit that lists all of the seller's creditors, classified as either secured or unsecured, and the amounts due to them. A copy of this affidavit form is included in the Appendix (Exhibit 19).

    If the affidavit shows the secured and unsecured creditors are not owed more than $2500 each, and the buyer has no knowledge that that is incorrect, the buyer can proceed to complete the transaction. However, if the amounts shown in the affidavit exceed $2500, generally speaking, the purchaser comes under an onus to obtain verification that those creditors are being provided for as part of the terms of the sale. Any purchaser who ignores that responsibility risks having the transaction attacked by creditors.

This is an example of a provincial statute that can also be used by a trustee in bankruptcy. In other words, in the example, Mario's creditors could use the statute to attack Metropolitan without first having to petition Mario's into bankruptcy; however, if Mario's *was* declared bankrupt, the trustee in bankruptcy could also pursue Metropolitan, using the provisions of the *Bulk Sales Act*.

## GIVING PREFERENTIAL TREATMENT TO A CREDITOR

In general terms, an improper preference occurs when a debtor with more than one creditor satisfies indebtedness to one creditor in circumstances where the other creditors will not be paid.

For example, Nick's Restaurant Supplies Inc. has assets of $10,000 in the bank, $7,000 in inventory, and not much else. On the other hand, Nick's has debts totalling $50,000 most of which is owed to his landlord, the government, and a variety of suppliers.[2] But $8000 of it is owed to Jane Smith who happens to be the sister of Nick Smith, the sole shareholder and director of Nick's Restaurant Supplies Inc. On June 1, Nick's issues a cheque for $8000 to Jane Smith, and on June 3, Nick's gives the other $2000 in its bank account to a trustee in bankruptcy as a retainer. Nick's then makes a voluntary assignment in bankruptcy with the idea that the other creditors who are owed $42,000 will have to be satisfied from the $7000 of inventory.

Obviously, there would be something badly wrong with our system if that kind of transaction could not be attacked and, in fact, it is easily attackable as a preference under both the *Bankruptcy and Insolvency Act* and the *Assignments and Preferences Act* (Ontario). However, the terms of the two statutes are not identical and the broad components of the offence that must be established under both are summarized and contrasted below.

Both the *Bankruptcy and Insolvency Act* and the *Assignments and Preferences Act* (Ontario) require that the debtor be "insolvent" or in "insolvent circumstances" at the time of the preference. The *Assignments and Preferences Act* (Ontario) relies on the common law definition of insolvency that focuses on the fair value of the debtor's property versus liabilities, whereas the *Bankruptcy and Insolvency Act* contains a more extensive definition of the term that

---

[2] Nick's has no secured creditors.

includes this concept but also includes the aspect of a general failure or inability to meet obligations as they become due.

It should also be stressed that the bald example of the payment made by Nick's Restaurant Supplies is only one type of preference. Both the *Bankruptcy and Insolvency Act* and the *Assignments and Preferences Act* (Ontario) make clear that a preference can be something more than just a payment. For example, the granting of a security interest or the transfer of title to property can also be a preference in certain situations. That is, suppose that instead of paying his sister, Nick Smith caused Nick's Restaurant Supplies Inc. to grant a general security agreement to her two days before the company went into bankruptcy. As already discussed at length, a *valid* security holder ranks ahead of ordinary unsecured creditors on a bankruptcy, but here the security would be struck out as constituting a preference. The same result would occur if Nick's had tried to just convey title to all of the inventory to Jane just before the bankruptcy.

## Proving Intent

A Supreme Court of Canada ruling has established that under the *Bankruptcy and Insolvency Act* it is necessary only to prove the intent of the debtor to prefer one creditor over the others and it is not necessary to also prove that the recipient of the preference also had that same intent. In other words, in our example it is irrelevant whether Jane Smith knew about, and intended to go along with, the attempt to prefer her position over that of the other creditors. Obviously, it would be harder to prove the offence if that additional element of "concurrent" intent of the creditor receiving the preference had to be established.

Under the *Bankruptcy and Insolvency Act,* a "rebuttable presumption" that the necessary intent element is present arises if the trustee can establish that:

1) the bankrupt was insolvent at the time of the transaction;

2) the transaction occurred within 3 months of bankruptcy if the bankrupt and the creditor receiving the (alleged) preference are not related or within 12 months of bankruptcy if they are; and

3)  the *effect* of the transaction was to confer a preference.

In other words, a rebuttable presumption means that the onus of proof has shifted. Thus, where one of these situations exists, the onus shifts to the debtor, or more practically speaking, to the creditor—who is trying to sustain or "enforce" the transaction that is being attacked—to show that it did not amount to a preference and that onus is no longer on the trustee or other creditor(s) attacking it.

There is no such rebuttable presumption under the *Assignments and Preferences Act* (Ontario) and so establishing the intent element is tougher—particularly in light of the "defences" discussed below.[3]

## What Is the Remedy?

If a preference is established, under the *Bankruptcy and Insolvency Act,* or under the *Assignments and Preferences Act* (Ontario) the transaction is void as against the trustee in bankruptcy, and the recipient of the preference (Jane Smith, in our example) will be directed to make the property received (i.e., the $8000) available to satisfy the other creditors.

## Defences

These types of transactions have been litigated for years, and in the many situations where transactions were *not* overturned as constituting a preference, it could be said that the debtor had a good "defence" to the allegation that a preference has been committed.

For example, under the *Bankruptcy and Insolvency Act* the following situations do not constitute preferences:[4]

1)  The transaction was made in a good faith expectation that it would enable the bankruptcy to continue in business.

2)  The creditor in question refused to supply more goods or services without receiving security for past advances.

---

[3] However, as discussed below, under "Limitation Periods," the Assignments and Preferences Act (Ontario) provides some assistance to the establishment of the intent aspect of the offence when the attack is launched quickly.

[4] Nor did they under its predecessor, the *Bankruptcy Act.*

3) The payment was made in the ordinary course and not with an intent to prefer.

4) New security was given in exchange for a new advance to the bankrupt.

5) The transaction was made in the 3- or 12- month period preceding bankruptcy referred to below, but the parties had properly agreed before that 3- or12- month period that the transaction would be done, and when it occurred the debtor was simply following through on something that he or she had legitimately already agreed to do.

The *Assignments and Preferences Act* (Ontario) contains specific sections that set out a series of "defences" to an allegation that a preference has occurred, some of which duplicate the situations just referred to with respect to the *Bankruptcy and Insolvency Act*. One of these "defences" in the *Assignments and Preferences Act* (Ontario) is so broad (the section talks about "any payment of money to a creditor"), however, that it may be necessary, as a practical matter, to establish that the creditor who received the preference was party to the intention that the other creditors should be mistreated. As noted, proving concurrence in this way is not necessary under the *Bankruptcy and Insolvency Act*.

## Limitation Periods

Under the *Bankruptcy and Insolvency Act* for the transaction to be deemed a preference, it must have occurred within 3 months of the effective date of bankruptcy if the bankrupt and the creditor are not "related" within the meaning of the Act, or within 12 months of that date if the parties are related. The effective date of the bankruptcy is the date on which a petition for a receiving order is filed, or the date on which an assignment is filed with the Official Receiver.

Under the *Assignments and Preferences Act* (Ontario) the limitation periods are on the one hand more stringent and on the other more liberal. On the stringent side there is a strong incentive to attack transactions within 60 days of their occurring because, in those cases, there is a presumption of the necessary intent. On the liberal side, it would appear that, in contrast to the 12 month outside "window" under the *Bankruptcy and Insolvency Act,* a transaction can be attacked under the *Assignments and Preferences Act* (Ontario) up to 6 years after it has occurred in accordance with the general *Limitations Act* (Ontario).

## FRAUDULENT CONVEYANCES

A fraudulent conveyance is a narrower concept than that of a preference.

Take this example. Jack is an entrepreneur who gets involved in many risky endeavours. He has always had more creditors than assets, and he has never really had much in the way of assets in his name. He has never owned a house or any land or even a new car. His creditors have chosen to deal with him because of his energy and his ideas; however, in October 1994 they began to lose patience with him. In fact, some of the creditors have started to sue Jack, and he has begun to consider bankruptcy as a way to stop the pressure and allow him to make a new start.

Jack's grandfather in England dies and unexpectedly leaves him a piece of property worth CN$100,000. The property is subject to a small—CN$20,000—mortgage. Jack's debts at that time are approximately $150,000 (all of which are due and payable), and he has assets worth maybe $30,000, which include money in the bank, some stocks and computer equipment.

Jack decides that he would still like to go bankrupt, but he does not want to share his new English property with his Canadian creditors. So, without telling any of his creditors or his prospective trustee in bankruptcy, he transfers title to the property to a company owned by his wife, in exchange for nothing more than the company agreeing to service the mortgage. That company is not among Jack's creditors. The next day Jack makes a voluntary assignment in bankruptcy.

## Definition

Jack has committed a fraudulent conveyance, as defined in both the *Assignments and Preferences Act* (Ontario) and the *Fraudulent Conveyances Act* (Ontario).[5]

---

[5] Again, both of these provincial statutes are available for use by trustees in bankruptcy.

The *Fraudulent Conveyances Act* (Ontario) defines a fraudulent conveyance as "a conveyance of real or personal property made with the intent to defeat, hinder, delay or defraud creditors ..." The term conveyance has, in turn, been interpreted widely in this context.

Under the *Assignments and Preferences Act* (Ontario) the definition of a fraudulent conveyance is pretty much the same as under the *Fraudulent Conveyances Act* (Ontario), but there is an added requirement that when the conveyance was made, the person making the conveyance (Jack in our example) was insolvent, unable to pay his or her debts in full, or knew himself or herself to be on the eve of insolvency.

## Proving Intent

Both the *Fraudulent Conveyances Act* (Ontario) and the *Assignments and Preferences Act* (Ontario) require that the fraudulent intent of the transferor be established.

The case law under the *Fraudulent Conveyances Act* (Ontario) shows that where certain disturbing circumstances or, as they are known, "badges of fraud" are found to exist the intent may be inferred. These badges of fraud include the following:

- The transfer was of all or substantially all of the transferor's property.
- The conveyance was secret.
- The consideration was grossly inadequate.
- There was a close relationship between the parties to the conveyance.

Arguably, all four of these badges of fraud examples apply to Jack's situation.

## What Is the Remedy?

Fraudulent conveyances are specifically dealt with in the two provincial statutes, the *Fraudulent Conveyances Act* (Ontario) and the *Assignments and Preferences Act* (Ontario), but not in the *Bankruptcy and Insolvency Act*. As such, the provincial statutes are geared to use by creditors of the person making the fraudulent conveyance (i.e., outside a formal bankruptcy). However, once that person goes bankrupt, the trustee in bankruptcy comes to represent those creditors and, given that the constitutionality of the provincial legislation has been settled, trustees in bankruptcy routinely pursue fraudulent conveyances under the *Fraudulent Conveyances Act* (Ontario) and the *Assignments and Preferences Act* (Ontario).

Under both statutes the remedy is an order directing the person who received the conveyance to make it available to satisfy the creditors' claims. In addition, these creditors (or a trustee in bankruptcy) are entitled to any proceeds received by the person making the conveyance, and they can also trace the property to the person who received it. If that person has subsequently resold or retransferred the property, they can still pursue it; however, they cannot upset another conveyance that was made "in good faith and for good consideration."[6] In other words, in our example, if Jack's wife's company had, in turn, sold the property for fair value (i.e., $100,000) to Bob, a person who knew nothing of Jack's fraudulent activities and who wanted the property for his own use, Bob's acquisition of title could not be overturned. However, Jack's trustee in bankruptcy could pursue the $100,000 that Bob paid to Jack's wife's company.

## Defences

The major exception or "defence" under both the *Fraudulent Conveyances Act* (Ontario) and the *Assignments and Preferences Act* (Ontario) is, in essence, the point just noted: namely, that conveyances made to a person who was acting in good faith, who paid good consideration for the property, and who had no knowledge of the other party's fraudulent intent, cannot be attacked. Also "saved" as exceptions under the *Assignments and Preferences Act* (Ontario) are conveyances that grant a security agreement in exchange for a contemporaneous advance of money and, similarly, a conveyance in exchange for a contemporaneous sale of goods of corresponding value to the asset conveyed.

---

6 "Good consideration" essentially means adequate or fair value.

## Limitation Period

It appears that fraudulent conveyances can be attacked, under both the *Fraudulent Conveyances Act* (Ontario) and the *Assignments and Preferences Act* (Ontario), for up to 6 years after they occur, in accordance with the general *Limitations Act* (Ontario).

## SETTLEMENTS: GIFTS WITH CONDITIONS

For many years the old *Bankruptcy Act* did not contain a definition of the term settlement and it was necessary to look to the case law. The new *Bankruptcy and Insolvency Act* has finally added a non-comprehensive definition of the term.

The simplest way to understand a settlement is to contrast it with an outright gift—which is, on the surface, a very similar transaction. Both gifts and settlements involve someone transferring something of value to someone else without receiving anything in return. With a gift the recipient is entitled to do whatever they want with the property. However, with a settlement the person making the transfer intends that the property stay in the same form or in some other specified form for the benefit of the recipient.

For example, suppose that one day Brian, a businessman, gives his daughter a gift of $100 because she did well on her mid-term exams; Brian also transfers his one-half interest in the house in which he lives with his family, to his wife. The first transaction is a gift because his daughter is free to do whatever she wants with the money. The second transaction is a settlement because Brian's intention, as discussed at length by him and his wife, is that no aspect of their lives will change as a result of this transfer, and the house is to be kept just as before so that Brian's wife and the rest of his family can continue to live in it for the same amount of time as they were already planning to live there.

Another example of a settlement—and one that is specifically addressed in the new definition section of the *Bankruptcy and Insolvency Act*—would be where Brian had a large insurance policy under which he was named as beneficiary and he changed this designation to his wife. Again, there is a specific intent on Brian's part that this asset will stay in the same form it was always in, but now for the benefit of his wife; the intent is not that his wife can "cash in" any value in the policy and use the proceeds for whatever she likes.

## Intent: Settlement or Gift?

The intent aspect is all important in identifying a settlement and differentiating it from a gift.

## What Is the Remedy?

The powerful remedy available if a settlement can be established is that the property transferred is deemed to be the property of the bankrupt notwithstanding the transfer. However, in this regard, it is vital to ensure that none of the "defences" are available and that the settlement occurred within one of the two limitation periods.

## Defences

The settlement remedies do not apply to settlements made before and in consideration of marriage or which are made in good faith and for good consideration.

## Limitation Periods

The *Bankruptcy and Insolvency Act* provides for two distinct limitation periods for attacking settlements. First, any settlement made within one year of bankruptcy is simply void. To use our example, if Brian transferred his interest in the house in which he lives to his wife on July 4, 1991, and went bankrupt on January 2, 1992, the settlement would not stand up against his trustee in bankruptcy.

The second limitation period is to the effect that a settlement made within five years of bankruptcy can also be attacked if the trustee can prove that at the time of the transfer:

1)  the bankrupt was unable to pay his debts without the aid of the property involved in the settlement; or

2)  that the bankrupt's interest in the property did not actually pass at the time of the execution of the settlement documents.

If Brian did not go bankrupt until January 1994, it would be up to his trustee to show that Brian was in debt in July 1991 and could not meet his obligations without having recourse to the equity value in his house or that the transfer that Brian intended to make to his wife at that time was somehow ineffective.

## REVIEWABLE TRANSACTIONS

A reviewable transaction is probably the easiest to understand of all of the types of transactions that can be reviewed by a trustee in bankruptcy.

In essence a reviewable transaction is a transaction between a bankrupt and someone not "at arms' length" from the bankrupt, in which something is transferred at a value much higher or lower than its fair market value.

An obvious example would be where Bad Moon Enterprises Ltd., a company that is in all sorts of financial trouble transfers a valuable painting for $100 to a numbered company ("Number Co.") owned by the same shareholders as Bad Moon's.

Another example would be where Bad Moon pays $10,000 to Number Co. in exchange for Number Co.'s providing consulting services to Bad Moon that have a value of, say, $500.[7]

## Intent

The intent or good faith of the parties is not relevant, nor is there any requirement that the bankrupt be insolvent at the time of the transaction.

## What Is the Remedy?

The court can give judgment to the trustee for the difference between the amount paid and the fair market value of the goods or services that changed hands. This judgment can then be enforced against the other party to the transaction.

The opinion of the trustee as to the value of the consideration will prevail unless the parties can establish a different value.

---

[7] These kinds of transactions also get the parties in trouble with the taxman.

## Limitation Period

To be attackable under the *Bankruptcy and Insolvency Act,* the reviewable transaction must have occurred within one year of the date of bankruptcy.

## IMPROPER CORPORATE DIVIDENDS

Both the Ontario *Business Corporations Act* and the *Canada Business Corporations Act* prohibit dividends to be declared by a company if "there are reasonable grounds for believing that" the corporation is unable to pay its liabilities as they become due (or would be unable after paying the dividend) or if the corporation cannot meet a basic "solvency test." The logic behind these provisions is obvious, and a point to note is that any director who improperly participates in the payment of dividends in contravention of these basic statutory provisions may be sued personally. Among the people who might pursue such a lawsuit is a trustee in bankruptcy of the company of which that person was a director.

## OPPRESSIVE CORPORATE CONDUCT

Both the *Canada Business Corporations Act* and the Ontario *Business Corporations Act* allow creditors and other interested parties to complain to the court that they have been "oppressed" by a corporation and people associated with the corporation.

More specifically, the *Canada Business Corporations Act* provides for a remedy whenever a corporation's business is being carried on, or the directors are exercising their powers, in a manner that is "oppressive or unfairly prejudicial to, or that unfairly disregards the interests of, any security holder, creditor, director or officer."

The Ontario *Business Corporations Act* definition is very similar al-- though it also encompasses a situation where it is "threatened" that corporate business or affairs will be carried out in an oppressive manner.

## What Is the Remedy?

These definitions of oppressive conduct feature the kind of broad, open-ended language that gives lawyers the creeps because it is so difficult to say where courts will draw the line in applying it. In turn, the court is given broad powers, where it has been satisfied that oppressive conduct has taken place, to make any kind of order it sees fit "to rectify the matters complained of."

The oppression remedy sections have frequently been applied in the context of "shareholder disputes," such as where the interests of a minority shareholder are being improperly ignored. In a particularly striking case, the majority shareholder charged management fees without authority and without the knowledge of the minority shareholder, thereby transferring most of the company's retained earinings to the majority shareholder. However, there is more than one precedent for the idea that, in appropriate circumstances, the sections can also be used by creditors of a company to upset what amounts to improper efforts to evade or hinder creditors.

## CRIMINAL FRAUD

The *Criminal Code of Canada* makes it an indictable offence for, in broad terms, anyone to transfer or conceal property, or to receive property from someone else, with an intent to defraud creditors. The punishment can be a stint in jail for up to two years.

So what is the difference between this statutory provision and the provisions already looked at—such as the fraudulent conveyance provisions of the *Fraudulent Conveyances Act* and the *Bankruptcy and Insolvency Act*? Basically, the *Criminal Code* is concerned with fraud that must be proven by the criminal standard of "beyond a reasonable doubt." In contrast, the various pieces of insolvency legislation we have looked at are concerned with conduct that may fall short of that standard, but that is still contrary to the public interest. One case described the distinction as one between actual fraud and "constructive or legal fraud."

In short, the distinction is subtle, but important. Also, although some creditors may derive satisfaction from seeing someone who has defrauded them go to jail, most would rather just get some or all of their money back. In that regard, the other statutory provisions we have looked at are more helpful than those in the *Criminal Code*.

# Corporate
# Reorganization

# Canada's Two Systems for Reorganization

O FTEN IN THE NEWS WE hear of large and well-known corporations in the United States filing for protection under "Chapter 11." This section of the U.S. *Bankruptcy Code* sets out a mechanism for a beleaguered company to try to reorganize its affairs before its creditors put the company into receivership or bankruptcy. Canada has legislation along the same lines.

The logic behind the process is obvious; what the company is saying to its creditors, in effect, is that they will all receive a disappointing recovery in a receivership and/or bankruptcy (say 5 or 40 cents on the dollar, depending on the ranking of the creditor in question), whereas if they all "bite the bullet" by agreeing to some form of compromise on their claim *now* and allowing the company to continue with less of a financial burden, there is a realistic, viable prospect that their ultimate recovery will be better (i.e., the 5-cents-on-the-dollar creditor gets 25 cents, and the creditor who was going to get 40 cents on the dollar moves up to a 65 or 70 cent recovery).

Of course, one of the centrepieces of the process is an evaluation by the creditors of how realistic and viable the prospect that the reorganized company can and will change its fortunes is. The only limit on the treatment of the creditors under a reorganization proposal or plan is the imagination of the person drafting it—the creditors must then decide whether the drafter's imagination is grounded in fact or fantasy.

However, while the logic behind the process may be simple, putting such an effort into effect can be enormously complicated, depending on the size of the debtor's operations. For example, it is a much more complicated matter to reorganize the affairs of a company like Algoma Steel[1] than those of a company that operates two dry cleaning stores.

What both the Canadian and the U.S. legislation try to do is set a framework within which the effort can at least be made to present such a plan to the creditors and, with an appropriate level of support, implement it. In doing so the legislation is obviously treading on extremely sensitive territory as far as the rights of both debtors and creditors are concerned. In other words, this subject elicits some of the most fundamental emotions in the already emotional area of how debt is repaid. Many creditors believe that any legal interference with their right to put a company into receivership or bankruptcy is a misguided, left-wing idea that should be wiped off the books. At the other extreme, many debtors would say that the legislation does not give them enough room to manoeuvre in what, from their viewpoint, is an altruistic, "beyond the call of duty" effort to *help* their creditors.

The U.S. legislation, which has a relatively long history, has always been perceived as very "pro debtor." That is, Chapter 11 is seen as a powerful tool in the hands of American corporations that have run into financial difficulty. I will return to that observation in discussing the Canadian situation, which has a much shorter history, but which is now rapidly evolving.

For many years the old Canadian *Bankruptcy Act* contained a reorganization section which was, in plain terms, completely useless. There were several reasons for that. First, with the explosion in the size and financial appetite of government since the Second World War, government claims came to represent a significant component of the debt of insolvent companies. The *Bankruptcy Act,* which became law in 1950, contained a provision to the effect that any reorganization—

---

[1] Notice that I picked as an example a company that was successful (at least to date) in its reorganization; many such efforts are unsuccessful. Examples of unsuccessful reorganization efforts include those of Olympia & York and Bargain Harold's.

or, to use the correct technical term, "proposal"—had to provide for payment in full of government claims. This section came to mean that, in most cases, a proposal could not include anything for the ordinary creditors because every dime of the company's scarce assets would have to go to the government. Even going through the motions of a proposal in those circumstances seemed pointless.

The second enormous flaw in the old *Bankruptcy Act* proposal provisions was that they did not require either secured creditors or landlords of the debtor to participate in the proceedings. In other words, the debtor had the right to present the proposal to only unsecured and government creditors, and the secured creditors and the landlords were free to pursue their normal remedies (as discussed in Chapters 1 and 2). With a company of any degree of sophistication, reorganization simply has to involve secured creditors and landlords.

A third weakness of the proposal provisions in the old *Bankruptcy Act* was that they did not prevent the termination or alteration of "executory" (i.e., unperformed) contracts involving the debtor while it was attempting to reorganize. For example, if a debtor needed the supply of certain goods or services while attempting to formulate a proposal but the contract with the supplier in question allowed the supplier to terminate the contract in the circumstances, the supplier's doing so could alone have precluded a successful proposal.

As a result of these shortcomings in the proposal provisions of the old *Bankruptcy Act*, when the recession hit at the end of the 1980s many lawyers went back to the books and discovered a statute that had been around since the 1930s: the *Companies' Creditors Arrangement Act*.

Under the *Companies' Creditors Arrangement Act*, an eligible[2] company can apply to the court for an order that stops or "stays" all proceedings by all creditors, including secured creditors, while the company formulates a reorganizational plan for submission to its creditors.

These stay orders are not always granted but when they are, they cover a broad "shopping list" of concerns that must be met by the

---

[2] Basically the eligibility requirement is that the company is "insolvent;" however, there are other, technical requirements as discussed ahead.

company while it is under court protection. For example, the orders normally provide that suppliers must continue supplying product that is essential to the company, regardless of any contractual right that the supplier would otherwise have to terminate the contract.

Once the stay order is in place, the *Companies' Creditors Arrangement Act* sets out very few rules on how the process should unfold. As a result, most of the major steps in the process require costly attendances in court to settle the issues. Consequently, the extreme expense of *Companies' Creditors Arrangement Act* proceedings kept them beyond the reach of many small Canadian businesses, and it was generally thought within the insolvency profession that only companies with a certain financial "critical mass" could afford to embark on the process. Part of the reality of the late 1980s and early 1990s was the fact that although the *Companies' Creditors Arrangement Act* had been on the books for a long time, it was only then being put into heavy use and the case law was developing at blinding speed. The process, it was found, was not for the faint-hearted or for companies that did not have a substantial war chest.

That imperfect situation was one of the main subjects of the comprehensive bankruptcy reform that culminated in the introduction of the *Bankruptcy and Insolvency Act* in November, 1992. The new legislation provides a new system for companies to try to reorganize that attempts to minimize trips to court before the process comes to a head and does so by setting out rules for many of the issues not addressed in the *Companies' Creditors Arrangement Act*.

In simplified terms, the lengthy "rules" in the *Bankruptcy and Insolvency Act* fit one of two categories:

1) there are rules designed to enhance the ability of a troubled company to survive while it is formulating a reorganization proposal to be submitted to its creditors; and

2) there are rules aimed at increasing the likelihood that the company formulating the proposal will ultimately be successful.

When the *Bankruptcy and Insolvency Act* was introduced, the *Companies' Creditors Arrangement Act* was not repealed,[3] and so

---

[3] *The Bankruptcy and Insolvency Act* contains a provision to the effect that it is to be reviewed three years after its November 1992 introduction. In other words, the govern-

companies that are in trouble can still pick one of two regimes under which to try to reorganize. In Chapter 15, the two statutes are compared in terms of the critical steps in each process.

Before embarking on those comparisons I will make one final, introductory observation: because the *Bankruptcy and Insolvency Act* tries hard to strike a balance between the rights of debtors and creditors, it allows access to the courts throughout the process of a reorganization attempt. As such, there is the potential for just as much expensive court work with a proposal under the *Bankruptcy and Insolvency Act* as there is with a reorganizational plan under the *Companies' Creditors Arrangement Act.*

That type of observation reflects one of my main objectives in this book, which is to point out the pitfalls and concerns for business people who want to use bankruptcy and insolvency legislation to help them in their lives. In pointing out such concerns I am necessarily focusing on some of the negative aspects of the law. On the positive side, many people feel that the *Bankruptcy and Insolvency Act,* which was the product of extensive effort by the politicians in consultation with Canada's insolvency professionals and international insolvency professionals, is a state-of-the-art package of balanced, fair legislation to enable troubled companies to attempt to reorganize that many other countries, including the United States, should envy.

---

ment is commited to avoiding a repeat of the situation where Canada's bankruptcy legislation is largely unamended for over four decades. It may be that upon that first review, the repeal of the *Companies' Creditors Arrangement Act* will be considered.

# A Step-by-Step Comparison of Canada's Two Reorganizational Systems

## DEALING WITH PROFESSIONAL ADVISERS

A company can never begin too early to work with its lawyers and insolvency professionals if a commercial reorganization becomes a possibility. Any detailed study of Canada's biggest successful and unsuccessful reorganizations of the last decade show that many of the ones that were unsuccessful were hampered because they were not started early enough.

Insolvency practitioners deal with reorganization efforts on a regular basis and can provide assistance in the following ways among others:

- identifying the problems facing the debtor and explaining what options are available to address them;

- breaking the creditors into the "classes" that will vote on the reorganization plan; and

- helping the company to understand what types of compromises those creditors must be asked to swallow, and providing information about whether other creditors in analogous circumstances have accepted such compromises.

In looking back on some insolvency situations, it is easy to see why, at the time, management thought that what turned out to be the start of an irreversible slide was merely a temporary problem with which they did not need outside help. However, if I can stress one point to companies experiencing difficulty in these very challenging times, it is to stay in close touch with their professional advisers in order to keep all options open to the greatest extent possible. No system of reorganizational laws can turn back the clock.

## THE ROLE OF THE MONITOR UNDER A PLAN AND THE TRUSTEE UNDER A PROPOSAL

Another important reason to enlist the help of an insolvency professional at the earliest possible time is that a person of that nature must be involved with the company while it is under protection from its creditors.[1]

In *Companies' Creditors Arrangement Act* proceedings, the person or firm is referred to as a "monitor," whereas under the *Bankruptcy and Insolvency Act,* the person is referred to as a trustee. Under the *Companies' Creditors Arrangement Act,* their duties as a watchdog over the insolvent company's affairs are spelled out in the initial court order. Under the *Bankruptcy and Insolvency Act,* they are in the specific sections in the statute and are referred to in the balance of this chapter.

Broadly speaking, the monitor or the trustee, as appropriate, fills a vital role as a qualified professional acting as a "buffer" between an insolvent company and its creditors during the delicate period in which a commercial reorganization is attempted. Sometimes the experience and prestige that these professionals bring to such a situation is enough to convince an otherwise panicky creditor to give the insolvent company a chance to "put something on the table."

## REQUIRED PRE-FILING ACTION

Under the *Bankruptcy and Insolvency Act,* no specific pre-filing action is required, other than the passing of the appropriate resolutions

---

[1] The insolvency professional will in most cases be a representative of a company which is licensed as a trustee in bankruptcy.

by the company's director(s). However, the *Companies' Creditors Arrangement Act* contains an anachronistic requirement that the company must have issued "bonds" (which include debentures) "under a trust deed or other instrument running in favour of a trustee."

Many readers will not even know what those words mean, and I can only say that in the 1930s, when the *Companies' Creditors Arrangement Act* was introduced, most companies financed their business needs by issuing bonds and debentures. In other words, if this book had been written in the 1930s, the Introduction to Part 1, which talked about the financial structure of a typical Canadian corporation, would have included a discussion about bonds or debentures issued under trust deeds.[2]

When numerous companies started getting into trouble in the late 1980s, their lawyers were confronted with this threshold requirement for the use of the *Companies' Creditors Arrangement Act*. Predictably, many companies created "instant trust deeds" (i.e., a day or two before the company sought court protection) and just as predictably many creditors of these companies argued that the *Companies' Creditors Arrangement Act* should not be available because these instant trust deeds were a sham and did not meet the requirements of the statute.

After some initial skirmishes, the courts came down on the side of the debtor companies and held that instant trust deeds were acceptable, and the fact that the debentures pursuant to these trust deeds had been issued just days before the company sought the protection of the court[3] did not disentitle an otherwise eligible and deserving company from that protection.

---

[2] Some sophisticated and usually public companies still make use of trust deeds. In the case of very large debt issues, the buyers or "subscribers" will often view it as an important consideration that their debentures are regulated by a trust deed under which the trustee is usually one of the large, institutional trust companies. However, to repeat, these instruments are almost never used anymore by private, Canadian business corporations.

[3] Typically, the trust deed is prepared, and two or three debentures are then issued pursuant to that trust deed for nominal consideration—say, $20 each—to some insiders of the company (i.e., the president or vice president and/or their spouses). In other words, it is classic situation of form over substance.

## REQUIREMENTS FOR FILING FOR COURT PROTECTION

In seeking court protection, the *Companies' Creditors Arrangement Act* requires that the debtor company have assets in Canada or be carrying on business in Canada, and be "insolvent." Indeed, the company must admit its insolvency in the initial court materials.

The *Bankruptcy and Insolvency Act* also requires that the company be "insolvent," which in the legislation's definition means that the debtor company owes at least $1000 and is unable to meet its obligations as they generally become due.

## INITIATING PROTECTION FROM CREDITORS

One of the major differences between the *Companies' Creditors Arrangement Act* and the *Bankruptcy and Insolvency Act* lies in the way the process starts for the debtor.[4]

Under the *Companies' Creditors Arrangement Act* the debtor must "earn" the initial protection from creditors by persuading a judge that he or she should grant a court order to that effect. Except in cases of real urgency the debtor should not go before the court "alone" or without any notice to the company's major creditors so that those creditors can argue against the granting of the stay order, if that is their position.[5]

In going to court, the company must be prepared to set out a preliminary outline showing what its reorganization plan will entail and how it will solve the problems of the company that have caused its insolvency. In other words, the company must demonstrate that it has made a proper analysis of how it got into trouble and that it has a plausible solution that addresses the problems uncovered by that analysis.

An interesting early case to consider the "threshold requirements" of the *Companies' Creditors Arrangement Act* was the *Bargain Harold's*

---

[4] As discussed below, however, once one scratches below the surface, one sees again that the distinction may be more formal than substantive.

[5] For a variety of reasons, which are discussed in this chapter, certain (even major) creditors may be willing to support a reorganizational effort at least at the early stage of the first court appearance to request a stay order.

case. In that case, a number of the major creditors of the company strenuously objected to the court imposing any form of stay against those creditors proceeding to enforce their security. The court held that although the onus was on those opposing creditors to show why the stay should *not* be granted, a number of factors in that case justified the conclusion that the stay should not be granted. Those factors included the following:

1) The debtor had not identified the precise nature of its financial problems.[6]

2) The debtor had no specific plan to salvage its operations.

3) The debtor needed further borrowing to continue, and no source of such funds had been identified.

4) The debtor had abandoned, or failed in, efforts to raise equity.

5) There was a complete lack of confidence, among the significant creditors, in the management of the company.

In other words, the court held that the debtor has to do more than just ask for relief from proceedings by creditors in order to get that relief.

Interestingly, under the *Bankruptcy and Insolvency Act* a debtor can obtain just such a stay of proceedings *automatically* by filing a one-page document called a notice of intention to make a proposal, a sample of which is included in the Appendix (Exhibit 20).

All that must be set out in the notice of intention—besides basic identifying information about the debtor—is the name of a licensed trustee in bankruptcy who has consented in writing to act as the trustee under the proposal and the names of all creditors with claims of $250 or more.

Thus, one can see at the outset how the *Bankruptcy and Insolvency Act* attempts to eliminate some of the court work by allowing the debtor to "get started" without an appearance in court. However, the act of filing a notice of intention sets the debtor on a course

---

[6] In somewhat striking terms, Mr. Justice Austin referred to an accountants' report and said, "translated to another medium, this language suggests that the patient is bleeding to death, but the doctors are unable to determine why."

that involves many responsibilities, as is the case if a stay order is obtained under the *Companies' Creditors Arrangement Act,* and those responsibilities begin as soon as that initial step has been taken under either piece of legislation.

For the sake of comparison, in the U.S. an automatic stay against proceedings by all creditors comes into effect when a company "files a petition" in a U.S. bankruptcy court pursuant to Chapter 11 of the U.S. *Bankruptcy Code.*

## Timing Requirements During the Sixty-Day Period Following Granting of the Stay

Under *Bankruptcy and Insolvency Act* reorganizational proceedings, the trustee must send a copy of the notice of intention to every known creditor of the debtor within 5 days of the filing of the notice.

Within 10 days of filing the notice of intention, the company must file a projected cash flow statement concerning the stay period (which has been reviewed by the trustee as to its reasonableness) as well as additional prescribed material.

Within 30 days of filing the Notice of Intention, the company is supposed to file the proposal itself. If these time limits are not met,[7] the company is deemed to have made an assignment in bankruptcy.[8]

Within 21 days of the introduction of the proposal, the creditors are supposed to vote on the proposal, and the Official Receiver is supposed to receive a package of prescribed materials, including notice of the meeting of creditors to vote on the proposal, the proposal itself, and voting materials, at least 10 days before the meeting.

Also, the trustee under a *Bankruptcy and Insolvency Act* proposal must file a report with the court and/or the Official Receiver upon learning of a material adverse change in the company's projected cash flow or financial circumstances, or before making any application to court to extend the stay period.

Under the *Companies' Creditors Arrangement Act,* there are no mandatory requirements during the first 60 days after the initial

[7] Subject to the court's extending the time limits, as discussed later in this chapter.

[8] The date of the bankruptcy is retroactive to the date of the filing of the notice of intention.

stay order has been granted. To the extent that there are any such requirements, they are provided for either in the initial court order or in subsequent court orders, if there are any. Indeed, it is up to the judge in each *Companies' Creditors Arrangement Act* case as to how long the stay will remain in effect. Typically, the stays are effective for at least 90 days, and they are often extended, by a further court order, if the debtor can convince the judge that an extension of the stay will increase the likelihood of the debtor putting together a plan that will be acceptable to its creditors.

Both the *Companies' Creditors Arrangement Act* and the *Bankruptcy and Insolvency Act* provide plenty of opportunity for the debtor company or any one or more of the creditors to go back to court during the two-month period following the stay and to ask a judge to exercise his or her discretion to vary the initial stay terms.

The *Bankruptcy and Insolvency Act* specifically lists a number of such "applications." For example, any party may apply to the court to shorten or lengthen the basic 30-day and 21-day periods referred to above. The *Bankruptcy and Insolvency Act* even goes on to say that where the debtor company is seeking an extension of the stay, such extensions may be granted in increments "not exceeding" 45 days for a maximum total stay of six months.[9]

Under the *Bankruptcy and Insolvency Act,* a secured creditor may also apply to have the stay lifted against particular secured assets. In those applications, the secured creditor will generally need to establish that he or she is otherwise going to be "materially prejudiced" by the stay or that it is otherwise equitable to do so.

Secured creditors can also apply for a court order shortening the *entire* stay (i.e., not just against particular secured assets) on

[9] Although a six-month stay may sound exceedingly long, under the *Companies' Creditors Arrangement Act* there is no such limitation period, and, indeed, some of Canada's biggest restructuring efforts under the *Companies' Creditors Arrangement Act* have involved stays in excess of six months. Under both statutes, if the company is under court protection for an extensive period, the court will, or should try to, ensure that the creditors' rights are being respected. For example, there is a proper treatment of all cash receipts and that—to the extent possible—those creditors' rights are not being further eroded. However, no creditor who is on the other side of such a proceeding would ever agree that his or her rights were sufficiently protected.

stipulated grounds that include "where the debtor has no viable prospect of formulating a successful proposal" and "where the debtor is not acting in good faith." Where there is one major secured creditor who has justifiably lost all faith in the management of the debtor, these sections can be used to attempt to require the debtor to appear in court to explain why it is realistic to think that a successful proposal can be completed.

Thus, although the court protection itself is automatic under the *Bankruptcy and Insolvency Act,* as opposed to the *Companies' Creditors Arrangement Act,* there are procedures under the *Bankruptcy and Insolvency Act* by which the debtor may quickly have to satisfy a court that the exercise is not a waste of time—that is, by addressing the same kinds of basic issues as were discussed in the *Bargain Harold's* case under the *Companies' Creditors Arrangement Act.*

Unlike the *Bankruptcy and Insolvency Act,* the *Companies' Creditors Arrangement Act* does not contain detailed sections dealing with the issue of "discretionary" timing requirements. However, a *Companies' Creditors Arrangement Act* proceeding is built around the court process and, in essence, anything that can be the subject of a court application during a stay under the *Bankruptcy and Insolvency Act* can also be submitted to a court overseeing a *Companies' Creditors Arrangement Act* reorganizational effort.

## SUPPLY CONTRACTS

As already noted, the initial stay order under most *Companies' Creditors Arrangement Act* proceedings will require the continuation of supply contracts, regardless of whether the contract specifically gives the supplier the right to terminate the contract for any one of several reasons including that the purchaser has not paid its bills for 100 days and/or is in default under another agreement that he or she has with the supplier. These orders usually list *all* the suppliers the debtor needs to continue in business while it tries to reorganize and thus include not only suppliers of things like raw materials but also suppliers of utilities and other services.[10]

---

[10] Obviously you cannot keep alive, and reorganize, a company which makes tires if it does not have an uninterrupted supply of rubber.

The *Companies' Creditors Arrangement Act* does not expressly say that courts have the power to make these kinds of orders. However, in one well-known case—which involved the large Quintette coal mine in British Columbia—the B.C. Court of Appeal said that such orders can be given under the section of the *Companies' Creditors Arrangement Act* that allows court orders prohibiting "proceeding[s] ... against the company ...."

Again, the *Bankruptcy and Insolvency Act* spells out in detailed language what has been "read into" the *Companies' Creditors Arrangement Act* by the courts. The *Bankruptcy and Insolvency Act* specifically says that during the stay period, or where an approved proposal is in effect, suppliers cannot terminate supply contracts,[11] and public utilities cannot discontinue service merely on the basis of the debtor's insolvency or because it sought protection under the *Bankruptcy and Insolvency Act*. Again, the *Bankruptcy and Insolvency Act* goes on to say that such creditors may seek a court order to the contrary so that, in the final analysis, the situation on this point is similar to that under the *Companies' Creditors Arrangement Act*.[12]

## LABOUR CONTRACTS

Companies can get their employment costs out of balance, as with any other corporate expenditure, and the need to adjust labour agreements can form one of the most basic—and most emotional—components of a restructuring effort.

With major companies, the problem can involve the need to rewrite union agreements, and just about any reorganizational effort involves the need for some employees to lose their jobs.

Under the *Bankruptcy and Insolvency Act,* employees are generally treated as unsecured creditors. However, certain employee

---

[11] Certain supply contracts are specifically exempted, including "eligible financial contracts." This term includes such esoteric, but not uncommon, agreements as currency or interest rate swap agreements and foreign exchange agreements.

[12] Interestingly, however, the situation is not identical under the two statutes: for example, there have been cases where *Companies' Creditors Arrangement Act* stay orders were effective to prevent the termination of "eligible financial contracts" as defined in the *Bankruptcy and Insolvency Act*.

claims are given specific priority. For example, a *Bankruptcy and Insolvency Act* proposal *must* provide for immediate payment of any unpaid wages for services performed during the six-month period prior to the filing of the notice of intention to make a proposal to both continuing employees and employees who are being terminated. The court must be "satisfied that the employer can and will make the payments." In the case of travelling sales people, an additional amount of up to $1000 of unpaid disbursements must also be paid.

In addition, under the *Bankruptcy and Insolvency Act,* many "employee-related" expenditures must also be paid as part of any proposal. For example, the proposal must provide for payment in full within 6 months of court approval of the proposal of all income tax, UI, and CPP withholdings with respect to each employee that were outstanding at the time the proposal process started.

Under the *Companies' Creditors Arrangement Act,* employees are also classified as unsecured creditors for amounts owing to them. Under both the *Companies' Creditors Arrangement Act* and the *Bankruptcy and Insolvency Act,* amounts could be owing by statute with respect to either termination pay or severance pay or as a result of any specific provisions in union contracts or other private contracts. Invariably, in complex reorganization, it has been necessary to enter into discussions with both the relevant union(s) and the Ministry of Labour.

## COMMERCIAL LEASES

Many places in the world—Tokyo and Los Angeles to name two—have had real estate collapses in the last few years. However, the boom and bust cycle of the past ten years in southern Ontario, particularly in Toronto, has been unprecedented in Canada. For approximately five years values marched steadily upwards, and during this boom period very few people[13] foresaw the equally merciless downturn of the next five years.

Over that wild ten-year cycle, both landlords and tenants have often found themselves on the wrong end of commercial leases in the sense that the leases were either well below or well above

---

[13] Including, obviously, many of the professionals in this field, such as real estate developers, landlords, brokers, appraisers, and bankers.

market values. For example, many companies that were tenants and in good health in the mid-1980s were also in an expansion mode and took on leases at rent levels that soon proved unsustainable. With the benefit of hindsight, one can criticize the thinking behind the idea that the company could ever meet the rent obligations. In any event, the situation that some of these companies found themselves in the early 1990s was one where the fundamental, core business that they had built in the mid-1980s was still viable, but was being smothered by the new lease obligations. Unless those lease obligations and the associated expenses could be stopped somehow (i.e., without a lot of other changes to the way the company did business), the entire business would be destroyed. Certainly, it is an issue that has figured prominently in many commercial reorganizations.

As usual, no explicit provision in the *Companies' Creditors Arrangement Act* deals with this issue. In some of the *Companies' Creditors Arrangement Act* cases, the tenant corporations simply abandoned their unfavourable leases. But this meant that the landlords then had potentially enormous claims for the loss of each lease, which could, in turn, give them a disproportionate voting power to kill the plan.

In the large Grafton Fraser reorganization under the *Companies' Creditors Arrangement Act*, the initial court orders allowed the tenants to terminate, rather than abandon, certain leases. Predictably, the landlords opposed these orders strenuously. The resulting litigation was ultimately resolved by negotiations between company management and the relevant landlords. These negotiations concluded in both outright terminations of certain leases and rent reductions. In an illustration of how "everything is negotiable" in corporate reorganizations, one of the large landlords ended up being a significant shareholder in the restructured company.

Again, the *Bankruptcy and Insolvency Act* tried to move away from the "law of the jungle" experience under the *Companies' Creditors Arrangement Act* by putting in a series of clear statutory provisions dealing with commercial leases. The *Bankruptcy and Insolvency Act* provides the following:

1) leases cannot be terminated by landlords during the stay period applicable to a tenant, merely because of the tenant's insolvency; and

2) while the stay is in effect, landlords cannot claim accelerated payments under their lease(s), even if rent was in arrears at the time the debtor filed for protection.

Also, the *Bankruptcy and Insolvency Act* contains a specific right for commercial tenants to terminate individual leases, on thirty days' notice and a payment of up to six months' accelerated rent in the case of each lease.[14] However, as with so many positive "rights" in the *Bankruptcy and Insolvency Act,* this one is subject to an offsetting right in favour of the landlord to a court order prohibiting such a termination.[15] If a landlord seeks this court order, the onus is expressly on the company to demonstrate that the repudiation of the lease is necessary to the viability of the overall proposal. In other words, the company must show that the termination is essential to the company's survival.

## BANKS AND OTHER SECURED CREDITORS

Secured creditors may be affected by reorganizational proceedings under both the *Bankruptcy and Insolvency Act* and the *Companies' Creditors Arrangement Act*. Under the *Companies' Creditors Arrangement Act,* the stay orders typically bind secured creditors and provide that a reorganizational plan may affect them. Just as typically, those secured creditors often move to vary the effect of those

[14] If less than six months are left on the lease, only rent for the number of months remaining must be paid. The payment is supposed to be made "immediately after court approval of the proposal." In practice, some companies negotiate "side deals" whereby the payment is for less than six months; by keeping the term out of the formal proposal, the companies do not ask the court to approve a proposal that contains less than the minimum statutory requirements. This is the kind of practice that may never be challenged because it is not causing financial damage to anyone who would be motivated to complain.

[15] In what is something of a loophole in the *Bankruptcy and Insolvency Act,* it appears that landlords can also get tenants to agree to give up this right to terminate leases. In practice, any such agreement would probably just give the landlord a little more power in negotiations with a tenant who needs to be rid of a lease.

orders on them—as discussed, for example, later in this chapter in the section on the creditor approval process.

Again, the *Bankruptcy and Insolvency Act* is more explicit. It says that the stay provisions bind secured creditors who have not begun to enforce their security prior to the filing of the originating proposal notice or, more importantly, who have not given notice of an intention to enforce security more than ten days before the originating proposal notice.

In other words, suppose that Thomas Enterprises Ltd. operates a chain of clothing stores and one of its main secured creditors is a bank that gave notice of its intention to enforce security against Thomas Enterprises on July 10. As mentioned earlier in this chapter, depending on the nature of its problems, Thomas Enterprises probably should have been in consultation with its professional advisers well before July 10. However, suppose that no such meetings took place until July 18 and that on July 20, after three days of discussion, Thomas Enterprises was still unsure of whether it should pursue a proposal under the *Bankruptcy and Insolvency Act*. If Thomas Enterprises does not formally file notice of its intention to make a proposal on that day, but instead decides to keep meeting to analyze the merits of such an effort, it will be too late to bind the bank. Even if the bank does not immediately start enforcing its security in accordance with its rights, a decision by Thomas to file a notice of intention to make a proposal on July 23 will not bind the bank.[16]

In addition, as discussed above, the *Bankruptcy and Insolvency Act* specifically allows secured creditors to apply to court to have certain types of security removed from the reorganization process and secured creditors routinely make such attempts under the *Companies' Creditors Arrangement Act* as well.

## GOVERNMENT CLAIMS

This may be the most important area of distinction between the *Companies' Creditors Arrangement Act* and the *Bankruptcy and Insolvency Act*—according to the most recent case law.

---

[16] In saying this, I am *not* advocating that a notice of intention to make a proposal be filed where the debtor company has not the firm intention of following through with a proposal.

For a long time, it was generally accepted that government creditors were subject to reorganizational efforts under the *Companies' Creditors Arrangement Act*. However, in a 1994 case called *Fine's Flowers,* the Ontario Court of Appeal held that the *Companies' Creditors Arrangement Act* does *not* bind the government.

The *Bankruptcy and Insolvency Act* specifically binds the government, subject to two major conditions. First, the company must keep its source deductions current during the period of the stay. Second, certain government claims—income tax, UI, and CPP—must be paid in full within six months of the approval of the proposal. However, subject to some uncommon exceptions that have already been referred to,[17] all other government claims rank merely as unsecured, ordinary claims.

## CASH FLOW DURING THE STAY PERIOD

One of the biggest problems a company embarking on a commercial reorganization in Canada must solve is how it will finance its operations during the stay period. By definition, companies that have come to the situation where they must try to reorganize have made extensive use of credit in the past to finance their day-to-day operations. As discussed in Chapter 1, this use of credit can take many forms, including the simple practice of not paying for supplies in cash.

As discussed earlier in this chapter, while both the *Bankruptcy and Insolvency Act* and *Companies' Creditors Arrangement Act* will require suppliers to continue to supply product to the debtor company during the stay, the practice under both statutes is to the effect that these products must be paid for immediately and in cash. No matter how badly a supplier has allowed arrears to pile up before the debtor filed for protection from creditors, that supplier is entitled to be paid in cash from that point forward.

The *Bankruptcy and Insolvency Act* contains a specific provision to the effect that the stay provisions do not require a supplier to continue to supply goods for anything other than "payments to be

---

[17] Such as statutory liens which have been properly registered and deemed trust claims where the funds have actually been segregated, as discussed in Chapters 3 and 12.

made in cash...or other valuable consideration." As usual, the *Companies' Creditors Arrangement Act* is silent on this issue, but the general practice is clearly in accordance with the specific terms of the *Bankruptcy and Insolvency Act*. This practice has also been reviewed in major *Companies' Creditors Arrangement Act* cases, such as the *Quintette Coal* case.

However, the outcomes of other *Companies' Creditors Arrangement Act* cases[18] suggest that under a *Companies' Creditors Arrangement Act* stay order suppliers could be required to supply on the terms that they had in place before the stay order. That is, if the suppliers had previously agreed to accept payment within ninety days of shipment, these cases say that they should continue to do so during the stay period. While, with respect, I do not agree with these decisions, I mention them as illustrations of the fact that virtually any issue surrounding a commercial reorganization can be the subject of costly litigation and that proceedings under the *Companies' Creditors Arrangement Act* are not identical to proceedings under the *Bankruptcy and Insolvency Act*.

So much for the use of "credit" generated by not paying suppliers quickly. What about the credit from banks and other creditors higher up in the chain of sources of credit discussed in Chapter 1? Can they be required to continue to play ball during a stay period by providing credit?

Again, the *Bankruptcy and Insolvency Act* at least tries to tackle this issue head on by providing that the stay provisions do not require the "further advance of money or credit." However, the first thing that many insolvency lawyers said when they saw this language was that arguably it was broad enough to mean that if a bank had agreed to make a certain amount of credit available (i.e., a credit facility of "up to $1,000,000"[19]) and only a portion (say, $700,000) of this credit line was drawn at the time that the borrower filed for protection, then the balance of the credit facility ($300,000 in the example) would have to be made available during the stay period.

---

[18] Such as the *Perfection Foods* case in Prince Edward Island and the *Steinberg* case in Quebec.

[19] As discussed in Chapter 1, such credit facilities are subject to a number of conditions.

To my knowledge, this liberal interpretation of the *Bankruptcy and Insolvency Act* section has not been accepted by a court, and certainly the practice under both the *Companies' Creditors Arrangement Act* and the *Bankruptcy and Insolvency Act* has been to the effect that undrawn credit facilities cannot be drawn on after the stay under either statute has started. Such drawings would obviously be to the disproportionate detriment of the creditor who made that credit facility available.

In some *Companies' Creditors Arrangement Act* cases—such as the *Dylex* case—the company obtained a fresh credit facility while under protection from creditors, on the condition that the court approved a "first charge" over all of the company's assets to support the repayment of the credit facility (i.e., regardless of what other registered security was already in place). This arrangement was opposed by certain other secured creditors but—in the kind of delicate balancing which must be done in these cases—the court approved the arrangement.

In summary, in Canada, a company has to look primarily to its cash flow or to specialized credit facilities to finance its operations during the stay period. In the U.S., on the other hand, under Chapter 11 proceedings, debtor companies have traditionally had more room to manoeuvre. Specifically, the U.S. *Bankruptcy Code* contemplates that companies that are "in Chapter 11" can raise unsecured credit, which is repaid ahead of other unsecured obligations of the company. In addition, under Chapter 11, the court can allow a company to obtain new secured financing, which will rank ahead of the company's financing which was secured on the date that court protection was sought.

These financing mechanisms under the U.S. *Bankruptcy Code* are often referred to as "debtor in possession" financing, and they are a powerful tool for companies trying to reorganize.

## THE CREDITOR APPROVAL PROCESS

Under both the *Companies' Creditors Arrangement Act* and the *Bankruptcy and Insolvency Act,* the creditors vote on the plan (to use the *Companies' Creditors Arrangement Act* term) or proposal (the

*Bankruptcy and Insolvency Act* term) by classes. Thus, how creditors are classified is a central issue under both statutes.[20]

Obviously, each creditor would like to be in their own class so that they have an effective veto power over the plan. Just as obviously, the debtor's natural instinct is to put as many creditors together as possible, for voting purposes, so that one or two "squeaky wheels" will be drowned out by the rest of the creditors in their class.

Again, the *Companies' Creditors Arrangement Act* offers little explicit guidance as to how the classes should be divided up, and it has fallen to the courts to impose some rules on the process. In general, the courts have tried hard to limit the number of classes, based on the proposition that creditors with similar interests should be treated as one class.

The *Bankruptcy and Insolvency Act* built on the *Companies' Creditors Arrangement Act* case law by stating specifically that secured creditors are to be classified according to the nature of their debt, the priority and nature of their security, the types of remedies available to the creditors in the absence of the proposal, the treatment of their claims under the proposal, and any other "prescribed criteria." However, as with the *Companies' Creditors Arrangement Act,* creditors who are unhappy with the way that the classes are set up under a *Bankruptcy and Insolvency Act* proposal, can apply to the court to review whether these guidelines have been observed.

Once the creditors have been classified for voting purposes, there is a distinct difference between the two Acts in the levels of support needed for the reorganization to pass. Under the *Companies' Creditors*

---

[20] Under both statutes there is a process whereby all creditors are required to submit a "proof of claim" form identifying the particulars of their claim. Under the *Bankruptcy and Insolvency Act* if a claim is disallowed, there is a mechanism for the creditor to appeal to the court. Under the *Companies' Creditors Arrangement Act,* the court order(s) governing the *Companies' Creditors Arrangement Act* proceeding will govern how the claims are treated. For example, the order might say that if a claim is reduced or disallowed, instead of there being an appeal process, the company will simply hold the vote—as discussed below—and only if the vote would have been decided differently if the claim had been allowed will the matter be considered further.

*Arrangement Act,* a majority in number representing at least three-quarters in the dollar value of the claims, is required with respect to each class of creditors. Under the *Bankruptcy and Insolvency Act,* the threshold per class is also a majority in number but the necessary dollar value represented by those creditors need only be two-thirds of the claims in that class. In certain situations, the difference between 75 percent and 66.6 percent of the dollar value of the claims in the class can represent the difference between the reorganization being approved or voted down.

The voting usually occurs at a meeting specifically held for that purpose. It is not necessary for the creditors to attend in person as voting by proxy is invariably allowed. However, these meetings often have something of the air of a political convention in that part of the drama is played out just before the voting and, as such, it is often a good idea for creditors to be at the meeting.

Every creditor reacts differently to reorganizational plans or proposals. Some companies have a policy to the effect that they will *never* vote in favour of any arrangement whereby they accept less than 100 cents on the dollar for a claim, if only because of the bad precedent that doing so would set. Certainly, some government agencies have taken that approach. However, sometimes these creditors will decide not to kill a proposal by simply not voting at all. In other words, they adhere to their policy of not voting in favour of a compromise but, by abstaining, they do not dilute the number of votes that are cast in favour of the plan or proposal and thereby they help its passage.

As already noted, the *Companies' Creditors Arrangement Act* requires passage by a majority of each class of creditors. In an apparent effort to facilitate proposals, the *Bankruptcy and Insolvency Act* provides that if the unsecured creditors approve of the proposal but some or all of the secured creditors do not, the proposal will not be defeated per se; however, the rights of the relevant secured creditors regarding their security will be reinstated. In practice, I do not know how useful this provision will be because typically if the secured creditors of an insolvent company are allowed to enforce their security[21] nothing will be left for the unsecured creditors. In

---

[21] As discussed in Parts 1, 2 and 3.

other words, I have trouble imagining the contents of a proposal that unsecured creditors could support by themselves regardless of whether the secured creditors withdraw their support from the company.

Chapter 11 of the U.S. *Bankruptcy Code* contemplates passage by one-half in number representing two-thirds of the dollar amount owed to the voting creditors.

## COURT APPROVAL

Both *Companies' Creditors Arrangement Act* plans and *Bankruptcy and Insolvency Act* proposals must receive formal court approval after they have been passed by the necessary majority of creditors. While it is rare that the court approval is not given in these circumstances, it is not unprecedented.

Under the *Companies' Creditors Arrangement Act,* the courts have generally looked at whether the plan demonstrates good faith and has a reasonable prospect of succeeding. In other words, the courts review the wisdom of what the creditors have voted to do. Similarly, the *Bankruptcy and Insolvency Act* specifically directs the court not to approve the proposal where the terms "are not reasonable or are not calculated to benefit the general body of creditors." However, once court approval is given under either Act, all of the creditors affected by the plan or the proposal are bound to live by its terms.

Remarkably, under Chapter 11, the U.S. Bankruptcy Court is able to approve a plan that has *not* been approved by various classes of creditors (unsecured *and* secured) if the Court concludes that the plan is nevertheless fair and equitable, and does not discriminate unfairly against the creditors who have voted against the plan. This mechanism—more "debtor friendly" than anything in Canadian law—is referred to among lawyers as the "cramdown" procedure under Chapter 11.

## OVERALL TIMING AND COSTS

Every reorganizational effort is different, and the timing and costs will depend on the complexity of the issues to be resolved. Most *Companies' Creditors Arrangement Act* proceedings take between three and six months, and the courts have often set stringent time limits where the business would otherwise substantially deteriorate. Ultimately, there is no strict time limit to *Companies' Creditors Arrangement Act* proceedings.

As already noted, the maximum stay available under the *Bankruptcy and Insolvency Act* is six months. So, the time frame for *Bankruptcy and Insolvency Act* proposals is generally in line with the majority of *Companies' Creditors Arrangement Act* proceedings. In the rare cases where more time is needed and the support of the creditors can be maintained over an extended period, the flexibility afforded by the *Companies' Creditors Arrangement Act* will be the only option.

The costs associated with the process can be very expensive. As there is about as much room for fighting in court under the *Bankruptcy and Insolvency Act* as under the *Companies' Creditors Arrangement Act,* the expense is there no matter which statute is used. Generally, though, *Companies Creditors Arrangement Act* proceedings are slightly more costly than those under the *Bankruptcy and Insolvency Act.*

## CONSEQUENCES OF THE FAILURE OF A PLAN OR PROPOSAL

There are three points at which a plan or proposal effort may fail:

1) before it ever comes to a vote, as, for example, when the company fails to prepare the plan, or complete another required step, within the time limits set by the relevant court order or the provisions of the *Bankruptcy and Insolvency Act;*

2) because the requisite majority of creditors do not vote in favour of the plan or proposal; and

3) when the company defaults in the performance of one of the terms of the plan or the proposal after it has been passed by the creditors and approved by the court.

In each case, the main effect of the failure is different under the *Bankruptcy and Insolvency Act* than under the *Companies' Creditors Arrangement Act.* Under the *Bankruptcy and Insolvency Act,* the company is deemed to have made an assignment in bankruptcy, retroactive to the date of the initiation of the proposal process, with all the finality that bankruptcy entails—as discussed in Part 3.

Under the *Companies' Creditors Arrangement Act* there is no such automatic bankruptcy if a plan fails. The main result is simply that the company stops enjoying the benefit of the stay, and the creditors are again entitled to exercise their legal remedies. However, in practice it is usually not as if the company just goes into some kind of free fall: one or more of these creditors will probably quickly move to have the company put into receivership and possibly bankruptcy as well. Thus, while the failure of a reorganizational effort under the *Bankruptcy and Insolvency Act* means that control of the company passes immediately to a trustee in bankruptcy, either such a trustee or a receiver is probably also soon put in place with respect to a company that fails to complete a reorganization under the *Companies' Creditors Arrangement Act*.

# Some Final Observations 16

I HOPE THAT THIS BOOK HAS achieved its goal of explaining in clear terms the broad structure of a corporate receivership, bankruptcy, and reorganizational effort and of alerting the reader to some of the major opportunities and risks that those processes present. In the end, however, no book can cover all the aspects of, and concerns associated with, an insolvency, and a reader will invariably need to turn to his or her lawyer for protection.

Let me give an example of how refined the law can be in this area. In Chapters 2, 8, and 12, I touched on the position of commercial landlords regarding a defaulting tenant and I pointed out the severe restrictions on the remedies that such a landlord has if his tenant becomes bankrupt. Predictably, many landlords try to obtain some form of protection from a third party against the consequences of a default by a commercial tenant. Such protection is usually obtained through a guarantee, an indemnity agreement, or a letter of credit.

One would think, if the tenant goes bankrupt such an agreement would be enforceable by a landlord. But the law in this area is to the effect that such agreements may not be enforceable when the tenant goes bankrupt. Briefly, what the cases focus on is whether the terms of the guarantee, indemnity, or letter of credit are defined solely by reference to the tenant's "obligations." If so, the guarantee or other agreement may fail when the tenant goes bankrupt because, by virtue of the *Bankruptcy and Insolvency Act,* at that point the tenant's obligations no longer exist—instead they have passed to the trustee in bankruptcy.

In other words, suppose that Bob Smith owns a company called Smith Enterprises Ltd. Smith Enterprises signs a lease with respect to a prime commercial location for ten years. Because Smith Enterprises is a new company, the landlord asks Bob Smith to sign a personal guarantee of the obligations of Smith Enterprises under the lease.

Now suppose that four months after the lease starts Smith Enterprises goes bankrupt and the trustee in bankruptcy quickly disclaims the lease. Obviously, the landlord will try to find a new tenant, but he is suddenly faced with the loss of the income from the lease which was otherwise going to be payable for over 9 1/2 more years.

In those circumstances, the landlord will be quick to pull out Bob Smith's personal guarantee. However, in what many readers must think is a bit of an absurd result, the guarantee will be worthless if what it says, in effect, is "I, Bob Smith, guarantee to perform the obligations of Smith Enterprises under its lease."

Although it seems a harsh or absurd result, many courts have come to this conclusion because, they say, the obligations of Smith Enterprises ceased when it went bankrupt and those obligations passed to the trustee in bankruptcy. In other words, to protect himself or herself, the landlord should draft its guarantee (or indemnity or letter of credit) in such a way that the obligations of Bob Smith are defined independently of any continued obligations of Smith Enterprises. Thus, these agreements typically provide that the guarantor is bound by a fresh, independent set of obligations in favour of the landlord if the tenant goes bankrupt.[1]

Obviously, that is an extremely picky legal point, and equally obvious is the fact that a book of this scope cannot get into that level of analysis because picky points like that are scattered throughout the insolvency process.

However, my point in closing is simply that while this book cannot act as a substitute for the kind of personalized legal advice that can

[1] It may be noted that there are some cases that have not followed this line of reasoning. In short, the law in this area is in a bit of a mess.

uncover those delicate points in any given situation, I hope that it has given the reader some understanding of the landscape in which those points occur and the pervasive extent to which that landscape forms part of the day-to-day world of many businesspeople.

# Appendix

The agreements included in the appendix are not presented as perfectly consistent legal precedents and they are certainly not presented as "ready to use" documents. (As noted elsewhere, this book is not intended as legal advice with respect to any particular fact situation.) However, they are offered as illustrations of some of the types of agreements referred to in this book.

# General Security Agreement

**THIS AGREEMENT** made as of the _____ day of _____, 19__.

**TO:** _____, a corporation incorporated under the laws of the Province of Ontario,

(the "Creditor")

OF THE FIRST PART

**FROM:** _____, a corporation incorporated under the laws of the Province of Ontario,

(the "Debtor")

OF THE SECOND PART

**THIS AGREEMENT WITNESSES** that, for good and valuable consideration, the Debtor agrees with the Creditor as follows:

# 1. INTERPRETATION

**1.1 Defined Terms.** In this Agreement, unless there is something in the context or subject matter inconsistent therewith,

(a) **"Accounts"** means all debts, book debts, amounts, claims, and moneys which now are, or which may at any time hereafter be, due or owing to or owed by the Debtor, whether or not earned by performance; excluding, to the extent that an assignment in favour of the Creditor is restricted by law, any such debts, amounts, claims and moneys due from the Government of Canada or any department or agency thereof or any Crown corporation; and including all securities, mortgages, bills, notes and other documents now held or owned, or which may be hereafter taken, held or owned, by or on behalf of the Debtor, in respect of the said debts, amounts, claims and moneys or any part thereof and all books, documents and papers recording, evidencing or relating to the said debts, amounts, claims and moneys or any part thereof;

(b) **"Banking Day"** means any day (other than a Saturday or a Sunday) on which banks generally are open for business in Toronto, Ontario;

(c) **"Chattel Paper"** means all present and future agreements made between the Debtor as secured party and others which evidence both a monetary obligation and a security interest in or a lease of specific goods;

(d) **"Collateral"** means all undertaking, property and assets of the Debtor, now owned or hereafter acquired and any proceeds from the sale or other disposition thereof, all of which includes without limitation, all Accounts, Inventory, Equipment, Intangibles, Documents of Title, Money, Chattel Paper, Instruments, Securities, Documents, Proceeds, and Leaseholds;

(e) **"Documents"** means all documents, including, without limitation, all computer records stored in any medium, books, invoices, letters, papers and other records, in any form evidencing or relating to the Collateral, all of which are herein called the "Documents";

(f)     **"Documents of Title"** means any writing now or hereafter owned by the Debtor that purports to be issued by or addressed to a bailee and purports to cover such goods and chattels in the bailee's possession as are identified or fungible portions of an identified mass, whether such goods and chattels are Inventory or Equipment, and which writing is treated in the ordinary course of business as establishing that the person in possession of such writing is entitled to receive, hold and dispose of the said writing and the goods and chattels it covers, and further, whether such writing is negotiable in form or otherwise, including bills of lading and warehouse receipts;

(g)     **"Equipment"** means all equipment now owned or hereafter acquired by the Debtor, including, without limitation, all machinery, fixtures, plant, tools, furniture, chattels, vehicles of any kind or description including, without limitation, motor vehicles, parts, accessories installed in or affixed or attached to any of the foregoing, all drawings, specifications, plans and manuals relating thereto, and any other tangible personal property which is neither Inventory nor Consumer Goods (as defined in the PPSA) and all items described in Schedule "A" hereto;

(h)     **"Event of Default"** shall have the meaning ascribed in Section 5;

(i)     **"Instruments"** means all present and future bills, notes and cheques (as such are defined pursuant to the *Bills of Exchange Act* (Canada)) of the Debtor, and all other writings of the Debtor that evidence a right to the payment of money and are of a type that in the ordinary course of business are transferred by delivery without any necessary endorsement or assignment and all letters of credit and advices of credit of the Debtor provided that such letters of credit and advices of credit state that they must be surrendered upon claiming payment thereunder;

(j)   **"Inventory"** means all goods or chattels now or hereafter forming the inventory of the Debtor including, without limitation, the goods, merchandise, raw materials, work in process, finished goods, goods held for sale or resale or lease or that have been leased or that are to be, or have been, furnished under a contract of service, and goods used in or procured for packing or packaging or used or consumed in the business of the Debtor;

(k)   **"Intangibles"** means all intangible property now owned or hereafter acquired by the Debtor and which is not Accounts including, without limitation, all contractual rights, goodwill, patents, trademarks, trade names, copyrights and other intellectual property of the Debtor and all other choses in action of the Debtor of every kind, whether due or owing at the present time or hereafter to become due or owing;

(l)   **"Leaseholds"** means subject to Section 2.3, all leases, now owned or hereafter acquired by the Debtor as tenant (whether oral or written) or any agreement therefor;

(m)  **"Money"** means all money now or hereafter owned by the Debtor, whether such money is authorized or adopted by the Parliament of Canada as part of its currency or by any foreign government as part of its currency;

(n)   **"Obligations"** means the aggregate of all indebtedness, obligations and liabilities of the Debtor to the Creditor, whether incurred prior to, at the time of, or subsequent to the execution hereof, including extensions and renewals, and whether the sum is from time to time reduced and thereafter increased or entirely extinguished and thereafter incurred again, and including, without limitation: unpaid prices for the Creditor's products and services delivered to the Debtor or the Debtor's customers; advances to the Debtor; all interest payable by the Debtor to the Creditor; obligations or liabilities of the Debtor under any present or future guarantee by the Debtor of the payment or performance or both of the debts, obligations or liabilities of a third party to the Creditor; and debts, obligations or liabilities of the Debtor under any agreement with the Creditor including, without limitation, this Agreement, or any invoice, purchase order, debt obligation or any other agreement whatsoever, whether it or they be in writing, and any and all expenses, including solicitor's fees on a solicitor and his own client basis, incurred by the Creditor in collecting the said obligations, indebtedness and liabilities from the Debtor and in preserving, exercising or enforcing any of its rights and remedies under this Agreement;

(o)     **"PPSA"** means the *Personal Property Security Act* (Ontario), as amended from time to time, and any regulations thereto;

(p)     **"Proceeds"** means all property in any form derived directly or indirectly from any dealing with the Collateral including, without limitation, property that indemnifies or compensates for the expropriation, destruction or damage of the Collateral or the proceeds therefrom and all proceeds of proceeds;

(q)     **"Securities"** means all present and future securities held by the Debtor, including shares, options, rights, warrants, joint venture interests, interests in limited partnerships, trust units, bonds, debentures and all other documents which constitute evidence of a share, participation or other interest of the Debtor in property or in an enterprise or which constitute evidence of an obligation of the issuer; including, without limitation, an uncertificated security within the meaning of Part VI (Investment Securities) of the *Business Corporations Act* (Ontario) and all substitutions therefor and dividends and income derived therefrom;

**1.2  Other Usages.** References to "this Agreement," "hereof," "herein," "hereto" and like references refer to this General Security Agreement and not to any particular Article, Section or other subdivision of this Agreement.

**1.3   Plural and Singular.** Where the context so requires, words importing the singular number shall include the plural and vice versa.

**1.4  Headings.** The division of this Agreement into Articles and Sections and the insertion of headings in this Agreement are for convenience of reference only and shall not affect the construction or interpretation of this Agreement.

**1.5  Currency.** Unless otherwise specified herein, all statements of or references to dollar amounts in this Agreement shall mean lawful money of Canada.

**1.6  Applicable Law.** This Agreement and all documents delivered pursuant hereto shall be governed by and construed and interpreted in accordance with the laws of the Province of Ontario and the laws of Canada applicable therein and the parties hereto do hereby attorn to the non-exclusive jurisdiction of the courts of the Province of Ontario.

**1.7  Prohibited Provisions.** In the event that any provision or any part of any provision hereof is deemed to be invalid by reason of the operation of any law or by reason of the interpretation placed thereon by a court, this Agreement shall be construed as not containing such provision or such part of such provision and the invalidity of such provision or such part shall not affect the validity of any other provision or the remainder of such provision hereof, and all other provisions hereof which are otherwise lawful and valid shall remain in full force and effect.

**1.8  Time of the Essence.** Time shall in all respects be of the essence of this Agreement.

**1.9  Schedules.** Each and every one of the schedules which is referred to in this Agreement and attached to this Agreement shall form a part of this Agreement.

## 2.   SECURITY INTEREST

**2.1   Grant of Security Interest.** As general and continuing security for the payment and performance of all Obligations, the Debtor hereby grants, assigns, conveys, mortgages, charges and creates to and in favour of the Creditor a security interest in the Collateral.

Whenever used elsewhere in this Agreement, the expression "security interest" refers to the security interest created in and/or the assignment created above, as the context may require or permit.

**2.2   Attachment of Security Interest.** The parties hereby agree that they intend the security interest to attach to the Collateral upon execution of this Agreement.

**2.3   Exception re: Leaseholds and Contractual Rights.** The last day of the term of any lease, sublease or agreement therefor is specifically excepted from the security interest created by this Agreement, but the Debtor agrees to stand possessed of such last day in trust for such person as the Creditor may direct and the Debtor shall assign and dispose thereof in accordance with such direction. To the extent that the security interest created by this Agreement in any contractual rights (other than Accounts) would constitute a breach under, or cause the acceleration of, such contract, to which the Debtor is a party, said security interest shall not be granted hereunder but the Debtor shall hold its interest therein in trust for the Creditor, and shall grant a security interest in such contractual rights to the Creditor forthwith upon obtaining the appropriate consents to the attachment of said security interest.

## 3.   COVENANTS OF THE DEBTOR

**3.1   Covenants.** The Debtor hereby covenants and agrees with the Creditor as follows:

(a)   The Debtor's name set out herein is the Debtor's full and exact name, and there is no form of the Debtor's name in any other language;

(b)    The Collateral is and will be kept in the Province of Ontario at the locations specified in Schedule "B", and the address on the front page hereof is where the Debtor keeps its records concerning accounts and contract rights;

(c)    The Debtor will promptly notify the Creditor in writing of any addition to, change in or discontinuance of its places of business or keeping of its records as shown at the beginning of this Agreement and in Subsection 3.1(b);

(d)    The Debtor is the duly registered and lawful owner and is now lawfully seized and possessed of its real and immoveable property, if any, and of all the Collateral subjected to the charges created by this Agreement; that it has good, right and lawful authority to mortgage, and charge and to grant security interests in the Collateral as provided in this Agreement; that the Collateral is free and clear of all liens, charges and encumbrances whatsoever; that it will preserve, warrant and defend the title to said Collateral and rights and every part thereof, as well as to all other Collateral hereafter acquired by the Debtor and which may for the time being and from time to time form part of the Collateral, for the benefit of the Creditor and against the claims and demands of all persons whomsoever;

(e)    The Debtor will at all times preserve, repair and keep in repair and good order and condition, or cause to be so preserved, repaired and keep in repair and good order and condition, up to a modern standard of usage and subject to reasonable wear and tear, all buildings, works, erections and Equipment used in or in connection with its business relating to the Collateral and which the Debtor considers necessary for the efficient operation thereof, and renew and replace, or cause to be renewed and replaced, all and any of the same which may become worn, dilapidated, unserviceable or inconvenient;

(f)    The Debtor shall, to the extent that it is able, pay when due all taxes and assessments upon the Collateral, upon this Agreement or upon any note or document evidencing the Obligations;

(g)     The Debtor shall keep the Collateral insured under policies with such provisions, for such amounts and by such insurers as are satisfactory to the Creditor from time to time, and will maintain such insurance with loss, if any, payable to the Creditor and will deliver copies of such policies to the Creditor;

(h)     The Debtor agrees to promptly notify the Creditor in writing of the acquisition by the Debtor of any personal property which is not of the nature or type described by the definition of Collateral, and the Debtor agrees to execute and deliver at its own expense from time to time amendments to this Agreement or additional security agreements as may be reasonably required by the Creditor in order that a security interest shall be granted in and shall attach to such personal property.

(i)     The Debtor shall prevent the Collateral from becoming an accession to any personal property not subject to the security interest created by this Agreement, or becoming affixed to any real property.

(j)     The Debtor shall deliver to the Creditor from time to time as the same are acquired by the Debtor all items of Collateral comprising Chattel Paper, Instruments, Securities and those Documents of Title which are negotiable.

(k)     The Debtor shall use its best efforts to obtain a written agreement from each landlord of the Debtor in favour of the Creditor and in form and substance satisfactory to the Creditor, whereby such landlord:
        (i) agrees to give notice to the Creditor of any default by the Debtor under the lease and a reasonable opportunity to cure such default prior to the exercise of any remedies by the landlord; and
        (ii) acknowledges the security interest created by this Agreement and the right of the Creditor to enforce the security interest created by this Agreement in priority to any claim of such landlord;

(l)  The Debtor shall notify the Creditor promptly of:
(i) any material change in the information contained herein, or in the schedules hereto, relating to the Debtor, the Debtor's business or the Collateral;
(ii) the details of any claims or litigation affecting the Collateral; and
(iii) any loss or damage to the Collateral; and

(m)  The Debtor shall at all reasonable times and from time to time allow the Creditor by or through any of its officers, agents, attorneys or accountants, to examine or inspect the Collateral wherever located and to examine, inspect or make extracts from the Debtor's books and records with respect to the Collateral.

**3.2  Performance of Covenants by the Creditor.** The Creditor may, in its sole discretion and upon notice to the Debtor, perform any covenant of the Debtor under this Agreement that the Debtor fails to perform and that the Creditor is capable of performing, including any covenant the performance of which requires the payment of money, provided that the Creditor will not be obligated to perform any such covenant on behalf of the Debtor and no such performance by the Creditor will require the Creditor further to perform the Debtor's covenants nor operate as a derogation of the rights and remedies of the Creditor under this Agreement.

## 4.  DEALING WITH COLLATERAL

**4.1  General Restrictions.** Except as specifically permitted herein, the Debtor shall not, without the prior written consent of the Creditor:

(a)  sell, lease or otherwise dispose of the Collateral or any part thereof;

(b)  release, surrender or abandon possession of the Collateral or any part thereof;

(c)  move or transfer the Collateral or any part thereof from its present location as specified in Schedule "B" hereto;

(d)   allow any insurance coverage on the Collateral to lapse, which coverage shall be for the full insurable value of the Collateral with the Creditor named as loss payee; or

(e)   enter into or grant, create, assume or suffer to exist any mortgage, charge, hypothec, assignment, pledge, lien or other security interest or encumbrance affecting any of the Collateral, other than the liens created under this Agreement, or as permitted in writing by the Creditor.

**4.2  Release by the Creditor.** The Creditor may, at its discretion, at any time release from the security interest created by this Agreement any part or parts of the Collateral or any other security or any surety for the Obligations either with or without sufficient consideration therefor without thereby releasing any other part of the Collateral or any person from this Agreement.

**4.3  Proceeds Held in Trust.** All Proceeds that are monies collected or received by the Debtor will be received by the Debtor in trust for the Creditor and will be forthwith paid to the Creditor. The Creditor shall not exercise its rights under this Section, and the Debtor's trust obligations under this Section need not be complied with, unless such Proceeds arise from a disposition of Collateral which is not permitted hereunder or unless and until the security hereby constituted becomes enforceable.

## 5.   DEFAULT AND ENFORCEMENT

**5.1  Enforceability of Security.** The security hereby constituted shall become enforceable upon the occurrence of any one or more of the following events:

(a)   if the Debtor defaults in payment or performance of any of the Obligations;

(b)   if an event of default occurs as specified in any other agreement between the parties;

(c)  the Debtor ceases to or threatens to cease to carry on its business or if a petition shall be filed, an order made or an effective resolution passed for its winding-up or liquidation;

(d)  the Debtor shall become insolvent or make a sale in bulk of its assets or seeks protection, makes a proposal or files on assignment under any insolvency legislation or is petitioned into bankruptcy, or if a custodian, a sequestrator, a receiver, a receiver and manager or any other officer with similar powers is appointed with respect to the Collateral, or any of its creditors take possession of or enforce its remedies over any of the Collateral; or

(e)  if the Creditor in good faith believes and has commercially reasonable grounds to believe that the prospect of payment or performance of the Obligations is or is about to be impaired or that the Collateral is or is about to be placed in jeopardy including upon the Debtor defaulting under any obligation to repay money, the payment of which is secured by the Collateral or other mortgaged property of the Debtor.

**5.2  Remedies.** At any time after the happening of any event by which the security hereby constituted becomes enforceable, the Creditor shall have the following rights, powers and remedies:

(a)  to appoint any person to be an agent or any person to be a receiver, manager or receiver and manager (herein called the "Receiver") of the Collateral and to remove any Receiver so appointed and to appoint another if the Creditor so desires; it being agreed that any Receiver appointed pursuant to the provisions of this Agreement shall have all of the powers of the Creditor hereunder, and in addition, shall have the power to carry on the business of the Debtor;

(b)  to make payments to parties having prior charges or encumbrances on the Collateral;

(c)  to enter onto any premises where the Collateral may be located;

(d)   to take possession of all or any part of the Collateral and any premises where such Collateral is located with power to exclude the Debtor, its agents and its servants from such Collateral and such premises;

(e)   to preserve, protect and maintain the Collateral and make such repairs to, replacements thereof and additions thereto as the Creditor shall deem advisable;

(f)   to enjoy and exercise all powers necessary or incidental to the performance of all functions provided for in this Agreement including, without limitation, the power to purchase on credit, the power to borrow in the Debtor's name or in the name of the Receiver and to advance its own money to the Debtor at such rates of interest as it may deem reasonable, provided that the Receiver shall borrow money only with the prior consent of the Creditor, and to grant security interests in the Collateral in priority to the security interest created by this Agreement, as security for the money so borrowed;

(g)   to sell, lease or dispose of all or any part of the Collateral whether by public or private sale or lease or otherwise and on any terms so long as every aspect of the disposition is commercially reasonable, including without limitation, terms that provide time for payment on credit; provided that,
(i) the Creditor or the Receiver will not be required to sell, lease or dispose of the Collateral, but may peaceably and quietly take, hold, use, occupy, possess and enjoy the Collateral without molestation, eviction, hindrance or interruption by the Debtor or any other person or persons whomever, for such period of time as is commercially reasonable;
(ii) the Creditor or the Receiver may convey, transfer and assign to a purchaser or purchasers the title to any of the Collateral so sold; and
(iii) subject to Section 5.8, the Debtor will be entitled to be credited with the actual proceeds of any such sale, lease or other disposition only when such proceeds are received by the Creditor or the Receiver in cash;

(h)   to enjoy and exercise all of the rights and remedies of a secured party under the PPSA;

(i)   to dispose of all or any part of the Collateral in the condition in which it was on the date possession of it was taken, or after any commercially reasonable repair, processing or preparation for disposition;

(j)   to sell or otherwise dispose of any part of the Collateral without giving any notice whatsoever where:
(i) the Collateral is perishable;
(ii) the Creditor or the Receiver believes on reasonable grounds that the Collateral will decline speedily in value;
(iii) the Collateral is of a type customarily sold on a recognized market;
(iv) the cost of care and storage of the Collateral is disproportionately large relative to its value;
(v) every person entitled by law to receive a notice of disposition consents in writing to the immediate disposition of the Collateral; or
(vi) the Receiver disposes of the Collateral in the course of the Debtor's business;

(k)   to notify the account debtors or obligors under any Accounts of the assignment of such Accounts to the Creditor and to direct such account debtors or obligors to make payment of all amounts due or to become due to the Debtor thereunder directly to the Creditor and to give valid and binding receipts and discharges therefor and in respect thereof and, upon such notification and at the expense of the Debtor, to enforce collection of any such Accounts, and to adjust, settle or compromise the amount or payment thereof, in the same manner and to the same extent as the Debtor might have done;

(l)   to commence, continue or defend proceedings in any court of competent jurisdiction in the name of the Creditor, the Receiver or the Debtor for the purpose of exercising any of the rights, powers and remedies set out in this Section, including the institution of proceedings for the appointment of a receiver, manager or receiver and manager of the Collateral; and

(m) at the sole option of the Creditor, provided notice is given in the manner required by the PPSA to the Debtor and to any other person to whom the PPSA requires notice to be given, to elect to retain all or any part of the Collateral in satisfaction of the Obligations.

**5.3 Special Rules re: Accounts.** After the security hereby constituted becomes enforceable,

(a) all Money or other form of payment received by the Debtor in respect of the Accounts shall be received in trust for the benefit of the Creditor hereunder, shall be segregated from other funds of the Debtor and shall be forthwith paid over to the Creditor in the same form as so received (with any necessary endorsement) to be held as cash collateral and applied as provided by Section 5.8; and

(b) the Debtor shall not adjust, settle or compromise the amount or payment of any Accounts, or release wholly or partly any account debtor or obligor thereof, or allow any credit or discount thereon.

**5.4 Receiver as Agent.** The Receiver shall be deemed to be the agent of the Debtor for the purpose of establishing liability for the acts or omissions of the Receiver and the Creditor shall not be liable for such acts or omissions and, without restricting the generality of the foregoing, the Debtor hereby irrevocably authorizes the Creditor to give instructions to the Receiver relating to the performance of its duties as set out herein.

**5.5 Expenses of Enforcement.** The Debtor shall pay to the Receiver the remuneration of the Receiver and all costs and expenses (including, without limitation, legal fees and disbursements on a solicitor and his own client basis) properly incurred by the Receiver pursuant to its appointment and the exercise of its powers hereunder, and shall pay to the Creditor and the Receiver as required all amounts of money (including interest thereon) borrowed or advanced by either of them pursuant to the powers set out herein, and the obligations of the Debtor to the Creditor and the Receiver pursuant to this Section 5.5 shall be payable on demand and shall bear interest at an annual rate of 6%, which interest shall be calculated and compounded monthly and payable on demand.

**5.6 Indulgences and Releases.** Either the Creditor or the Receiver may grant extensions of time and other indulgences, take and give up securities, accept compositions, grant releases and discharges, release any part of the Collateral to third parties and otherwise deal with the Debtor, debtors of the Debtor, sureties and others and with the Collateral and other security as the Creditor or the Receiver may see fit without prejudice to the Obligations or the right of the Creditor and the Receiver to repossess, hold, collect and realize the Collateral.

**5.7 No Liability for Failure to Exercise Remedies.** The Creditor and the Receiver shall not be liable or accountable to the Debtor or to any other person for any failure to exercise any of the rights, powers and remedies set out in Section 5.2, and shall not be bound to commence, continue or defend proceedings for the purpose of preserving or protecting any rights of the Creditor, the Receiver, the Debtor or any other party in respect of the same.

**5.8 Proceeds of Disposition.** Subject to the claims, if any, of the prior secured creditors of the Debtor, all moneys received by the Creditor or by the Receiver pursuant to Section 5.2 shall be applied as follows:

(a) first, in payment of all costs and expenses incurred by the Creditor in the exercise of all or any of the powers granted to it under this Agreement and in payment of all of the remuneration of the Receiver and all costs and expenses properly incurred by the Receiver in the exercise of all or any of the powers granted to it under this Agreement, including, without limitation, the remuneration, costs and expenses referred to in Section 5.5;

(b)  second, in payment of all amounts of money borrowed or advanced by either of the Creditor or the Receiver pursuant to the powers set out in this Agreement and any interest thereon;

(c)  third, in payment of the Obligations, provided that if there are not sufficient moneys to pay all of the Obligations, the Creditor may apply the moneys available to such part or parts thereof as the Creditor, in its sole discretion, may determine; and

(d)  fourth, in payment of any surplus in accordance with applicable law.

**5.9 Debtor Liable for Deficiency.** If the monies received by the Creditor or the Receiver pursuant to Section 5.2 are not sufficient to pay the claims set out in Section 5.8, the Debtor shall immediately pay the Creditor the amount of such deficiency.

**5.10 Restriction on Debtor.** Upon the Creditor taking possession of the collateral or the appointment of a Receiver, all the powers, functions, rights and privileges of the Debtor or any officer, director, servant or agent of the Debtor with respect to the Collateral shall, to the extent permitted by law, be suspended unless specifically continued by the written consent of the Creditor; however, all other powers, functions, rights and privileges of the Debtor or any officer, director, servant or agent of the Debtor shall be unaffected by such events.

**5.11 Rights Cumulative.** All rights and remedies of the Creditor set out in this Agreement shall be cumulative and no right or remedy contained herein is intended to be exclusive but each shall be in addition to every other right or remedy contained herein or in any existing or future security document or now or hereafter existing at law or in equity or by statute. The taking of a judgment or judgments with respect to any of the Obligations shall not operate as a merger of any of the covenants contained in this Agreement.

**5.12 Care by the Creditor.** The Creditor shall be deemed to have exercised reasonable care in the custody and preservation of any of the Collateral in the Creditor's possession if it takes such action for that purpose as the Debtor requests in writing, but failure of the Creditor to comply with any such request shall not be deemed to be (or to be evidence of) a failure to exercise reasonable care, and no failure of the Creditor to preserve or protect any rights with respect to such Collateral against prior parties, or to do any act with respect to the preservation of such Collateral not so requested by the Debtor, shall be deemed a failure to exercise reasonable care in the custody or preservation of such Collateral.

**5.13 Standards of Sale.** Without prejudice to the ability of the Creditor to dispose of the Collateral in any manner which is commercially reasonable, the Debtor acknowledges that a disposition of Collateral by the Creditor which takes place substantially in accordance with the following provisions shall be deemed to be commercially reasonable:

(a) Collateral may be disposed of in whole or in part;

(b) the purchaser or lessee of such Collateral may be a customer of the Creditor;

(c) the disposition may be for cash or credit, or part cash and part credit; and

(d) the Creditor may establish a reserve bid in respect of all or any portion of the Collateral.

**5.14 Application by Debtor re: Receiver.** The Debtor hereby irrevocably waives its right to make an application to any court with respect to the appointment, powers or remuneration of the Receiver.

## 6.   GENERAL

**6.1   Waiver.** Any breach by the Debtor of any of the provisions contained in this Agreement or any default by the Debtor in the observance or performance of any covenant or condition required to be observed or performed by the Debtor hereunder, may only be waived by the Creditor in writing, provided that no such waiver by the Creditor shall extend to or be taken in any manner to affect any subsequent breach or default or the rights resulting therefrom.

**6.2 The Creditor as Attorney.** The Debtor hereby irrevocably appoints the Creditor and any person further designated by the Creditor to be the attorney of the Debtor for and in the name of the Debtor to execute and do any deeds, documents, transfers, demands, assignments, assurances, consents and things which the Debtor is obliged to sign, execute or do hereunder and, after the happening of any event by which the security hereby constituted becomes enforceable, to commence, continue and defend any proceedings authorized to be taken hereunder and generally to use the name of the Debtor in the exercise of all or any of the powers hereby conferred on the Creditor.

**6.3 Further Assurances.** The Debtor shall do, execute, acknowledge and deliver or cause to be done, executed, acknowledged and delivered, such further acts, deeds, mortgages, transfers and assurances as the Creditor shall reasonably require for the better assuring, charging, assigning and conferring unto the Creditor a security interest in the Collateral or property intended to be charged hereunder, or which the Debtor may hereafter become bound to charge in favour of the Creditor, for the purpose of accomplishing and effecting the intention of this Agreement.

**6.4 Continuing Security.** The security interest constituted hereby shall be deemed to be a continuing security for the Obligations until all of the Obligations from time to time are paid and performed in full and any and all commitments of the Creditor in favour of the Debtor have been cancelled under the Credit Agreement and otherwise.

**6.5 No Obligation to Advance.** Neither the execution nor delivery of this Agreement shall obligate the Creditor to advance any moneys to the Debtor.

**6.6  Consumer Goods.** Notwithstanding any other clause in this Agreement, in no event shall goods that are used or acquired for use primarily for personal, family or household purposes form part of the Collateral.

**6.7  Notices.** All notices and other communications provided for herein shall be in writing and shall be personally delivered to an officer or other responsible employee of the addressee or sent by facsimile, charges prepaid, at or to the applicable address or tele-facsimile number, as the case may be, of the party set opposite its name below or at or to such other address or addresses or telefac-simile number or numbers as either party may from time to time designate to the other party in such manner. Any communication which is personally delivered as aforesaid shall be deemed to have been validly and effectively given on the date of such delivery if such date is a Banking Day and such delivery was made during normal business hours of the recipient; otherwise, it shall be deemed to have been validly and effectively given on the Banking Day next following such date of delivery. Any communication which is transmitted by telefacsimile as aforesaid shall be deemed to have been validly and effectively given on the date of transmission if such date is a Banking Day and such transmission was made during normal business hours of the recipient; otherwise, it shall be deemed to have been validly and effectively given on the Banking Day next following such date of transmission.

In the case of the Debtor:

_____

Attention: _____

In the case of the Creditor:

_____

Attention: _____

**6.8  Assignment.** The Creditor may assign or transfer this Agreement, any of its rights hereunder or any part thereof.

**6.9  Successors and Assigns.** This Agreement shall enure to the benefit of the Creditor and its successors and assigns and shall be binding upon the Debtor and its successors and assigns.

**6.10 Entire Agreement.** This Agreement and the agreements referred to herein and any document, agreement or instrument delivered pursuant to such agreements constitute the entire agreement between the parties hereto and supersede any prior agreements, undertakings, declarations, representations and undertakings, both written and verbal, in respect of the subject matter hereof.

**6.11 Receipt of Copy of Agreement.** The Debtor hereby acknowledges receipt of an executed copy of this Agreement.

**IN WITNESS WHEREOF** the Debtor has executed this Agreement.

_____

Per: _____

# EXHIBIT 2

## Assignment of Book Debts

**TO:** _____

(the "Creditor")

**THE UNDERSIGNED** _____, (the "Assignors") agree to each for good and valuable consideration hereby assign, transfer, and set over unto the Creditor all debts, accounts, choses in action, claims, demands, and moneys now due and owing or accruing due or which may hereafter become due or owing to the Assignors, together or separately, including (without limiting the foregoing) all moneys which may become payable to the Assignors by _____ together with all contracts, securities, bills, notes, lien notes, judgments, chattel mortgages and all other rights, benefits and documents now or hereafter taken, vested in or held by the Assignors in respect of or as security for such debts, accounts, choses in action, claims, demands, and moneys hereby assigned or intended so to be or any part thereof and the full benefit and advantage thereof, and all rights of action, claim, or demand which the Assignors now have or may at any time hereafter have against any person or persons, firm or corporation in respect thereof.

**AND THE ASSIGNORS** hereby nominate, constitute, and appoint the Creditor to be the true and lawful attorney of the Assignors in the name of the Assignors to ask, demand, and receive of and from any and all debtors of the Assignors the debts severally owing or which may become owing from them, and on non-payment of the same or any part thereof to commence and prosecute any action or proceeding for the recovery of the same and to use all other lawful remedies which the Assignors could or might have used for such recovery, and on receipt or recovery to sign and give good and effectual receipt or receipts for the same with full power from time to time to appoint a substitute or substitutes for all or any of the purposes aforesaid, and in case of any difficulty or dispute with any debtor of the Assignors to submit such difficulty or dispute to arbitration in such manner as the Creditor shall see fit and to compound, compromise, and accept part in satisfaction for payment of the whole of any debt hereby assigned or to grant an extension of time for payment thereof either with or without security; all as the Creditor in its absolute discretion shall deem expedient, and the Assignors hereby agree to ratify whatsoever the Creditor shall lawfully do or cause to be done in the premises and to indemnify the Creditor of and from all loss, costs, charges, and expenses by reason of any such proceeding.

**THE ASSIGNORS** hereby further assign, transfer, and set over unto the Creditor each and all the book or books of record and otherwise, together with all papers, documents, and writings whatsoever which shall at any time during the continuance of this Indenture be in the possession, power, custody, or control of the Assignors relating or referring to the said book debts, claims and rights hereby assigned or intended so to be or in any way representing or evidencing same.

**THE ASSIGNORS** further hereby covenant, promise and agree to and with the Creditor to well and truly execute or cause to be executed all or any such further or other document or documents as shall or may be required by the Creditor to more completely or fully vest in the Creditor the said book debts, claims, and rights hereby assigned or intended so to be and the right to receive the said moneys or to enable the said the Creditor to recover same and will from time to time prepare and deliver to the Creditor all deeds, books, vouchers, promissory notes, bills of exchange, accounts, letters, invoices, papers, and all other documents in any way relating to the said book debts, claims, and rights hereby assigned.

**PROVIDED** and it is hereby distinctly understood and agreed that these presents are and shall be a continuing collateral security to the Creditor for the general balance due at any time by the Assignors to the Creditor and all indebtedness for which the Assignors now are or may hereafter be liable to the Creditor and all renewals thereof, and substitutions therefor and all bills of exchange, promissory notes, cheques, and other instruments whatsoever in any way representing or securing the same and all future bills, notes, or other instruments which may at any time hereafter be given or taken in renewal of or in substitution therefor either in whole or in part or as in any wise representing the said indebtedness or any part thereof together with all costs, charges, and expenses to which the Creditor shall be put in connection therewith or in connection with the collection or recovery of any of the book debts, claims, or rights hereby assigned, notwithstanding any change in the nature or form of said indebtedness or in the bills, notes, or other obligations representing the same or any part thereof or in the names or the parties to such bills, notes, or other obligations so held as collateral thereto.

**PROVIDED ALWAYS** and it is hereby distinctly agreed that these presents are and shall be continuing and collateral security to the present and any future indebtedness of the Assignors to the Creditor and shall not create any merger of the said indebtedness in respect of any sum or sums so owing or which may hereafter become owing or any bill of exchange, promissory note, or other security given for the same or any part or parts thereof or of any contract in respect thereof and shall not operate as a release to the Assignors or suspend, impair, or otherwise affect the rights and remedies of the Creditor from time to time in respect of any such indebtedness and further shall not in any way operate as a release to or affect the rights of the Creditor as against any third party or parties liable for such indebtedness or any part or parts thereof or upon any bill of exchange, promissory note, or other security or contract representing the same or any part thereof or which may be taken as security therefor or for any part thereof.

## IT IS FURTHER UNDERSTOOD AND AGREED that:

(i)   the agreement between the parties is that the existing indebtedness of the Assignors to the Creditor as well as all future indebtedness, no matter how secured, shall be treated as secured hereby; and

(ii)   the said existing indebtedness shall be treated as continuing notwithstanding new transactions with the Assignors, the intention of the parties being that this present existing indebtedness may remain undischarged, except as to any amount by which the total indebtedness of the Assignors to the Creditor may be actually reduced below the present amount of same.

**IT IS HEREBY DECLARED AND AGREED** by and between the parties hereto that the word "Creditor" wherever used throughout this Agreement shall extend to and include the legal representatives, successors and assigns of the "Creditor" and the word "Assignors" wherever used throughout this Agreement shall extend to and include the successors and assigns of the Assignors.

**THIS INSTRUMENT** shall be governed and construed in accordance with the laws of the Province of Ontario, and the Assignors expressly attorn to the courts and laws of the said Province. This agreement constitutes the entire agreement among the parties with respect to the subject matter hereof and may only be amended by written instrument executed by the Assignors and the Creditor.

**IN WITNESS WHEREOF** the undersigned have hereunto executed this Assignment this _____ day of _____ , 19____.

**SIGNED SEALED and DELIVERED**      )
**in the presence of**                               )
                                                                )
_____            )_____
                                                                )
                                                                )
_____            )_____

# EXHIBIT 3

# Inventory Security Agreement

**THIS AGREEMENT** made as of the _____ day of _____, 19__.

**TO:** _____, a corporation incorporated under the laws of the Province of Ontario,

    ("the Creditor")

                             OF THE FIRST PART

**FROM:** _____, a corporation incorporated under the laws of the Province of Ontario,

    (the "Debtor")

                             OF THE SECOND PART

**THIS AGREEMENT WITNESSES** that, in consideration of the Creditor selling its products to the Debtor on terms of credit and for other good and valuable consideration, the Debtor agrees with the Creditor as follows:

# ARTICLE 1
## INTERPRETATION

**1.1 Defined Terms.** In this agreement, unless there is something in the context or subject matter inconsistent therewith,

**"Banking Day"** means any day (other than a Saturday or a Sunday) on which banks generally are open for business in Toronto, Ontario;

**"Collateral"** means all Inventory and Proceeds;

**"Event of Default"** shall have the meaning ascribed thereto in Section 4;

**"Inventory"** means all goods, products or chattels now or hereafter provided by the Creditor to the Debtor, including, without limitation, products of the Creditor described in Schedule "A" annexed hereto;

**"Obligations"** means the aggregate of all indebtedness, obligations and liabilities of the Debtor to the Creditor, whether incurred prior to, at the time of, or subsequent to the execution hereof, including extensions and renewals, and including, without limitation: unpaid prices for products of the Creditor, goods, chattels and services delivered to the Debtor or the Debtor's customers; advances to the Debtor; all interest payable by the Debtor to the Creditor; obligations or liabilities of the Debtor under any present or future guarantee by the Debtor of the payment or performance or both of the debts, obligations or liabilities of a third party to the Creditor; and debts, obligations or liabilities of the Debtor under any agreement with the Creditor including, without limitation, this Agreement, and any promissory note, invoice purchase order, debt obligation or any other agreement whatsoever, whether it or they be in writing;

**"PPSA"** means the *Personal Property Security Act* (Ontario), as amended from time to time, and any regulations thereto;

**"Prime Rate"** means the rate of interest per annum charged by the _____ Bank to its customers in Toronto, Ontario for loans of Canadian dollars, as the same is adjusted from time to time.

**"Proceeds"** means all property in any form derived directly or indirectly from any dealing with the Collateral including, without limitation each and every account, debt, claim and demand of every nature and kind which may hereafter become due, owing or accruing to the Debtor relating to dealings by the Debtor in the goods, products and chattels supplied by the Creditor and all rights, interests and benefits of the Debtor thereto and property that indemnifies or compensates for the expropriation, destruction or damage of the Collateral or the proceeds therefrom and all proceeds of proceeds;

**1.2 Other Usages.** References to "this agreement", "hereof", "herein", "hereto" and like references refer to this Inventory Security Agreement and not to any particular Article, Section or other subdivision of this agreement.

**1.3 Plural and Singular.** Where the context so requires, words importing the singular number shall include the plural and vice versa.

**1.4 Headings.** The division of this agreement into Articles and Sections and the insertion of headings in this agreement are for convenience of reference only and shall not affect the construction or interpretation of this agreement.

**1.5 Currency.** Unless otherwise specified herein, all statements of or references to dollar amounts in this agreement shall mean lawful money of Canada.

**1.6 Applicable Law.** This agreement and all documents delivered pursuant hereto shall be governed by and construed and interpreted in accordance with the laws of the Province of Ontario and the laws of Canada applicable therein and the parties hereto do hereby attorn to the non-exclusive jurisdiction of the courts of the Province of Ontario.

**1.7 Prohibited Provisions.** In the event that any provision or any part of any provision hereof is deemed to be invalid by reason of the operation of any law or by reason of the interpretation placed thereon by a court, this agreement shall be construed as not containing such provision or such part of such provision and the invalidity of such provision or such part shall not affect the validity of any other provision or the remainder of such provision hereof, and all other provisions hereof which are otherwise lawful and valid shall remain in full force and effect.

**1.8 Time of the Essence.** Time shall in all respects be of the essence of this agreement.

**1.9 Schedules.** Each and every one of the schedules which is referred to in this agreement and attached to this agreement shall form a part of this agreement.

# ARTICLE 2
## SECURITY INTEREST

**2.1 Grant of Security Interest.** As general and continuing security for the payment and performance of all Obligations, the Debtor hereby grants to the Creditor a security interest in the Collateral and agrees that title in and to the Inventory shall remain in the Creditor until the price therefor has been paid by the Debtor in full.

**2.2 Attachment of Security Interest.** The parties hereby agree that they intend the security interest to attach to the Collateral upon execution of this agreement.

## ARTICLE 3
## COVENANTS OF THE DEBTOR

**3.1  General Restrictions.** Except as specifically permitted herein, the Debtor shall not, without the prior written consent of the Creditor:

(a)  sell, lease or otherwise dispose of the Collateral or any part thereof, except in the ordinary course of the Debtor's business;

(b)  release, surrender or abandon possession of the Collateral or any part thereof;

(c)  move or transfer the Collateral or any part thereof from its present location as specified in Schedule "B" hereto;

(d)  allow any insurance coverage on the Collateral to lapse, which coverage shall be for the full insurable value of the Collateral with the Creditor named as loss payee; or

(e)  enter into or grant, create, assume or suffer to exist any mortgage, charge, hypothec, assignment, pledge, lien or other security interest or encumbrance affecting any of the Collateral.

**3.2  Performance of Covenants by the Creditor.** The Creditor may, in its sole discretion and upon notice to the Debtor, perform any covenant of the Debtor under this agreement that the Debtor fails to perform and that the Creditor is capable of performing, including any covenant the performance of which requires the payment of money, provided that the Creditor will not be obligated to perform any such covenant on behalf of the Debtor and no such performance by the Creditor will require the Creditor further to perform the Debtor's covenants nor operate as a derogation of the rights and remedies of the Creditor under this agreement.

# ARTICLE 4
# DEFAULT AND ENFORCEMENT

**4.1 Enforceability of Security.** The security hereby constituted shall become enforceable in each and every one of the following events:

(a) if the Debtor defaults in payment performance of any of the Obligations;

(b) the failure or inability of the Debtor to pay any of its debts or liabilities as the same fall due;

(c) the occurrence of a default by the Debtor under any agreement, instrument or writing entered into by the Debtor with any person;

(d) the Debtor making or agreeing to make an assignment, disposition or conveyance, whether by way of sale or otherwise, of its assets in bulk;

(e) the abandonment by the debtor of the Collateral or any part thereof;

(f) the Debtor ceases to or threatens to cease to carry on its business;

(g) the Debtor seeks protection, makes a proposal or files an assignment under any insolvency legislation or is petitioned into bankruptcy or any of its creditors take possession of or enforces its remedies over any of the Collateral;

(h) the filing of an application or petition or the passing of a resolution for the winding-up or dissolution of the Debtor, or the granting or issuing of an order for the winding-up or dissolution of the Debtor;

(i) an execution, sequestration or any other process of any court or other tribunal becoming enforceable against the Debtor or a distress or analogous process being taken or issued against the

Debtor or levied upon the property of the Debtor or any part thereof including, without limitation, a warrant of distress for any rent or taxes in respect of any premises occupied by the Debtor or in respect of any premises in or upon which the Collateral or any part thereof may at any time be situate;

(j) the appointment of a receiver, receiver and manager, agent, liquidator or other similar administrator of any part(s) of the Collateral or the taking by a secured party or any other encumbrancer of possession of the Collateral or any part(s) thereof;

(k) the Debtor removing or attempting to remove all or any part of the Collateral out of Ontario without having first obtained the written consent of the Creditor, provided that where the purchase order with respect to certain Collateral indicates that the ultimate destination of such Collateral is outside of Ontario and the Creditor provides the Debtor with such Collateral, the Creditor is deemed to have consented to the removal of such Collateral out of Ontario; and

(l) if the Creditor in good faith believes and has commercially reasonable grounds to believe that the prospect of payment or performance of the Obligations is or is about to be impaired or that the Collateral is or is about to be placed in jeopardy.

**4.2 Remedies.** At any time after the happening of any event by which the security hereby constituted becomes enforceable, the Creditor shall have all of the remedies of a secured party under the PPSA and the right to appoint any person to be an agent or any person to be a receiver, manager or receiver and manager (herein called the "Receiver") of the Collateral and such Receiver shall have all of the powers of the Creditor hereunder, and in addition, shall have the power to carry on the business of the Debtor.

**4.3 Receiver as Agent.** The Receiver shall be deemed to be the agent of the Debtor for the purpose of establishing liability for the acts or omissions of the Receiver and the Creditor shall not be liable for such acts or omissions and, without restricting the generality of the foregoing, the Debtor hereby irrevocably authorizes the Creditor to give instructions to the Receiver relating to the performance of its duties as set out herein.

**4.4  Expenses of Enforcement.** The Debtor shall pay to the Receiver the remuneration of the Receiver and all costs and expenses (including, without limitation, legal fees and disbursements on a solicitor and his own client basis) properly incurred by the Receiver pursuant to its appointment and the exercise of its powers hereunder, and shall pay to the Creditor and the Receiver as required all amounts of money (including interest thereon) borrowed or advanced by either of them pursuant to the powers set out herein, and the obligations of the Debtor to the Creditor and the Receiver shall be payable on demand and shall bear interest at an annual rate equal to the Prime Rate plus three percent (3%), which interest shall be calculated and compounded monthly and payable on demand.

**4.5  Indulgences and Releases.** Either the Creditor or the Receiver may grant extensions of time and other indulgences, take and give up securities, accept compositions, grant releases and discharges, release any part of the Collateral to third parties and otherwise deal with the Debtor, debtors of the Debtor, sureties and others and with the Collateral and other security as the Creditor or the Receiver may see fit without prejudice to the Obligations or the right of the Creditor and the Receiver to repossess, hold, collect and realize the Collateral.

**4.6  No Liability for Failure to Exercise Remedies.** The Creditor and the Receiver shall not be liable or accountable to the Debtor or to any other person for any failure to exercise any of the rights, powers and remedies herein set out and shall not be bound to commence, continue or defend proceedings for the purpose of preserving or protecting any rights of the Creditor, the Receiver, the Debtor or any other party in respect of the same.

**4.7  Proceeds of Disposition.** Subject to the claims, if any, of the prior secured creditors of the Debtor, all moneys received by the Creditor or by the Receiver shall be applied as follows:

(a)  first, in payment of all costs and expenses incurred by the Creditor in the exercise of all or any of the powers granted to it under this agreement and in payment of all of the remuneration of the Receiver;

(b)  second, in payment of all amounts of money borrowed or advanced by either of the Creditor or the Receiver;

(c)  third, in payment of the Obligations; and

(d)  fourth, in payment of any surplus in accordance with applicable law.

**4.8  Debtor Liable for Deficiency.** If the monies received by the Creditor or the Receiver are not sufficient to pay the claims of the Creditor, the Debtor shall immediately pay the Creditor the amount of such deficiency.

**4.9  Rights Cumulative.** All rights and remedies of the Creditor set out in this agreement shall be cumulative and no right or remedy contained herein is intended to be exclusive but each shall be in addition to every other right or remedy contained herein or in any existing or future security document or now or hereafter existing at law or in equity or by statute. The taking of a judgment or judgments with respect to any of the Obligations shall not operate as a merger of any of the covenants contained in this agreement.

**4.10 Standards of Sale.** Without prejudice to the ability of the Creditor to dispose of the Collateral in any manner which is commercially reasonable, the Debtor acknowledges that a disposition of Collateral by the Creditor which takes place substantially in accordance with the following provisions shall be deemed to be commercially reasonable:

(a)   Collateral may be disposed of in whole or in part;

(b)   the purchaser or lessee of such Collateral may be a customer of the Creditor;

(c)   the disposition may be for cash or credit, or part cash and part credit; and

(d)   the Creditor may establish a reserve bid in respect of all or any portion of the Collateral.

## ARTICLE 5
## GENERAL

**5.1 Waiver.** Any breach by the Debtor of any of the provisions contained in this agreement or any default by the Debtor in the observance or performance of any covenant or condition required to be observed or performed by the Debtor hereunder, may only be waived by the Creditor in writing, provided that no such waiver by the Creditor shall extend to or be taken in any manner to affect any subsequent breach or default or the rights resulting therefrom.

**5.2 The Creditor as Attorney.** The Debtor hereby irrevocably appoints the Creditor and any person further designated by the Creditor to be the attorney of the Debtor for and in the name of the Debtor to execute and do any deeds, documents, transfers, demands, assignments, assurances, consents and things which the Debtor is obliged to sign, execute or do hereunder and, after the happening of any event by which the security hereby constituted becomes enforceable, to commence, continue and defend any pro-ceedings authorized to be taken hereunder and generally to use the name of the Debtor in the exercise of all or any of the powers hereby conferred on the Creditor.

**5.3 Further Assurances.** The Debtor shall do, execute, acknowl-edge and deliver or cause to be done, executed, acknowledged and delivered, such further acts, deeds, mortgages, transfers and assurances as the Creditor shall reasonably require for the better assuring, charging, assigning and conferring unto the Creditor a security interest in the Collateral or property intended to be charged hereunder, or which the Debtor may hereafter become bound to charge in favour of the Creditor, for the purpose of accomplishing and effecting the intention of this agreement.

**5.4  Continuing Security.** The security interest constituted hereby shall be deemed to be a continuing security for the Obligations until all of the Obligations from time to time are paid and performed in full and any and all commitments of the Creditor in favour of the Debtor have been cancelled.

**5.5  No Obligation to Advance.** Neither the execution nor delivery of this agreement shall obligate the Creditor to advance any moneys to the Debtor.

**5.6  Successors and Assigns.** This agreement shall enure to the benefit of the Creditor and its successors and assigns and shall be binding upon the Debtor and its successors and assigns.

**5.7  Entire Agreement.** This agreement and the agreements referred to herein and any document, agreement or instrument delivered pursuant to such agreements constitute the entire agreement between the parties hereto and supersede any prior agreements, undertakings, declarations, representations and undertakings, both written and verbal, in respect of the subject matter hereof.

**5.8  Receipt of Copy of Agreement.** The Debtor hereby acknowledges receipt of an executed copy of this agreement.

**IN WITNESS WHEREOF** the Debtor has executed this agreement.

Per: _____

Name:

Title:

[I have authority to bind the corporation]


Per: _____

Name:

Title:

[I have authority to bind the corporation]

# EXHIBIT 4

# Notice of Retention

## NOTICE PURSUANT TO SECTION 65(2)
## OF THE *PERSONAL PROPERTY SECURITY ACT* (ONTARIO)

**TO:** [debtor, all guarantors, all PPSA creditors and everyone else with an interest in the collateral of whom the Lender is aware]

Attn: _____

**AND TO:** _____

Attn: _____

**TAKE NOTICE** that pursuant to a _____ dated _____, 19__ and a _____ dated _____, 19__ (collectively the "**Security**") all made between _____ carrying on business as _____ (the "**Company**") and _____ (the "**Secured Party**"), the Secured Party intends to accept and retain the collateral in satisfaction of the obligation secured unless the collateral is redeemed.

1.    The collateral consists of all personal property of the Company, including the personal property of the Company used in connection with or generated by its operation of its division located at _____ _____.

2.    The principal amount required to satisfy the obligation of the Company secured by the Security as at the _____ day of _____, 19\_\_ is $\_\_\_\_, together with interest thereon from _____, 19\_\_ to and including _____, 19\_\_ of $_____, and interest thereon from and including _____,19\_\_ until payment in full at the rate per annum of _____ per cent.

3.    The Secured Party's address where payment should be made is:

[Mailing Address]

Attention:   _____

Telephone:   _____

4.    Upon payment of the amounts due as above described, you may redeem the said collateral. Upon payment, the payor will be credited with any rebates or allowances to which the Company is entitled by law or under any agreement with the Secured Party.

5.    Unless the amounts due as above described are paid by the _____ day of _____, 19\_\_, the said collateral will be accepted by the Lender in satisfaction of the debts of the Company.

Allow ten days for deemed receipt by registered mail plus 30 days thereafter.

**DATED** at Toronto this _____ day of _____, 19\_\_.

**THE LENDER CORPORATION**
By its solicitors:

Per: _____

# Notice to Account Debtors

EXHIBIT 5

Direct Line—59

April 24, 1995

Attention: Chief Financial Officer

Dear Sirs:

We are the solicitors representing _____ in the matter of the assignment to _____ by _____ of a _____ promissory note of _____, together with the principal and all accrued interest thereon, a copy of which promissory note is annexed hereto (the "Promissory Note").

You are hereby directed to make all further payments otherwise due to _____ pursuant to the Promissory Note to _____ at the following address:

A copy of the assignment made by _____ in favour of _____ is enclosed for your records.

Would you please acknowledge this assignment and redirection of funds by signing and returning to us the enclosed copy of this letter.

Yours very truly,

Enclosures

The foregoing is hereby acknowledged the _____ day of ____, 19__.

Per:_____

EXHIBIT 6

# PPSA
# Notice of Sale

## NOTICE PURSUANT TO SECTION 63 OF
### THE *PERSONAL PROPERTY SECURITY ACT* (ONTARIO)

To:  [debtor, all guarantors, all PPSA creditors and anyone else with an interest in the collateral of whom the Lender is aware]

Attn:

And to:

Attn:

**TAKE NOTICE** that pursuant to a _____ dated _____, 19__ and a _____ dated _____, 19__ (collectively the "Security") all made between _____ carrying on business as _____ (the "Company") and _____ Bank (the "Secured Party"), the Secured Party intends to dispose of the collateral thereby secured unless the collateral is redeemed.

1.    The collateral consists of all personal property of the Company, including the personal property of the Company used in connection with or generated by its operation of the _____ located at _____.

2.    The principal amount required to satisfy the obligation of the Company secured by the Security as at the _____ day of _____, 19__ is $_____, together with interest from _____, 19__ to and including _____, 19__ of $_____ and interest thereon from and including _____, 19__ until payment in full at the rate per annum of ___ %.

3.    The Secured Party's address where payment should be made is:

_____

    Attention:

    Telephone:

4.    The estimated expenses of the Secured Party pursuant to Section 63(1) of the said Act are _____ Dollars ($_____).

5.    Upon payment of the amounts due as above described, you may redeem the said collateral. Upon payment, the payor will be credited with any rebates or allowances to which the Company is entitled by law or under any agreement with the Secured Party.

6.    Unless the amounts due as above described are paid by the _____ day of _____, 19__, the said collateral will be disposed of and the Company will be liable for any deficiency.

7.    Unless payment of the amounts due as above-described is received on or before the _____ day of _____, 19__, there will be a private sale, public tender or public auction of the said collateral.

**DATED** at Toronto this _____ day of _____, 19____.

_____ **BANK**

By its solicitors: _____

Per: _____

_____ [Telephone]

**Allow 10 days for deemed receipt by registered mail plus 15 days thereafter.**

# EXHIBIT 7

# PPSA Notice to Remove Fixtures

**NOTICE PURSUANT TO SECTION 34(5) OF
THE *PERSONAL PROPERTY SECURITY ACT* (ONTARIO)**

**To:**   [debtor, all guarantors, all persons with an interest in the real property as determined by a subsearch of title]

Attn:

And to:

Attn:

   **TAKE NOTICE** that pursuant to a _____ dated _____, 19___ and a _____ dated _____, 19__ (collectively the "Security") all made between _____ carrying on business as _____ (the "Company") and _____ Bank (the "Secured Party"), the Secured Party intends to remove fixtures charged by the Security from the real property occupied by the Company described herein unless the obligations of the Company to the Secured party are satisfied.

1.   The principal amount required to satisfy the obligation of the Company secured by the Security as at the _____ day of _____, 19___ is $_____, together with interest thereon from _____, 19__ to and including _____, 19__ of $_____ and interest thereon from and including _____, 19__ until payment in full at the rate per annum of _____%.

3.   The real property to which the fixtures are affixed is municipally known as _____, Ontario and the legal description of the said real property is as follows:

4.   The Secured Party's address where payment should be made is:

_____

Attention:

Telephone:

5.   Unless the amounts due as above described are paid by the _____ day of _____, 19__, the said fixtures will be removed from the real property herein described.

DATED at Toronto this _____ day of _____, 19____.

_____ BANK

By its solicitors: _____

Per: _____

_____ [Telephone]

**Allow 10 days for deemed receipt by registered mail plus 10 days thereafter.**

# EXHIBIT 8

# Notice of Sale Under Charge/Mortgage

**NOTICE OF SALE UNDER CHARGE/MORTGAGE**

**TO:** _____ **[chargor/mortgagor]**

**AND TO: The parties shown on Schedule "A" attached hereto.**

TAKE NOTICE that default has been made in payment of the moneys due under a certain charge/mortgage dated the ____day of _____, 19_____ made

BETWEEN:

_____ **[chargor/mortgagor]**,

Chargor/Mortgagor

-and-

_____ **[chargee/mortgagee]**,
a trust company incorporated
under the laws of Canada,

Chargee/Mortgagee

-and-

_____            Guarantor

-and-

_____            Consenting Spouse

on the securtiy of ALL AND SINGULAR that certain parcel or tract of land and premises situate, lying and being in the [city] of _____, [municipality] of _____and being comprised of _____ [legal description], registered in the _____ [registry office] (No. _____ ), which charge/mortgage was registered on the _____day of _____, 19___ in the _____[registry office] (No. _____) as Instrument No. _____(the "Charge/Mortgage").

    AND _____ [chargee/mortgagee] hereby gives you notice that the amounts now due on the Charge/Mortgage for principal money, interest and costs, respectively, are as follows:

| | |
|---|---|
| Principal money | $_____ |
| Interest as of | |
| _____, 19_____ | _____ |
| Cost of these proceedings | _____ |
| | |
| TOTAL | $_____ |

    AND UNLESS the said sums, together with interest theron at the rate of _____% per annum calculated _____ and any further costs and disbursements incurred in these proceedings, are paid on or before the _____ day of _____, 19___, _____[chargee/mortgagee] shall sell the property covered by the said Charge/Mortgage under the provisions contained in it.

    THIS NOTICE is given to you as you appear to have an interest in the charged/mortgaged property and may be entitled to redeem the same.

DATE at _____, this _____ day of _____, 19___.

_____ **[chargee/mortgagee]**
By its solicitors and authorized agents,

_____

Per:_____

# Extract from section 428 of the *Bank Act* (Canada)

EXHIBIT 9

**(7) Sale of goods on non-payment of debt.** In the event of non-payment of any debt, liability, loan or advance, as security for the payment of which a bank has acquired and holds a warehouse receipt or bill of lading or has taken any security under section 427, the bank may sell all or any part of the property mentioned therein or covered thereby and apply the proceeds against that debt, liability, loan or advance, with interest and expenses, returning the surplus, if any, to the person by whom the security was given.

**(8) Idem.** The power of sale referred to in subsection (7) shall, unless the person by whom the security mentioned in that subsection was given has agreed to the sale of the property otherwise than as herein provided or unless the property is perishable and to comply with the following provisions might result in a substantial reduction in the value of the property, be exercised subject to the following provisions, namely,

(a)    every sale of such property other than livestock shall be by public auction after

(i) notice of the time and place of the sale has been sent by registered mail to the recorded address of the person by whom the security was given, at least ten days prior to the sale in the case of any such property other than products of the forest, and at least thirty days prior to the sale in the case of any such property consisting of products of the forest, and

(ii) publication of an advertisement of the sale, at least two days prior to the sale, in at least two newspapers published in or nearest to the place where the sale is to be made stating the time and place thereof; and

(b)    every sale of livestock shall be made by public auction not less than five days after

(i) publication of an advertisement of the time and place of the sale in a newspaper, published in or nearest to the place where the sale is to be made, and

(ii) posting of a notice to writing of the time and place of the sale, in or at the post office nearest to the place where the sale is to be made.

and the proceeds of such a sale of livestock, after deducting all expenses incurred by the bank and all expenses of seizure and sale, shall first be applied to satisfy privileges, liens or pledges having priority over the security given to the bank and for which claims have been filed with the person making the sale, and the balance shall be applied in payment of the debt, liability, loan or advance, with interest and the surplus, if any, returned to the person by whom the security was given.

# EXHIBIT 10

# Memorandum Re:
# Directors and Officers Liability

The following is a summary of certain commonly encountered statutes and the potential sources of liability. There are literally hundreds of statutes that can impose liability on directors and officers. The two main sources of liability are:

(a)  offences, for which fines and penalties (such as imprisonment) are imposed. Offences may be specifically set forth or there may be a general offence for a breach of provisions of the legislation; and

(b)  pencuniary or monetary obligations on a director or officer. For example, the *Business Corporations Act* provides that directors who approve certain transactions contrary to the legislation, such as providing financial assistance to a shareholder without a prescribed solvency test being met, are jointly and severally liable to repay amounts lost by the corporation as a result of such actions being taken. Another example is the provision whereby directors may be personally liable for up to six-months' wages of employees.

It is also important to note that much of the legislation that imposes liability also sets forth detailed conditions upon which a director or officer may be relieved from liability and that in most cases a due diligence defence is available. Therefore, the summary below does not tell the whole story.

PART I – ENVIRONMENTAL LEGISLATION

| STATUTE | SUMMARY OF CERTAIN SOURCES OF LIABILITY |
|---|---|
| Environmental Protection Act | - Failure to take reasonable care to prevent discharge of contaminants (even if there has been no discharge)<br>- Failure to report discharge of contaminants |
| Ontario Water Resources Act | - Failure to take reasonable care to prevent the discharge of material into water that may impair the quality of the water<br>- Failure to report a discharge of material that may impair water quality<br>- Consuming water in excess of prescribed amounts without a permit |
| Pesticides Act | - Failure to take reasonable care to prevent harmful effects of pesticides on the environment<br>- Discharging a pesticide that causes or is likely to cause harm to the environment |
| Ontario Mining Act | - Failure to take reasonable care to ensure compliance with requirements of the legislation concerning mine rehabilitation and closure |
| Canadian Environmental Protection Act | - Breach of the legislation, including manufacturing or importing of prohibited substance, and failure to report or take measures to notify the public as required in certain circumstances |
| Dangerous Goods Transportation Act | - Transportation of dangerous goods without applicable prescribed safety requirements and safety marks |
| Transportation of Dangerous Goods Act, 1992 | - Handling, transporting or importing dangerous goods without applicable prescribed safety requirements |
| Fisheries Act | - Harmful alteration, disruption or destruction of fish habitat |

## PART – CORPORATE AND SECURITIES LEGISLATION

| STATUTE | SUMMARY OF CERTAIN SOURCES OF LIABILITY |
|---|---|
| *Canada Business Corporations Act* | - Improper purchase, redemption or acquisition of shares, payment of a commission, payment of a dividend, giving of financial assistance, payment of an indemnity or payment to a shareholder<br>- Issuance of shares for less than fair money equivalent<br>- Insider trading<br>- Liability to employees for wages<br>- Breach of duty of care<br>- Breach of the legislation |
| *Ontario Business Corporations Act* | - Improper purchase, redemption or acquisition of shares, payment of a commission, payment of a dividend, giving of financial assistance, payment of an indemnity, or payment to a shareholder<br>- Issuance of shares for less than fair money equivalent<br>- Insider trading<br>- Liability to employees for wages<br>- Breach of duty of care<br>- Breach of the legislation |
| *Securities Act* | - Misrepresentation in document filed with the Commission or distributed to the public<br>- Insider trading and tipping<br>- Policy 9.1 may create a source of liability if not complied with |
| *Bankruptcy and Insolvency Act* | - Breach of provisions of the legislation<br>- Payment of dividends or redemption of shares within the 12-month period preceding bankruptcy if the corporation was insolvent or became insolvent |
| *Corporations and Labour Unions Return Act* | - Failure to file returns or comply with the legislation |
| *Investment Canada Act* | - Non-compliance with the legislation |
| *Competition Act* | - Commission of certain offences by the corporation, including failure to comply with order of Competition Tribunal, and with respect to restricted trade practices<br>- Failure to comply with other provisions of legislation |

| Construction Lien Act | - Breach of trust by the corporation |
|---|---|
| Business Names Act | - Breach of the legislation, such as business name registration requirements |
| Corporations Information Act | - Breach of the legislation, including filing of notices |

## PART III – OBLIGATIONS TO EMPLOYEES

| STATUTE | SUMMARY OF CERTAIN SOURCES OF LIABILITY |
|---|---|
| Canada Business Corporations Act | - Possible liability for six-months' wages of employees, including vacation pay and bonuses |
| Ontario Business Corporations Act | - Possible liability for six-months' wages of employees, including vacation pay and bonuses |
| Corporations Act | - Possible liability for six-months' wages of employees, including vacation pay and bonuses |
| Canada Corporations Act | - Possible liability for six-months' wages of employees, including vacation pay and bonuses |
| Employment Standards Act | - Possible liability for six-months' wages of employees, including vacation pay and bonuses |
| The Occupational Health and Safety Act | - Liability for breach of the legislation |
| Hazardous Products Act | - Liability for breach of the legislation |
| Human Rights Code | - Infringement of the Human Rights Code |
| Canadian Human Rights Act | - Engaging in discriminatory practices contrary to the legislation |
| Pay Equity Act | - Contravening certain sections of the legislation, such as intimidating or discriminating against a person who makes disclosure or exercises a right under the legislation |
| Labour Relations Act | - Liability for breach of the legislation |
| Canada Labour Code | - Liability for breach of the legislation |

## PART IV – PENSION LEGISLATION

| STATUTE | SUMMARY OF CERTAIN SOURCES OF LIABILITY |
|---|---|
| *Pension Benefits Standards Act, 1985* | - Liability for breach of the legislation, including failure to remit amounts required to be remitted to a pension fund |
| *Pension Benefits Act* | - Liability for breach of the legislation, including failure to remit amounts required to be remitted to a pension fund |

## PART V – OBLIGATIONS TO GOVERNMENT FOR TAXES AND SOURCE DEDUCTIONS

| STATUTE | SUMMARY OF CERTAIN SOURCES OF LIABILITY |
|---|---|
| *Canada Pension Plan Act* | - Failure to deduct and remit appropriate amounts |
| *Unemployment Insurance Act* | - Failure to deduct and remit appropriate amounts |
| *Income Tax Act, Excise Tax Act (GST), Retail Sales Tax Act* | - Failure to deduct and remit appropriate amounts, and failure to pay taxes |

## PART VI – NON-SHARE CAPITAL CORPORATIONS – CHARITIES

| STATUTE | SUMMARY OF CERTAIN SOURCES OF LIABILITY |
|---|---|
| *Corporations Act* | - Liability for employee wages<br>- Breaches of other provisions of the legislation |
| *Canada Corporations Act* | - Liability for employee wages<br>- Breaches of other provisions of the legislation |
| *Charities* | - Higher duty of care imposed on directors of a charitable corporation |

## PART VII – FEDERAL FINANCIAL INSTITUTIONS LEGISLATION

| STATUTE | SUMMARY OF CERTAIN SOURCES OF LIABILITY |
|---|---|
| *Bank Act, Trust and Loan Companies Act, Insurance Act* | - Issuance of shares or subordinated indebtedness for improper consideration<br>- Improper purchase or redemption of shares, reduction of capital, payment of a dividend, payment of an indemnity or related party transaction<br>- Liability to employees for wages<br>- Breach of duty of care<br>- Breach of the legislation |

# EXHIBIT 11

## Corporate Searches

1. **General Corporate Searches**
   (a) Identify any companies which amalgamated with each to form the current company.
   (b) Identify any changes in name of the current company.

2. ***Personal Property Security Act* Searches**

3. ***Bank Act* Security Searches**

4. **Bankruptcy Searches**
   (a) Bankruptcy Court
   (b) Official Receiver

5. **Executions**

6. **Bills of Sale**

7. **Bulk Sales**

# Notice of Intention to Enforce Security

EXHIBIT 12

TO:_____, an insolvent person

Take notice that:

1. _____, a secured creditor, intends to enforce its security on the property of the insolvent person described below: [Describe the property to which the security relates.]

2. The security that is to be enforced is in the form of _____ [provide particulars of the security].

3. The total amount of indebtedness secured by the security is $_____.

4. The secured creditor will not have the right to enforce the security until after the expiry of the 10-day period following the sending of this notice, unless the insolvent person consents to an earlier enforcement.

Dated at _____ this ____ day of _____, 19__.

[Name of Secured Creditor]

[Name and Title of Signing Officer]

# Demand for Repossession of Goods

In the matter of the bankruptcy (or receivership) of the property of _____

To:_____,
purchaser (*or trustee or receiver*)

I, _____,
of _____ (*address*),
(*or* as _____ of
_____,) supplier, hereby
demand access to and repossession of the goods described below,
which were sold and delivered to _____, the
purchaser, on the dates and in accordance with the terms indicated
in the attached documents:

*(Attach copies of documents of sale (i.e., invoice, delivery slip, etc.) and
provide a description of the goods that is sufficient to enable them to
be identified.)*

The purchaser, having made an assignment that was filed with
the Official Receiver on _____, (*or* having

been declared bankrupt by a receiving order made on
_____, *or* a receiver having been appointed
in respect of the purchaser's property on _____)
or the trustee (*or* receiver) is required to release the goods
described above in accordance with subsection 81.1(1) of the *Bankruptcy and Insolvency Act.*

  Dated at _____ this _____ day
of _____.


         _____
         Supplier

EXHIBIT 14

# Agreement of Purchase and Sale

**THIS AGREEMENT** made this _____ day of _____, 19__.

**BETWEEN:**

_____, as receiver and manager of the undertaking and property and assets of _____
(hereinafter called the **"Vendor"**)

OF THE FIRST PART

**AND:**

_____, a corporation incorporated under the laws of the Province of Ontario,
(hereinafter called the **"Purchaser"**)

OF THE SECOND PART

**WITNESSES:**

_____

_____

## 1.   Sale and Purchase of Assets

The Vendor agrees to sell, and the Purchaser agrees to purchase for the purchase price of _____ Dollars ($_____) ("**Purchase Price**"), subject to the adjustments set out in paragraph 5, upon the terms and subject to the conditions hereinafter set forth, the undertaking and all the property and assets of _____ ("**Corporation**") except cash on hand which undertaking and property and assets comprise the following and are hereafter referred to as the "**Assets**":

(a)   All accounts receivable of the Corporation.

(b)   All inventory and stock-in-trade including raw materials, work-in-process and finished goods of the Corporation.

(c)   The lands and buildings owned by the Corporation municipally known as _____, Toronto, Ontario and more particularly described in Schedule "A" annexed hereto.

(d)   All machinery, equipment and vehicles of the Corporation including, without limitation, that more particularly described in Schedule "B" annexed hereto.

(e)   Save as aforesaid, the undertaking and all other property and assets of whatsoever nature and kind and wheresoever found belonging to the Corporation including, without limitation, any existing goodwill, patents, patent applications, inventions, trade marks, trade names, industrial rights and designs.

## 2.   Payment of Purchase Price

The Purchaser shall pay the Purchase Price as follows:

(a)   _____ Dollars ($_____) upon execution of this Agreement as a deposit ("**Deposit**") to be credited toward the Purchase Price at the Time of Closing (as hereinafter defined) and to be held by the Vendor in trust until the Time of Closing.

(b)   _____ Dollars ($_____), subject to the adjustments

set out in herein, including those in paragraph 5 and further adjusted to give effect to paragraph 6, together with the moneys payable under paragraph 4, at the Time of Closing.

The Deposit shall be invested by the Vendor in an interest-bearing term deposit with a Canadian chartered bank. If the transaction of purchase and sale contemplated by this Agreement ("**Transaction**") fails to close, interest earned on the Deposit shall follow disposition of the Deposit in accordance with this Agreement or as may be required by law. If the Transaction closes, the Vendor shall be entitled to the interest earned on the Deposit which interest shall not be credited toward the Purchase Price.

3.    **Allocation**
      The Purchase Price shall be allocated as follows:

      (a) Assets described in paragraph 1(a) - $____

      (b) Assets described in paragraph 1(b) - $____

      (c) Assets described in paragraph 1(c) - $____

      (d) Assets described in paragraph 1(d) - $____

      (e) Assets described in paragraph 1(e) - $____

4.    **Taxes**
      The Purchaser shall pay at the Time of Closing, in addition to the Purchase Price, all applicable federal and provincial taxes exigible in connection with the Transaction including, without limitation, goods and services tax, Ontario retail sales tax and land transfer tax. Alternatively, where applicable, the Purchaser shall have the option to furnish the Vendor with appropriate purchase exemption certificates together with an indemnity saving the Vendor harmless from any liability in respect of such taxes.

5.    **Adjustments**
      Such adjustments as are normally made between a vendor

and purchaser shall be made as of the Effective Date (as hereinafter defined) to the balance of the Purchase Price due at the Time of Closing including, without limitation, municipal realty taxes, local improvements, water rates, public utilities and prepaid items. No adjustment shall be made for insurance which shall be arranged separately by the Purchaser.

### 6.   Effective Date

The Transaction shall be effective as of the opening of business on _____, 19__ ("**Effective Date**"). If the Transaction is completed in accordance with this Agreement the management and operation of the business of the Corporation by the Vendor (which the Vendor undertakes to carry on in the ordinary and usual course) on and after the Effective Date shall be for the account of the Purchaser, and the Purchaser shall be entitled to the benefit of all revenues and receipts from the carrying on of such business and shall be responsible for all expenses, outgoings and liabilities made or incurred by the Vendor in carrying on such business in the ordinary and usual course. The Purchaser's responsibility shall extend to the Vendor's reasonable fees and legal fees during such period but not, for greater certainty, the Vendor's fees and legal fees applicable to documenting and completing the Transaction. The Vendor may deduct such expenses, outgoings and liabilities from such revenues and receipts. All moneys received by the Vendor on account of the Assets described in subparagraph 1(a) except to the extent required to pay such expenses, outgoings and liabilities shall be held in trust by the Vendor to be paid to the Purchaser upon completion of the Transaction.

### 7.   Receiver Obligations

The Purchaser shall receive the benefit of, and shall assume the responsibilities under, all contracts, agreements, obligations to employees, obligations under existing licence arrangements, purchase orders and forward commitments (collectively, "**Receiver Obligations**") to which the Vendor is entitled or under which the Vendor is liable in the ordinary and usual course of business from and after the Effective Date as a result of the management and operation of the business of the Corporation in such ordinary and usual course. The Purchaser will indemnify and save harmless the Vendor from and against all claims, demands, losses, damages, costs, charges and expenses at any time made against or incurred by the Vendor under or by virtue of the Receiver Obligations.

## 8.  Conditions - Purchaser

The obligation of the Purchaser to complete the Transaction is subject to the following conditions being fulfilled or performed at or prior to the Time of Closing:

(a)  Subject to paragraph 11, title to the Assets being free from any mortgage, charge, lien, security interest or other encumbrance.

(b)  All representations and warranties of the Vendor contained in this Agreement shall be true and the Vendor shall have delivered to the Purchaser satisfactory evidence to that effect (provided that acceptance of that evidence and completion of the Transaction shall not be a waiver of such representations and warranties).

(c)  The Vendor shall have carried on the Corporation's business on and after the Effective Date in the ordinary and usual course.

(d)  The Vendor shall have performed each of its obligations under this Agreement.

(e)  The furnishing by the Vendor at its expense of certificates of mechanical fitness concerning any motor vehicles included in the Assets.

(f)  [as appropriate] _____
_____
_____

The foregoing conditions are for the exclusive benefit of the Purchaser and any condition may be waived by it in whole or in part, any such waiver to be binding on it only if made in writing.

**9.   Conditions - Vendor**

The obligation of the Vendor to complete the Transaction is subject to the following conditions being fulfilled or performed at or prior to the Time of Closing:

(a)   The furnishing to the Vendor of an irrevocable letter of credit or other instrument of guarantee by a Canadian chartered bank (in form and substance satisfactory to the Vendor) securing the Vendor against the performance by the Purchaser of its obligations under paragraph 7.

(b)   All representations and warranties of the Purchaser contained in this Agreement shall be true and the Purchaser shall have delivered to the Vendor satisfactory evidence to that effect (provided that acceptance of that evidence and completion of the Transaction shall not be a waiver of such representations and warranties).

(c)   The Purchaser shall have performed each of its obligations under this Agreement.

(d)   [as appropriate] _____

_____

_____

_____

The foregoing conditions are for the exclusive benefit of the Vendor and any condition may be waived by it in whole or in part, any such waiver to be binding on it only if made in writing.

**10.  Planning Act**

This Agreement is conditional upon compliance with the *Planning Act* of Ontario.

## 11.  Title

The Purchaser shall be allowed, at its expense, until _____,
19__ to examine the title to the Assets described in paragraph 1(c)
and to satisfy itself that there are no outstanding municipal work
orders or deficiency notices affecting those Assets and that the present use of those Assets may be continued. If the Vendor shall
through any cause be unable or unwilling to answer or comply with
any requisition or objection which the Purchaser will not waive,
this Agreement shall be at an end (notwithstanding any intervening
negotiations or litigation or any attempt to remove or comply with
the same) and the Deposit with accrued interest shall be returned
to the Purchaser but without any other compensation. The Vendor
shall not encumber the Assets following the date hereof and will
not sell or dispose of the Assets between the date hereof and the
Date of Closing other than in the ordinary and usual course of business. The Vendor shall not be required to furnish or produce any
abstract, deed, declaration or other document or evidence of title
except those in its possession.

## 12.  Risk

The Assets shall be and remain at the risk of the Vendor until
the Time of Closing. If, prior to the Time of Closing, the Assets
shall be substantially damaged or destroyed by fire or other casual-
ty, then, at its option, the Purchaser may decline to complete the
Transaction. Such option shall be exercised within fifteen (15) days
after notification to the Purchaser by the Vendor of the occurrence
of the loss or damage in which event this Agreement shall be terminated automatically and the Purchaser shall be entitled only to a
return of the Deposit with accrued interest but without any other
compensation. If the Purchaser does not exercise such option it
shall complete the Transaction and shall be entitled to an assignment
of the proceeds of insurance referable to such loss or damage.
Where any damage is not substantial, the Purchaser shall complete
the Transaction and shall be entitled to an assignment of the proceeds of insurance referable to such damage. If any dispute arises
under this paragraph as to whether damage or destruction is substantial, such dispute will be determined by an arbitrator mutually
acceptable to the parties. If the parties fail to agree on an arbitrator,

either may, after such party has notified the other of such failure to agree, give notice to the other party that it wishes to submit the dispute to arbitration by a single arbitrator in accordance with the *Arbitrations Act* of Ontario. The name of an arbitrator shall be proposed in such notice and if the other party is not agreeable to such proposed arbitrator, section 8 of such Act shall be applicable. The decision of the arbitrator which shall be final and binding on the parties shall be made as soon as possible following his appointment and his fees and expenses shall be borne equally by the parties.

### 13. Possession of Property

The Vendor shall remain in possession of the Assets until the Date of Closing. In no event shall title to the Assets pass to the Purchaser until the Vendor has executed and delivered the instruments referred to in paragraph 14.

### 14. Closing

The completion of the Transaction shall take place at the offices of _____, Ontario, on the _____ day, 19__ (such date or such earlier or later date as may be agreed being herein referred to as the "**Date of Closing**") at _____ o'clock in the _____noon (which time is herein referred to as the "**Time of Closing**"). At the Time of Closing the Vendor shall deliver to the Purchaser such deeds of conveyance, bills of sale and assignments as may be requisite to convey the Assets to the Purchaser. Such instruments shall contain covenants of the Vendor to the effect only that the Vendor has the right to convey and has done no act to encumber the Assets.

### 15. Vendor's Capacity

The Vendor acts in its capacity as receiver and manager of the Corporation and, except as regards its representations in paragraph 17, shall have no personal or corporate liability under or as a result of this Agreement.

### 16. Investment Canada Act

The Purchaser represents to the Vendor that it is not a non-Canadian as defined in the *Investment Canada Act*.

### 17.  Vendor's Representations
The Vendor represents and warrants to the Purchaser that:

(a)  the security held by _____ pursuant to which the Vendor was appointed receiver and manager of the Corporation, being a debenture of the Corporation dated _____, 19__, is valid and effective security;

(b)  the Vendor has been validly appointed as such receiver and manager and has full right, power and authority to enter into this Agreement and to convey the Assets; and

(c)  the Vendor is not a non-resident within the meaning of the *Income Tax Act* of Canada.

### 18.  Tender
Any tender of documents or money hereunder may be made upon the Vendor or the Purchaser or their respective solicitors on the Date of Closing. Money may be tendered by cheque certified by a chartered bank of Canada, trust company of Canada or Province of Ontario savings office or by a bank draft.

### 19.  "As is, Where is"
The Purchaser confirms that it has entered into this Agreement on the basis that the Vendor does not guarantee title to the Assets, that the Purchaser has inspected the Assets, that the Assets are purchased by the Purchaser on an "as is, where is" basis and that no warranty or condition is expressed or can be implied as to title, encumbrances, description, fitness for purpose, merchantability, quantity or quality thereof or in respect of any other matter or thing whatsoever. Without limiting the generality of the foregoing, the Assets are specifically offered as they will exist on the Date of Closing and with no adjustment to be allowed to the Purchaser for any changes in the condition or quantities of the items comprising the Assets from the date of this Agreement to the Date of Closing except that the portion of the Purchase Price applicable to the Assets described in paragraph 1(b) shall be adjusted based on an inventory to be taken jointly by the Vendor and Purchaser at the

close of business on the last business day next preceding the Effective Date. The amount of such adjustment shall be the difference between the portion of the Purchase Price allocated to such Assets by paragraph 3 and ___ per cent (___%) of the cost of such Assets as determined by such inventory. Any dispute in connection with such inventory shall be arbitrated in the same manner as the dispute referred to in paragraph 12.

### 20. Notice

Any notice, demand, acceptance, request, election or waiver required or permitted to be given hereunder ("**Notice**") shall be in writing and shall be deemed to be sufficiently given:

(a)  if personally delivered to _____or other officer of the Vendor in Toronto, or to _____or other officer of the Purchaser, as the case may be; or

(b)  if mailed (at any time other than during a general discontinuance of postal services due to strike, lockout or otherwise) by registered mail, postage prepaid, addressed to the party to whom the same is given as follows:
(i) in the case of the Vendor:
(ii) in the case of the Purchaser:

Any notice shall be deemed to have been given to and received by the party to whom it is addressed if delivered, when delivered, and if mailed, on the second bank business day after the mailing thereof in Canada. Either party may by Notice given as aforesaid designate a changed address to which a Notice to such party shall be given and any Notice to such party shall thereafter be delivered or sent to such address.

### 21. Time of Essence

Time shall, in all respects, be of the essence hereof.

### 22. Currency

All references herein to money amounts are to Canadian currency.

## 23. Further Assurances

Each of the parties shall, from time to time and at the request of the party requesting the same, do all such further acts and things and execute and deliver such further instruments and documents as may be necessary or desirable to give effect to this Agreement.

## 24. Obligations to Survive

The obligations, representations and warranties of the parties hereto shall survive the completion of the Transaction.

## 25. Headings

The headings contained in this Agreement shall not affect the meaning or interpretation of this Agreement.

## 26. Number and Gender

Where the context so requires, words importing the singular number include the plural and vice versa, and words importing gender shall include the masculine, feminine and neuter genders.

## 27. Entire Agreement

This Agreement constitutes the only agreement between the parties with respect to the subject matter hereof and supersedes any and all prior negotiations and understanding. This Agreement may not be amended or modified in any respect except by written instrument.

## 28. Law Governing

This Agreement shall be governed by and construed in accordance with the laws of the Province of Ontario and the laws of Canada applicable therein.

## 29. Successors and Assigns

This Agreement shall be binding upon and enure to the benefit of the parties hereto and their respective successors and assigns.

**IN WITNESS WHEREOF** the parties have executed this Agreement as of the day and year first above written.

_____, as Receiver and Manager of

_____

Per: _____

[Authorized Signing Officer]


Per: _____

[Authorized Signing Officer]

EXHIBIT 15

# Bill of Sale

**THIS INDENTURE** made as of the _____ day of _____19__.

**BETWEEN:**

_____, as Receiver and Manager of the undertaking
and property and assets of _____
(hereinafter called the "**Vendor**")

OF THE FIRST PART

- and -

_____, a corporation incorporated under the laws
of the Province of Ontario
(hereinafter called the "**Purchaser**")

OF THE SECOND PART

**WHEREAS** by a general security agreement dated the ____ day
of _____, _____ notice of which was registered pursuant to the provisions of the *Personal Property Security Act,* (the "**PPSA**") and a general assignment of book debts dated the ____ day of ____, 19__
notice of which was registered pursuant to the provisions of
the PPSA (hereinafter collectively referred to as the "**Security**

**Documentation**") created and issued by _____ (the "**Corporation**") and assigned and pledged or hypothecated by the Corporation to _____ (the "**Lender**") as general and continuing collateral security for the payment and fulfilment of all debts and liabilities of the Corporation to the Lender, the Corporation mortgaged and charged in favour of the Lender its undertaking and all its property and assets as more fully set out in the Security Documentation;

**AND WHEREAS** default was made under the Security Documentation on the _____ day of _____, 19\_\_;

**AND WHEREAS** _____ was appointed as Receiver (and Manager) of the assets of the Corporation by the Lender on the _____ day of _____, 19\_\_ pursuant to the provisions of the Security Documentation;

**AND WHEREAS** every person entitled to receive from the Lender a notice of disposition pursuant to section 63(4) of the PPSA has, after the date of default referred to above, consented in writing to the immediate disposition of the collateral subject to the Security Documentation;

**AND WHEREAS** the Purchaser has agreed to purchase, on the terms and conditions more particularly set out herein, all raw materials, work in progress, finished goods and other inventory owned or used by the Corporation, as listed in Schedule A annexed hereto (hereinafter referred to as the "**Purchased Assets**");

**NOW THEREFORE THIS INDENTURE WITNESSES** that in consideration of the premises and the sum of Two Dollars ($2.00) of lawful money of Canada now paid by the Purchaser to the Vendor and other good and valuable consideration (the receipt and adequacy whereof is hereby acknowledged), the Vendor doth hereby grant, sell, convey, assign, transfer and set over unto the Purchaser, its successors and assigns, the Purchased Assets which are located at the locations more particularly described in Schedule B annexed, hereto to hold the Purchased Assets unto and to the use of the Purchaser.

The Vendor releases to the Purchaser all its right, title and interest in and to the Purchased Assets.

The Vendor covenants with the Purchaser that it has the right to sell, and that it has done no act to encumber, the Purchased Assets.

The Vendor represents and warrants to the Purchaser as follows and acknowledges that the Purchaser is relying upon the following representations and warranties in connection with its purchase of the Purchased Assets:

1. the recitals set forth in this indenture are true and accurate in all respects;

2. the Lender has not released, discharged, assigned or encumbered the Security Documentation or the indebtedness secured thereby;

3. the Vendor was duly appointed as receiver of the Corporation and such appointment has not been revoked;

The Vendor hereby covenants and agrees that it will at the request of the Purchaser at any time or times hereafter do, execute, acknowledge and deliver, or cause to be done, executed, acknowledged and delivered all such reasonable further acts, deeds, assignments, transfers, conveyances, consents, assurances and other documents and take all such other action as may be required for the better assigning, transferring, granting and assisting in transferring to the Purchaser title to and possession of the Purchased Assets.

Save as aforesaid nothing herein contained shall be deemed to be a representation, warranty, guarantee or covenant, express or implied, on the part of the Vendor for any cause, matter or thing whatsoever.

Each of the Purchased Assets is sold on an "as is, where is" basis. The Purchaser has inspected the Purchased Assets and no representation, warranty or condition is expressed nor can be implied as to description, fitness for purpose, merchantability, quantity, condition or quality thereof or in respect of any matter or thing whatsoever and the Purchaser shall be deemed to have relied entirely on his own investigation and inspection. Without limiting the generality of the foregoing, it is expressly acknowledged and agreed by the Purchaser that it has taken delivery of each of the items comprising the Purchased Assets.

This Indenture shall enure to the benefit of and be binding upon the parties hereto and their respective corporate successors.

**IN WITNESS WHEREOF** this Indenture has been executed by the parties as of the day and year first above written.

_____, as Receiver of

_____

Per: _____
       [Authorized Signing Officer]

       Name: _____

       Title: _____

Per: _____
       [Authorized Signing Officer]

       Name: _____

       Title: _____

EXHIBIT 16

# Questions to be Put to an Officer of a Bankrupt Corporation

## Questions to be put to an Officer of the Bankrupt Corporation by the Official Receiver

### Introduction to Official Receiver

The following question or questions to a like effect are to be put by the Official Receiver. Such questions should be expanded or supplemental by Official Receiver in an endeavour to extract from the examination the maximum amount of essential information and to determine as nearly as possible the true cause of the bankruptcy, the disposition of the property and the conduct of the bankrupt corporation. The books, statements, etc., of the bankrupt corporation should be on hand for reference or as the basis of a more detailed examination of any phase of the corporation's business or conduct which the Official Receiver may deem warranted.

1. Are you an officer of the corporation referred to in these proceedings?
2. Have you been made aware of your duties pursuant to sections 158 and 159 of the *Bankruptcy and Insolvency Act?*
3. What is your full name and what position do you hold in the corporation?

4. What is the full name of the corporation and what is the address of its head office?

5. When and under what law or Act of Parliament was it incorporated?

6. What is the authorized capital of the corporation?

7. What amount of the capital has been subscribed and what amount of the subscribed capital has been paid in full?

8. What amount of the capital was paid in cash and what was the consideration for any other issue of the share capital?

9. Did the corporation have a share register containing particulars of the allotment, issue and transfer of all shares?

10. Does it disclose the amount paid on each share of the corporation whether by cash or otherwise?

11. What is the total amount, if any, unpaid on the shares of the corporation and by whom are such amounts owing?

12. What are the names of the principal shareholders?

13. What are the names of the directors and officers of the corporation?

14. Has the corporation any wholly owned subsidiary corporation? If so, give particulars.

15. Has the bankrupt corporation or its subsidiaries ever been in bankruptcy before or make a proposal or arrangements with the creditors?

16. When did the bankrupt corporation commence business?

17. What was the nature of its business?

18. Was a proper set of books maintained and are they written up to date?

19. Were the books audited annually?

20. What is the name of the auditor and when was the last audited statement drawn up?

21. Have all proper returns been made to the various government agencies requiring same?

22. When did the corporation first become aware of its insolvency?

23. Did the corporation continue to carry on business and contract liabilities after it became aware of its insolvency?

24. Has the corporation made any payments, returned any goods, delivered any property or given security to any of its creditors

during the three months preceding the date of its bankruptcy or since it became aware of its insolvency, except in the ordinary course of business? If so, given particulars.

25. Has the corporation within the twelve months preceding the date of its bankruptcy

    (a) executed any bill of sale or chattel mortgage or pledged any of its property?

    (b) sold, disposed of or removed any of its property except in the ordinary course of trade?

    If so, give particulars.

26. Has the corporation made or been a party to any settlement of property within the five years preceding the date of its bankruptcy. If so, give particulars.

27. What are the causes of the bankruptcy of the corporation?

28. What were the sales for the past three years and what percentage of the sales represented the profit or mark up?

29. When did the operations of the corporation last show a profit?

## Note to Official Receiver

The additional questions put by the Official Receiver and the answers thereto should be entered in the space provided below or on a sheet to be attached hereto.

I, _____ of the _____ of _____ in the Province of _____, make oath and say that to the best of my knowledge and belief the above answers are true in every respect.

SWORN before me at the _____ )
of _____ in the Province of )
_____ this _____ )
day of _____, 19____ )     _____
Official Receiver in and for Bankruptcy )     (Signature)
Division No. _____ of the Bankruptcy )
District of _____ )

# EXHIBIT 17

# Proof of Claim (Property)

In the matter of the bankruptcy (*or* proposal) of _____ _____ of _____, debtor, and the claim of _____, claimant, and _____, trustee.

All notices or correspondence regarding this claim to be forwarded to the following address:_____ _____

I, _____, of the _____ of _____ in the Province of _____.

DO HEREBY CERTIFY:

1.   That I am the claimant herein, (*or* that I am _____ _____ of _____).
         (state position or title)          (name of claimant)

2.   That I have knowledge of all the circumstances connected with the claim hereinafter referred to.

3.    That on the _____ day of _____, 19___, the debtor herein

(a)   caused to be filed a proposal lodged in accordance with the *Bankruptcy and Insolvency Act* with the trustee,

(b)   made an assignment in accordance with the *Bankruptcy and Insolvency Act* to the trustee, (*delete if inapplicable*)

(c)   was declared bankrupt by a receiving order filed on the said date.

4.    That, on the said date, the property enumerated in the document(s) hereto attached and marked "A" (and "B") was in possession of the bankrupt, and still remains in the possession of the bankrupt and (or) the trustee.

5.    That the claimant hereby claims the said property, or interest therein, by virtue of the document(s) hereto attached and marked "A", namely:

*(Set out particulars of all documents serving as proof of claim, giving*
*(i) the grounds on which the claim is based, and*
*(ii) sufficient particulars to enable the property to be identified; if these particulars do not appear on the face of these documents, attach an additional statement marked "B" setting them forth.)*

6.    That the claimant is entitled to demand from the trustee the return of the property enumerated in the aforementioned document(s).

7.    That I hereby demand that the trustee return to me (or the claimant whom I represent) the property enumerated in the aforementioned document(s) within fifteen (15) days after the filing hereof, or within fifteen (15) days after the first meeting of the creditors of the debtor herein, whichever is the later.

SWORN before me at the          )

_____ of _____, )

in the _____ of _____, )          _____

this _____ day of _____, 19__)          [Signature of claimant]


_____

A Commissioner, etc.


**WARNING:** *Subsection 201(1) of the **Bankruptcy and Insolvency Act** prescribes severe penalties for making any false claim, declaration or statement of account.*

# EXHIBIT 18

## Proof of Claim

In the matter of the bankruptcy (or proposal or receivership of the property) of _____ *(name of debtor)* of _____ *(city and province)* and the claim of _____, creditor.

All notices or correspondence regarding this claim to be forwarded to the following address:

I, _____ *(name of creditor)* of _____ *(city and province)*, do hereby certify:

1.  That I am a creditor of the above-named debtor, (or that I am _____ *(state position or title)* of _____ *(name of creditor)*.

2.  That I have knowledge of all the circumstances connected with the claim referred to in this form.

3.  That the said debtor was at the date of the bankruptcy (or the proposal or the receivership), namely the _____ day of _____,

19__, and still is indebted to the above-named creditor (referred to in this form as "the creditor") in the sum of $_____, as shown by the statement of account (or affidavit) attached hereto and marked "Schedule A", after deducting any counterclaims to which the debtor is entitled. *(The attached statement of account or affidavit must specify the vouchers or other evidence in support of the claim.)*

4.    *(Check and complete appropriate category)*

A. (    ) UNSECURED CLAIM

That in respect of the said debt, I do not hold any assets of the debtor as security and

*(Check appropriate description)*

(    ) I do not claim a right to a priority.

(    ) I claim a right to a priority under section 136 of the *Bankruptcy and Insolvency Act. (Set out on an attached schedule details to support priority claim.)*

B. (    ) SECURED CLAIM

That in respect of the said debt, I hold assets of the debtor valued at $_____ as security, particulars of which are as follows:

*(Give full particulars of the security, including the date on which the security was given and the value at which the creditor assesses the security, and attach a copy of the security documents.)*

C. (    ) CLAIM BY FARMER, FISHERMAN, OR AQUACULTURIST

That I hereby make a claim under subsection 81.2(1) of the *Bankruptcy and Insolvency Act* for the unpaid amount of $___. *(Attach a copy of sales agreement and delivery documents.)*

5.   That to the best of my knowledge and belief, I am *(or the above-named creditor is) (or am not or is not)* related to the debtor within the meaning of section 4 of the *Bankruptcy and Insolvency Act.*

6.   That the following are the payments that I have received from and the credits that I have allowed to the debtor within the three months *(or, if the creditor and the debtor are related within the meaning of section 4 of the Bankruptcy and Insolvency Act, within the 12 months)* immediately preceding the date of bankruptcy:

*(Provide details of payments and credits)*

      Dated at _____ this _____ day of _____, 19\_\_.


_____    _____

Witness                                      Creditor

NOTE: If an affidavit is attached, it must have been sworn to before a person qualified to take affidavits.

**WARNINGS:**

**A trustee may, pursuant to subsection 128(3) of the *Bankruptcy and Insolvency Act,* redeem a security on payment to the secured creditor of the debt or the value of the security as assessed, in a proof of security, by the secured creditor.**

**Subsection 201(1) of the *Bankruptcy and Insolvency Act* provides severe penalties for making any false claim, proof, declaration or statement of account.**

# EXHIBIT 19

## *Bulk Sales Act* Affidavit

### STATEMENT AS TO SELLER'S CREDITORS

Statement showing names and addresses of all unsecured trade creditors and secured trade creditors of _____ (the "seller") of _____, in _____, _____ and the amount of the indebtedness or liability due, owing, payable or accruing due or to become due by the seller to each of them.

### UNSECURED TRADE CREDITORS

| Name of Creditor | Address | Amount |
|---|---|---|
|  |  |  |
|  |  |  |

### SECURED TRADE CREDITORS

| Name of Creditor | Address | Amount | Nature of Security | Due or becoming due on the date fixed for the completion of the sale |
|---|---|---|---|---|
|  |  |  |  |  |
|  |  |  |  |  |
|  |  |  |  |  |

## AFFIDAVIT

I, _____, of the _____ of
_____, in the _____
of _____, make oath (or affirmation)
and say:

1.   That the foregoing statement is a true and correct statement

     (a) of the names and addresses of all the unsecured trade
creditors of the said _____ and of the amount of
the indebtedness or liability due, owing, payable or accruing due or
to become due and payable by the said _____ to
each of the said unsecured trade creditors; and

     (b) of the names and addresses of all the secured trade credi-
tors of the said _____ and of the amount of the
indebtedness or liability due, owing, payable or accruing due or to
become due and payable by the said corporation to each of the
said secured trade creditors, the nature of their security, and
whether they are or in the event of sale will become due and
payable on the date fixed for the completion of the sale.

2.   That I am _____ of
_____ and have personal knowledge of the facts
herein deposed to.

SWORN before me at the            )

_____ of _____,)

in the Province of Ontario        )    _____

this _____ day of ____, 19__ )

_____

**A Commissioner, etc.**

# Notice of Intention to Make a Proposal

Take notice that:

1. I, _____, an insolvent person, pursuant to subsection 50.4(1) of the *Bankruptcy and Insolvency Act*, intend to make a proposal to my creditors.

2. _____ *(name of trustee)*, of _____*(address of trustee)*, a licensed trustee, has consented to act as trustee under the proposal and a copy of the consent is attached hereto.

3. A list of the names of the known creditors with claims amounting to $250 or more and the amounts of their claims is attached.

4. Pursuant to section 69 of the *Bankruptcy and Insolvency Act*, all proceedings against me are stayed as of the date of filing this notice with the Official Receiver in my locality.

Dated at _____ this _____ day of _____, 19__.

Per: _____
                                   Authorized Signing Officer


To be completed by Official Receiver:

Filing Date:


                        _____
                                   Official Receiver

# Glossary

Please note that these are not precise legal definitions, but practical, working definitions.

ASSIGNMENT—(in bankruptcy) the document, and the process, by which a company voluntarily goes into bankruptcy. This process is discussed in Chapter 11, starting on page 113.

ATTACHMENT—the basic steps that must occur for a creditor to have a security agreement that is capable of being "perfected" within the requirements of the *Personal Property Security Act*. See the definition of "perfection" below and the discussion of the idea of "attachment," starting on page 6.

*BANK ACT*—a federal statute that, among other things, provides for a special type of security interest that may only be taken by banks. See the discussion starting on page 25.

*BANKRUPTCY AND INSOLVENCY ACT*—the federal statute which, among other things, regulates corporate bankruptcies and receiverships in Canada, and provides a framework for a company to attempt a commercial reorganization.

BULK SALE—a certain type of sale, by a company, that is out of the ordinary course of its business. In order to protect the creditors of the selling company, such sales are regulated by the *Bulk Sales Act,* which is discussed starting on page 142.

COLLATERAL—assets that belong to a borrower and that the borrower "pledges" or agrees to grant a security interest in, to secure the borrower's obligations to repay certain debt to a certain creditor or creditors. If the borrower defaults in the loan arrangements with the creditor(s), the collateral is then made available to the creditor(s) to be used towards recovery of the debt, all subject to various legal limitations.

COMMERCIAL REORGANIZATION—an effort by an insolvent company to reorganize its finances in order to avoid bankruptcy and/or receivership. This process is discussed in Chapter 15.

*COMPANIES' CREDITORS ARRANGEMENT ACT*—the more flexible, but potentially more costly, of the two mechanisms available in Canada for a company to attempt a commercial reorganization. This statute is reviewed in Chapters 14 and 15.

CONSIDERATION—in a legal sense means the value in exchange for which an asset is transferred or some action is taken. Sometimes an examination of whether a transaction will stand up to later scrutiny focuses on whether it was supported by adequate consideration.

CONSTRUCTION LIEN—a right given to people who supply goods or services that go towards improving a piece of real property. The right is designed to help those people to get paid for their services and is described starting on page 46.

CRYSTALLIZATION (of a floating charge)—the point at which the floating charge ceases to be merely floating and is, instead, immediately enforceable by the creditor who holds the charge.

DEEMED TRUSTS—trusts that are imposed, or "deemed to exist," by statute. See the discussion starting on page 36.

DEFENDANT—in a civil lawsuit, the party being sued.

DIRECTOR LIABILITY—the ways in which individual directors who run business corporations are personally liable for certain obligations incurred by those corporations, if they are not paid by the company. See Exhibit 13 in the Appendix and the discussion starting on page 32.

DISCLAIMER—termination by a trustee in bankruptcy of a lease, which had been entered into by a (now) bankrupt tenant. This process is discussed starting on page 132.

DISTRESS—the power of a commercial landlord to seize certain property of his or her tenant and to sell it in order to pay rent arrears. See the discussion starting on page 30.

DUE DILIGENCE—the investigation that must often be done by parties involved in insolvency situations in order to protect their interests. See the discussion starting on page 98.

ELIGIBLE FINANCIAL CONTRACTS—certain contracts which are not stayed when an insolvent company seeks protection from creditors under the *Bankruptcy and Insolvency Act*. See the discussion on page 173.

ESTATE (in bankruptcy)—in essence, the total property owned or to be owned by a company, which passes to the trustee in bankruptcy when that company is declared bankrupt.

FIXED CHARGE—a security interest that applies to a particular asset at all times. The asset is not supposed to be sold without the security interest being paid off. An example is a security interest over a particular piece of production equipment.

FIXTURE—a piece of personal property that has been annexed to real property and is regarded as part of the land. As discussed starting on page 8, **fixtures** are given special treatment under the *Personal Property Security Act*. While so far no case has demonstrated conclusively how permanently something has to be annexed to the land to be considered a fixture, the term seems to include property that is annexed in both a removable and unremovable manner.

FLOATING CHARGE—a security interest that "floats" over a group of assets—such as accounts receivable and/or inventory—that can be sold or converted into money and used by the debtor as long as the floating charge has not crystallized.

FORECLOSURE—a remedy whereby a creditor accepts title to his or her collateral in full satisfaction of the debt.

FRAUDULENT CONVEYANCE—an improper transfer of an asset, designed to defeat creditors. See the discussion starting on page 149.

GARNISHMENT—a procedure whereby money payable by one party (A) to another (B) can be applied to satisfy B's obligations to his or her creditors. See the discussion starting on page 59.

GENERAL ASSIGNMENT OF BOOK DEBTS—a specific type of security agreement used under the *Personal Property Security Act*. See Exhibit 2 in the Appendix and the discussion starting on page 10.

GENERAL SECURITY AGREEMENTS—broad-ranging security agreements used under the *Personal Property Security Act*. See Exhibit 1 in the Appendix and the discussion starting on page 9.

GOODWILL—an asset carried on the books of many companies; essentially it reflects the value of the name or reputation which the company has built up (or purchased).

GUARANTEE—an agreement whereby one party agrees to perform the obligations of another party. An example is where a shareholder of a company agrees to be liable for the borrowings of the company.

INDEMNITY AGREEMENT—an agreement whereby one party agrees to make good any expenditures that someone else (A) is put to as a result of the default, by a third party, in performing his or her obligations to A.

INFORMATION PACKAGE—the material often assembled by receivers to assist persons interested in buying some or all of the assets of the company in receivership. See the discussion starting on page 80.

LETTER OF CREDIT—an agreement by the issuer—typically a bank—to give credit to another person or to make a payment to that person, in certain circumstances, at the request of a third person, who is a customer of the bank.

MORTGAGE—an agreement whereby real property is pledged as security for the repayment of a debt. See the discussion starting on page 15.

MORTGAGEE—the creditor, or secured party, under a mortgage.

*MORTGAGES ACT*—Ontario statute that regulates the taking and enforcement of mortgages.

MORTGAGOR—the person who owes the debt secured by a mortgage.

NOTICE DISPUTING PETITION—the document whereby a company who is resisting being put into involuntary bankruptcy puts its case to the court. See the discussion starting on page 116.

NOTICE OF GARNISHMENT—the document whereby a creditor with a judgment against a debtor enforces the garnishment remedy in order to recover the judgment. See the discussion starting on page 59.

NOTICE OF INTENTION TO ENFORCE SECURITY—the ten-day notice that must be served by creditors seeking to enforce security over all or substantially all of the assets of a business debtor. See the form in the Appendix on page 66 and the discussion starting on page 17 in Chapter 5.

NOTICE OF INTENTION TO MAKE A PROPOSAL—the document whereby an insolvent company gains protection from its creditors under the proposal provisions of the *Bankruptcy and Insolvency Act*. See the discussion starting at page 168.

PERFECTION (of a *Personal Property Security Act* interest)—the steps necessary to make the interest enforceable against a third party (i.e., someone other than the debtor). The most common method of perfection is registration, as discussed on page 6.

PERSONAL PROPERTY—broadly, every type of property that does not include real estate or real property.

*PERSONAL PROPERTY SECURITY ACT*—Ontario statute that governs the taking or giving and the enforcement of security interests in collateral which is personal property.

PETITION (for a receiving order)—the formal document whereby a creditor (or creditors) of an insolvent company asks the court to declare that company bankrupt, on the basis that the company has committed an act of bankruptcy. See the discussion starting on page 114.

PLAINTIFF—the party claiming relief in a lawsuit.

PLAN—the terms of a commercial reorganization attempted pursuant to the *Companies' Creditors Arrangement Act*. This is discussed in Chapter 15.

PREFERENCE—the improper satisfaction, by a debtor, of one creditor over another creditor or other creditors. See the discussion starting at page 145.

PROMISSORY NOTE—means a written promise to pay a sum of money on stipulated terms, including on demand.

PROOF OF CLAIM—the written proof of a debt that must be submitted by a creditor in a bankruptcy. There is a separate proof of claim form for a beneficiary of trust property held by a bankrupt. See the forms in the Appendix (Exhibits 17 and 18) and the discussion starting on page 120. The term "proof of claim" also refers to the proof of debt that must be submitted for voting purposes in a commercial reorganization, as discussed in Chapter 15.

PROPOSAL—the term used to describe a commercial reorganization under the *Bankruptcy and Insolvency Act,* as discussed in Chapter 15.

PURCHASE MONEY SECURITY INTEREST—a special type of security interest under the *Personal Property Security Act* that allows the creditor a first claim on assets that he or she has, in essence, provided the financing for, regardless of how many other secured creditors were in place before such financing was provided. See the discussion starting at page 10.

REAL PROPERTY—land and generally anything erected or growing on, or affixed to, land. See the definition of **fixture** above.

RECEIVER—one who has been appointed, under security documentation, to take possession or control of all or substantially all of the inventory, accounts receivable, or property of a commercial borrower. See the discussion starting at page 73. Receivers may also be appointed by the Court, as discussed starting on page 83.

RECEIVING ORDER—the court order declaring a company involuntarily bankrupt. See the discussion starting at page 116.

REPAIRERS' AND STORERS' LIEN—refers to a right that exists for the benefit of those who provide repair or storage services. See the discussion starting on page 44.

REVIEWABLE TRANSACTION—both a general category of transactions that can be attacked by the creditors of a debtor who engaged in such transactions and a specific type of such transaction in which property is dealt with at a price conspicuously more or less than fair market value. See the discussions on the general and the particular kinds starting on page 154.

SECURED CREDITOR—a creditor who holds a proper and enforceable security interest over collateral.

SECURITY INTEREST—an interest in a property that allows the property to be sold or otherwise dealt with if the owner of the property fails to honour his or her obligations to the creditor who enjoys the benefit of the security interest.

SETTLEMENT—a transaction that is similar to a gift which is distinguished from a gift because the donor intends that the property be kept in a specific form, for the benefit of the recipient. See the discussion starting on page 152.

SEVERANCE PAY—an obligation that arises on the termination of certain relatively senior employees. See the discussion on page 136.

SPECIAL RESOLUTION (under the *Bankruptcy and Insolvency Act*)—generally, a resolution passed by a majority in number and three-fourths in the dollar value of the claims of creditors with proven claims; note, however, that the necessary resolution for passage of a proposal under the *Bankruptcy and Insolvency Act* by each class of creditor is a majority in number and only two-thirds of the dollar value.

STATUTE—an act or a law of the federal or provincial legislature.

STATUTORY LIENS—in effect, security interests deemed to exist by statute, not by private contract.

TERMINATION PAY—arises when employees are terminated. The obligation varies depending on whether the termination is accompanied by other terminations within defined periods; see the discussion on page 136.

THIRTY-DAY GOODS—a term used to refer to goods that may be subject to certain rights by an unpaid supplier who delivered the goods within 30 days of a receivership or a bankruptcy. See the discussion starting on page 90.

TRADE CREDITOR—an ordinary (normally unsecured) creditor of a business corporation.

TRUST DEEDS—instruments under which companies may issue bonds and/or debentures. As discussed starting on page 167 trust deeds are a requirement for companies seeking to use the *Companies' Creditors Arrangement Act*.

TRUSTEE IN BANKRUPTCY—a federally licensed person or company authorized to receive and administer all of the property of a bankrupt company. See page 123.

WRIT OF SEIZURE AND SALE—an instrument that allows a creditor who has obtained a judgment against a debtor to direct the sheriff to seize and sell certain assets of the debtor to satisfy the debt. See the discussion starting on page 58.

# Index

# About the Author

**JEFFREY CARHART** is a corporate and commercial lawyer with Miller Thomson; his practice handles many commercial financings and insolvencies. He represents a wide variety of clients: banks, trust and insurance companies, commercial financing institutions, receivers and trustees in bankruptcy, as well as corporate and individual borrowers. Mr. Carhart has written several articles published in *The Canadian Bankruptcy Reports* (Carswell), has been involved in many professional speaking programs: The Canadian Institute, Canadian Bar Association, Insight seminars, and is an instructor in the Debtor/Creditor Law section of the Bar Admission Course.